W0006348

Contemporary Boat Migration

Challenging Migration Studies

This provocative new series challenges the established field of migration studies to think beyond its policy-oriented frameworks and to engage with the complex and myriad forms in which the global migration regime is changing in the twenty-first century. It proposes to draw together studies that engage with the current transformation of the politics of migration, and the meaning of 'migrant', from the below of grassroots, local, transnational and multi-sited coalitions, projects and activisms. Attuned to the contemporary resurgence of migrant-led and migration-related movements, and anti-racist activism, the series builds on work carried out at the critical margins of migration studies to evaluate the 'border industrial complex' and its fall-outs, build a decolonial perspective on global migration flows, and critically reassess the link between (im)migration, citizenship and belonging in the cross-border future.

Series Editors:

Alana Lentin, Associate Professor in Cultural and Social Analysis at Western Sydney University

Gavan Titley, Senior Lecturer in Media Studies at the National University of Ireland, Maynooth

Titles in the Series:

Radical Skin, Moderate Masks: De-radicalising the Muslim and Racism in Post-racial Societies
Yassir Morsi

Contemporary Boat Migration: Data, Geopolitics, and Discourses
Edited by Elaine Burroughs and Kira Williams

The Undeported: The Making of a Floating Population of Exiles in France and Europe
Carolina Sanchez Boe (forthcoming)

Race in Post-racial Europe: An Intersectional Analysis
Stefanie C. Boulila (forthcoming)

Contemporary Boat Migration

Data, Geopolitics and Discourses

Edited by Elaine Burroughs
and Kira Williams

ROWMAN &
LITTLEFIELD
INTERNATIONAL

London • New York

Published by Rowman & Littlefield International Ltd
Unit A, Whitacre Mews, 26–34 Stannary Street, London SE11 4AB
www.rowmaninternational.com

Rowman & Littlefield International Ltd.is an affiliate of Rowman & Littlefield
4501 Forbes Boulevard, Suite 200, Lanham, Maryland 20706, USA
With additional offices in Boulder, New York, Toronto (Canada), and Plymouth (UK)
www.rowman.com

British Library Cataloguing-in-Publication Data
A catalogue record for this book is available from the British Library

ISBN: HB 978-1-7866-0514-6

Library of Congress Cataloging-in-Publication Data Available
ISBN: 978-1-78660-514-6 (cloth : alk. paper)
ISBN: 978-1-78660-515-3 (electronic)

Contents

SECTION THREE: DISCOURSES 113

Figures and Tables

FIGURES

TABLES

Chapter 1

Introduction: Challenging Migration Studies through Addressing Critical Gaps in Studying Migration by Boat

Elaine Burroughs and Kira Williams

INTRODUCTION

In recent years, with the fleeing of people from a range of conflict zones and the increased restricted access to areas such as the European Union (EU) and countries like the United States, Canada and Australia, international human migration by boat has become more frequent, sensationalised and precarious. Migration by boat has gained significant attention from a range of actors, including enforcement authorities, political elites, media and non-/inter-governmental organisations. Indeed, this book was written during a turbulent time, in which the topic of migration by boat was presented by many in positions of elite status as a 'crisis'. The sea has increasingly become a space of hope/desperation for migrants, as well as a place of geopolitical conflict over territory and sovereignty (Mountz 2013).

For these reasons, this edited book aims to explore how migration by boat is researched, the geopolitical focus on it and the way in which it is discursively represented. This collection re-orientates the focus of the current literature on migration by boat – that is, from humanitarian and legal realities (e.g., Carling and Hernandez-Carretero 2011; Gammeltoft-Hansen 2008) to the empirical relationship between data and methodologies, legal regimes and geopolitics and discourses. What also concerns us in this volume is the intertwined relationship between these three distinct elements. The book originated as the result of a paper session where we identified major gaps in studying migration by boat in 2016. The key objective of this collection is to offer a platform for new and established scholars to explore migration by boat through these three under-researched entities.

This chapter briefly outlines what the book is, why we made it, how it addresses current important issues in migration studies, what its wider benefits are and what to expect inside. As previously referred to, it generally studies three crucial, yet understudied, issues in contemporary migration by boat: data and methodology, legal regimes and geopolitics and discourses. We approach these issues using empirically focused, novel methods through specific case studies. The chapters in this volume are interdisciplinary in nature and are drawn from key disciplines in the field of migration studies, including geography, sociology, political studies and linguistics. Furthermore, the contexts examined here emerge from a range of geographical contexts (Europe, Canada and Australia). Although a range of geographical locations are examined, this book does not provide an exhaustive account of the topic of migration by boat. Rather, it explores it through three specific lenses. Furthermore, not only does each chapter examine a specific case in relation to the core topic of migration by boat, each chapter also relates to the other chapters within this book; therefore, although each chapter stands in its own and can be read in this way, the book can also be read as a single inter-related entity that examines migration by boat through the themes of data, geopolitics and discourse.

Three major benefits of the book are its general contribution to studying migration by boat, providing evidence on this issue for contemporary political debates, and, last, in giving critical insight into social theory and human rights law. The book has three sections: section 1 explores data and methodology in two chapters, section 2 uncovers legal regimes and geopolitics in three chapters and section 3 studies discourses on migration by boat in three chapters. We then summarise and build on our general findings in a final chapter.

ORIGIN AND HISTORY OF THE BOOK

We first met and discussed migration by boat and border enforcement in late 2015. We found that the issue's contemporary relevance and relative deficiency in empirical papers warranted the creation of a paper session to explore these topics, which we led at the American Association of Geographers 2016 annual meeting in Chicago, the United States. At this time, and as further described later in this book, we identified three core topics in studying migration by boat which needed immediate empirical research: data and methodology, legal regimes and geopolitics and discourses. Based on this insightful dialogue between us, the presenters, many of whom are contributors in this volume, and the audience, we agreed to co-edit a volume to address these topics insofar as we could for wider scholarship.

We solicited contributions to this volume based on those three themes. We quickly received proposals not only from those who presented at our panel but also from a number of influential scholars in the field who also saw an urgency for these research projects. We reviewed our accepted proposals, making modifications to more tightly fit them to this book's themes. It turned out that Rowman & Littlefield International, our ultimate publisher, actively sought submissions like ours for its 'Challenging Migration Studies' series. This series challenges migration studies as past scholars have established it; it calls for new theory, methodologies and data to move us beyond policy-oriented frameworks in order to engage the complex changes in the global migration regime. Given our book's goals of filling and expanding critical gaps in current migration studies literature with respect to migration by boat, we agreed that 'Challenging Migration Studies' was a perfect fit and submitted our later accepted proposal to Rowman & Littlefield International.

GENERAL DESCRIPTION AND JUSTIFICATION OF THE BOOK

This is an edited book that focuses on crucial, yet understudied, issues in contemporary migration by boat through three themes: data and methodology, legal regimes and geopolitics and discourses. All contributors approach these issues using empirically focused, novel methods through specific case studies. The book begins by looking at core problems and ways forward in data and methodologies to study migration by boat. It then proceeds to employ examples of these new data and methodologies to empirically study the complex legal regimes and geopolitics of migration by boat. Finally, the book considers how elite and media discourses entangle themselves within these legal regimes and geopolitics using new evidence and approaches.

While the migration of people by boat is a long-standing phenomenon, journeys have become more frequent and precarious as states illegalise entry. As migration at sea becomes more common, it has gained attention from a range of actors. The sea has thus become a space of hope/desperation for migrants as well as conflict over territory and sovereignty (Mountz 2013), representing wider social debates in and beyond Australia, Canada, the EU and the United States (Castles and Miller 1998; Samers 2010). Current literature on migration by boat reflects these debates, primarily concentrating on the humanitarian and legal realities of migration by boat and border enforcement at sea (e.g., Carling and Hernandez-Carretero 2011; Gammeltoft-Hansen 2008); however, few studies have analysed their empirical relationship or systematic connections. This edited volume aims to fill this gap and thereby address three important, overlapping themes of these debates.

The first theme explores data and methodologies on migration by boat, its discourses and its enforcement. It identifies appropriate research methodologies and sources to gather these data (e.g., operations, interceptions, deaths).

Current data are missing or insufficient to empirically describe these phenomena; furthermore, availability typically varies by topic and region, and data are gathered in different ways by a wide variety of institutions (e.g., states, universities, think-tanks). Even where data do exist, differences in definitions, recording, power relations, reluctance to report and data destruction hinder aggregation to achieve a larger sample size or wider geographic scale. We must overcome these issues in order to understand migration by boat. We therefore provide novel insights into and propose new methods.

A number of scholars have specifically worked around data issues on human migration at sea (Carling 2007; Weber and Pickering 2011; Williams and Mountz 2016). Think-tanks and NGOs have also contributed to our wider knowledge (e.g., De Bruycker et al. 2013). Although important, these projects typically did not focus on methodological problems, publish their data or contribute to a longer, more sustained research on migration by boat, its discourse or its enforcement. A number of data-focused and sustained projects have also emerged online in the past decade (Border Crossing Observatory 2015; Hutton 2014; Spijkerboer et al. 2015). While these projects have shared their data and information on their use of innovative methodologies online, they have yet to fully publish their methodological details or findings in an academic setting. In bringing together these strands of research, then, this edited book addresses the following critical questions: how can research designs tackle issues of data paucity on migration at sea, especially at larger scales? How do we study secretive and obfuscated research subjects, like migrants at sea and state enforcement operations? What are the findings from projects which have taken on these issues? What can we learn from their methodological innovations and results? We argue that in order to understand the concept of migration by boat, especially its geopolitics and discourses, we require new and improved data and methodologies.

The second theme builds upon the first by focusing on the relationship between data on migration by boat and governance and geopolitics of the 'border'. A large body of work currently exists which analyses the legal status of international migration at sea and, on a more limited level, its enforcement (e.g., Barnes 2004; Pugh 2004). Only a limited number of scholars have explored the empirical relationship between legal regimes, geographies, geopolitics and migration by boat, its discourse and enforcement (Klepp 2011; Lutterbeck 2006; Mainwaring 2012; Mountz 2010). There is currently a lack of literature which makes a strong connection between empirical work on migration by boat and the legalities and politics of migration. Given our existing literature, what are the more specific relationships between legality, geography and migrant outcomes at sea? How do states, migrants or discourse bring them about in practice? How do these practices work in specific regions or locations, especially those relatively understudied in previous research? Are there broader, empirical connections between these patchworks from which we can learn something new? What are the wider impacts of these conclusions for migration on land or by air?

Building upon the two themes already outlined, the third theme identifies and analyses how elite discourses represent migration by boat. While many authors have examined how migration is broadly represented in elite discourses, few have specifically looked at migration by boat. This small cohort of literature has concentrated on the regions of Australasia (Bogen and Marlowe 2015; Holtom 2013; Kampmark 2007; McKay, Thomas and Blood 2011; O'Doherty and Lecouter 2007; Slattery 2003), Canada (Ashutosh and Mountz 2012) and the EU (Bacas 2013; Bruno 2016; Campesi 2011). Existing research on migration by boat indicates that discourses play an important role in the categorisation of migrants through a particular frame in order to legitimise the governance and geopolitics of human migration at sea. This literature has also shown that these discursive representations can have an impact on public opinion.

This edited book extends current literature on discourses of migration by boat in two key ways. First, we focus on discursive data and methods – that is, discourses from the news media, political outlets and online sources – rather than papers that take a more theoretical approach. We ask: what are the key discourses that construct migration by boat, and what is their function? Second, we extend approaches to discourses of migration by boat by explicitly linking data on human migration at sea (e.g., deaths, apprehensions) and the governance of this type of migration with discursive and visual representations. Key questions include what are the links, if any, between data on migration by boat and discursive representations? What are the relationships between representations of migration by boat and border geopolitical practices?

KEY BENEFITS OF THE BOOK

We argue that by addressing this critical yet understudied issue in migration studies, this book has three major benefits. First, the exploration of migration by boat in contemporary society is an under-researched area within migration studies. Of the literature that does exist, it tends to focus on the legalities of the situation; this book therefore addresses three themes that are currently understudied within this topic, namely empirical data and methods, legal regimes and geopolitics and discourses. Most distinctly, this book empirically explores the relationship between these three themes, and bringing these three themes together alone is a novel contribution of this volume. The book therefore addresses a critical gap within migration studies, and also within the study of migration by boat, by offering a number of approaches in undertaking research on migration by boat empirically and utilising novel methods. We aim to contribute to future research on data gathering, analysis and methodologies.

Second, migration by boat is a relevant issue in contemporary politics. Despite heavy interest by policymakers and publics alike, we currently have a notable lack of scientific evidence to support how migration by boat works or how best to respond to it. This book aims to offer scientific evidence to better understand how migration by boat works – in particular in relation to geopolitics and discourses. By offering empirical analysis of discourses of migration by boat, this book explores the linkages between discourses and broader political agendas. There is a continually growing demand for these empirical details, which this book provides in a coherent, logical and critical way.

Third, migration by boat and its enforcement provide critical insight into social theory and human rights law. Due to the extreme violence which occurs in trying to manage movement by boat, what happens to migrants at sea often reveals the power of people, space and politics. A migrant boat at sea quickly becomes a place where social forces, especially geopolitics, converge and can so be better understood. To understand and measure these forces, however, we must combine social theory with improved data and methodologies to adjust to the particular empirical difficulties of studying this often-obfuscated issue. We argue that it is our combination of theory, evidence in case studies and new methodologies which will help create a new agenda to push this much-needed research forward.

BOOK CONTENTS

We separate the book into three sections, with one section for each theme: data and methodology, legal regimes and geopolitics and discourses. Section 1 contains two chapters which explore data and methodologies for studying migration by boat, its surrounding geopolitics and related state border enforcement. Despite its contemporary relevance, the study of migration by boat currently lacks specialised approaches to understand it. This gap has at least two sources: the difficulty in collecting primary sources of data and the focus of research on applied theory and case studies as opposed to methodology itself.

Scholars in the past two decades in particular have had to design and innovate new ways to study the complex socio-economic, legal, political and spatial dimensions of the phenomena of migration by boat; however, these new and useful methods often become lost because they remain underdeveloped and undershared. Contributors Alison Mountz and Kira Williams therefore explore these new ways forward in addition to pointing out existing data-related and methodological problems. In sum, chapters 2 and 3 help contribute to future research on migration by boat by taking on two strong barriers to current scholarship: data gaps and methodological limitations. In doing so, they help form the basis of further discourse and research.

Section 2 has three chapters which explore the geopolitics and legal regimes surrounding contemporary migration by boat. While section 1 introduced us to and showed issues in studying migration by boat, chapters by Giuseppe Campesi, Paolo Cuttitta and Joanne van Selm decompose its complex political and social realities. Previous work in the field has often shown the consequences of governance institutions on the everyday lives of migrants; however, scholars have yet to contribute a nuanced understanding of the legal regimes and geographies of migration by boat, and, in particular, how these play out in international geopolitics.

Although a large body of work currently exists which analyses the legal and political status of migration at sea, and, on a more limited level, its related border enforcement, only a small number of scholars have delved into the empirical relationship between legal regimes, geographies and geopolitics of migration by boat. This section therefore brings together three case studies related to these phenomena by leading researchers in the field. By its conclusion it addresses a number of critical questions in current studies of migration by boat: what are the more specific relationships between legality, geography and migrant outcomes at sea? How do states, migrants or discourse bring them about in practice? How do these practices work in specific regions or locations? Are there broader, empirical connections between these patchworks from which we can learn something new? This section therefore contributes to scholarship by connecting the analytical and empirical gaps between the legal regimes, geographies and geopolitics with migration by boat.

Section 3 also reviews an important but understudied issue through three chapters: how elite and media discourses represent migration by boat. Though many authors have examined how such discourses broadly and theoretically represent migration, few have specifically looked in detail or at migration by boat more generally. Given that existing research indicates that discourses play an important role in the legal, political and spatial classification of migrants, and that section 2 shows how such constructions affect everyday lives, a nuanced, empirical understanding of discourses of migration by boat is extremely useful.

Through these chapters, Elaine Burroughs, Marco Binotto and Marco Bruno and Andonea Dickson contribute to discourses of migration by boat in two key ways. First, they focus on discursive data and methods – that is, they make use of empirical evidence related to discourses from news media, political outlets and online sources – rather than solely taking a theoretical approach. They specifically address questions to identify key discourses which construct migration by boat and their functions. Second, they extend existing approaches to discourses on migration by explicitly linking empirical data on human migration by boat and its governance with discursive and visual representations. This section thus analyses the links between data on migration by boat and discourse, as well as the relationships between representations of migration by boat with border enforcement practices, thereby giving critical insight into discourses on migration by boat.

In our final chapter, 'Conclusion: Problems, Answers and Ways Forward in Studying Migration by Boat', we summarise the knowledge learnt from this book and how it responds to the core problems we identified. We then proceed to offer potential paths forward in researching this topic in order to challenge and enhance migration studies as a field. It is our hope and expectation that you will find this edited volume useful in furthering the critical understanding of, and research on, migration by boat.

BIBLIOGRAPHY

Ashutosh, Ishan, and Mountz, Alison, 'The Geopolitics of Migrant Mobility: Tracing State Relations through Refugee Claims, Boats, and Discourses', *Geopolitics* 17, no. 2 (2012): 335.

Bacas, Jutta, 'Perceiving Fences and Experiencing Borders in Greece: A Discourse on Irregular Migration across European Borders', *Journal of Mediterranean Studies* 22, no. 2 (2013): 319.

Barnes, Richard, 'Refugee Law at Sea', *International and Comparative Law Quarterly* 53, no. 1 (2004): 47.

Bogen, Rachel, and Marlowe, Jay, 'Asylum Discourse in New Zealand: Moral Panic and a Culture of Indifference', *Australian Social Work* 70, no. 1 (2017): 104.

Border Crossing Observatory, 'Australian Border Deaths Database', 2013, accessed 1 July 2017. http://artsonline.monash.edu.au/thebordercrossingobservatory/

Bruno, Marco, ' "Framing Lampedusa": The Landing Issue in Italian Media Coverage of Migrations, between Alarmism and Pietism', in *Public and Political Discourses of Migration: International Perspectives*, edited by Haynes, Amanda, Power, Martin, Devereux, Eoin, Dillane, Aileen, and Carr, James (London: Rowman and Littlefield, 2016).

Campesi, Giuseppe, 'The Arab Spring and the Crisis of the European Border Regime: Manufacturing Emergency in the Lampedusa Crisis', Fiesole: EUI working paper (2011).

Carling, Jorgen, 'Control and Migrant Fatalities at the Spanish-African Borders', *International Migration Review* 42, no. 2 (2007): 42.

Carling, Jorgen, and Hernandez-Carretero, Maria, 'Protecting Europe and Protecting Migrants? Strategies for Managing Unauthorised Migration from Africa', *The British Journal of Politics and International Relations* 13, no. 1 (2011): 42.

Castles, Steven, and Miller, Mark, *The Age of Migration: International Population Movements in the Modern World*, second edition (New York: Guildford Press, 1998).

de Bruycker, Philippe, di Bartolomeo, Anna, and Fargues, Philippe, 'Migrants Smuggled by Sea to the EU: Facts, Laws and Policy Options', *Migration Policy Centre* (2013), accessed 1 July 2017. http://www.migrationpolicycentre.eu/docs/MPC-RR-2013-009.pdf

Gammeltoft-Hansen, Thomas, 'The Refugee, the Sovereign and the Sea: EU Interdiction Policies in the Mediterranean', Danish Institute for International Studies working paper (2008): 6. http://www.econstor.eu/bitstream/10419/44650/1/560120990.pdf

Holtom, Bridget, ' "Boat People" in Australia: Press, Policy and Public Opinion', Research Project BEES (BEES0007) (2013), accessed 1 July 2017. http://geoview.iag.org.au/index.php/GEOView/article/view/29

Hutton, Margaret, 'Database of Asylum Seeker Boats', 2014, accessed 1 July 2017. http://www.sievx.com/dbs/boats/

Kampmark, Binoy, ' "Spying for Hitler" and "Working for Bin Laden": Comparative Australian Discourses on Refugees', *Journal of Refugee Studies* 19, no. 1 (2006): 1.

Klepp, Silja, 'A Double Bind: Malta and the Rescue of Unwanted Migrants at Sea, a Legal Anthropological Perspective on the Humanitarian Law of the Sea', *International Journal of Refugee Law* 23, no. 3 (2011): 538.

Lutterbeck, Derek, 'Policing Migration in the Mediterranean', *Mediterranean Politics* 11, no. 1 (2006): 59.

Mainwaring, Cetta, 'Constructing a Crisis: The Role of Immigration Detention in Malta', *Population, Space and Place* 18, no. 6 (2012): 687.

McKay, Fiona, Thomas, Samantha, and Blood, Warwick, ' "Any One of These Boat People Could Be a Terrorist for All We Know!' Media Representations and Public Perceptions of 'Boat People' Arrivals in Australia', *Journalism* 12, no. 5 (2011): 607.

Mountz, Alison, 'Political Geography: Reconfiguring Geographies of Sovereignty', *Progress in Human Geography* 37, no. 6 (2013): 829.

Mountz, Alison, *Seeking Asylum: Human Smuggling and Bureaucracy at the Border* (Minneapolis: University of Minnesota Press, 2010).

O'Doherty, Kieran, and Lecouter, Amanda, ' "Asylum Seekers", "Boat People" and "Illegal Immigrants": Social Categorisation in the Media', *Australian Journal of Psychology* 59, no. 1 (2007): 1.

Pugh, Michael, 'Drowning Not Waving: Boat People and Humanitarianism at Sea', *Journal of Refugee Studies* 17, no. 1 (2004): 50.

Samers, Michael, 'An Emerging Geopolitics of "Illegal" Immigration in the European Union', *European Journal of Migration and Law* 6, no. 1 (2010): 27.

Slattery, Kate, 'Drowning Not Waving: The 'Children Overboard' Event and Australia's Fear of the Other', *Media International Incorporating Culture and Policy* 109, no. 1 (2003): 93.

Spijkerboer, Thomas, Last, Tamara, Cuttitta, Paolo, Baird, Theodore, and Ulusoy, Orcun, 'Human Costs of Border Control', 2015, accessed 1 July 2017. http://www.borderdeaths.org/

Weber, Leanne, and Pickering, Sharon, *Globalization and Borders: Deaths at the Global Frontier* (London: Palgrave Macmillan, 2011).

Williams, Kira, and Mountz, Alison, 'Rising Tide: Analyzing the Relationship between Externalization and Migrant Deaths and Boat Losses', in *Externalizing Migration Management: Europe, North America and the Spread of Remote Control*, edited by Zaiotti, Ruben (London: Routledge, 2016).

Section One

DATA AND METHODOLOGY

This part of the book explores data and methodologies for studying migration by boat, its surrounding geopolitics and related state border enforcement. Despite its contemporary relevance, the study of migration by boat currently lacks specialised approaches to understand it. This gap has at least two sources: the difficulty in collecting primary sources of data and the focus of research on applied theory and case studies as opposed to methodology itself. Scholars in the past two decades in particular have had to design and innovate new ways to study the complex socio-economic, legal, political and spatial dimensions of the phenomena of migration by boat; however, these new and useful methods often become lost because they remain underdeveloped and undershared. This section therefore explores these new ways forward in addition to pointing out existing data-related and methodological problems.

In the following chapters by Alison Mountz and Kira Williams, we find that current data on migration by boat are often missing or insufficient to adequately describe it. Drawing from her research related to island detention and migration at sea, for example, Mountz shows how at the onset of her projects her research team could neither find nor agree upon a definition of what was a migrant boat. Williams likewise shares how even basic requests for information about migration by boat to states can become many times more complicated and obfuscated than expected. Examples like these are all too common in studying migration by boat. In her chapter, Williams identifies more general data-related problems in the field: differences in definitions, differences in recording, power relations, reluctance to report and even intentional data destruction. Mountz discusses the complex vulnerability and ethical concerns surrounding working with such data for migrants, bureaucrats and scholars alike. These barriers raise a daunting challenge to future researchers. What can we do to handle these issues to facilitate our own as well as future research?

Mountz and Williams each proceed by identifying and expanding on new methodological paths for research on migration by boat. Mountz specifically formulates ten innovative strategies with examples of how they have been used by recent scholarship. She poignantly argues and elaborates on how and why these strategies can overcome current methodological issues while not exposing migrants to further harm. Williams takes a slightly different approach: she forms a basis for a more generalised approach to studying migration by boat combining a number of existing methodologies. Through this approach, she demonstrates how a combination of methodologies addresses not only the limitations of individual methodologies but also most of the data-related issues identified earlier.

In sum, chapters 2 and 3 help contribute to future research on migration by boat by taking on two strong barriers to current scholarship: data gaps and methodological limitations. In doing so, they help form the basis of further discourse and research.

Chapter 2

Methodological Approaches to Researching Boat Migration: Moving Vessels and Emotional Landscapes

Alison Mountz

INTRODUCTION

Boats move, carrying untold people to oft-unknown destinations. Boats transport and hide. They are shapeshifters. They are vehicles and stories unfolding; they occupy newspaper articles. Boat journeys are the stuff of myth, legend, adventure, tragedy and heroism. In the world of human migration and mobility studies, they are the opposite of first-class plane travel. They move slowly, offer harder and riskier passage, but do not require passports or visas. Once, they carried slaves down below. Today, they carry migrants instead. Packed in poor conditions, these are moves of despair and hope which tie marine vessels inexorably to landscapes of emotion. Not surprisingly, boats carrying migrants and displaced people are the subject of front-page news articles, poetry, memoirs, movies, memories and novels. Consider Vietnamese-Canadian author Kim Thúy's (2012) evocative book *Ru*, a poetic, autobiographical novel about the journey from Vietnam to Canada via Malaysia by boat. In this passage, the narrator's connection to her own small children recalls a family on the boat that had carried her to Canada as a child:

> swept up in the love of a mother sitting across from me in the hold of our boat, clutching a baby with a head covered in scabs and stinking sores. I have held that picture in my head for days and perhaps nights as well. One small bulb hanging from a cord held in place by a rusty nail cast a weak light, always the same, through the hold.

Years later, when she becomes an adult and a mother, the narrator remembers this time anew.

Ru conveys the ambiguity of time and space, the disorientation of passage on a boat captained by others: 'There was no way to know if we were rearing skyward or plunging to the depths. Heaven and hell met in a single embrace within the belly of our ship. Heaven held out the promise of change, a new future, a new story for our lives'. Thúy also commits the emotional landscapes of boat migration to text, fear prominent among them:

> Hell, though, became our fears: pirates, hunger, intoxication on biscuits soaked in motor oil, lack of water, not being able to stand again, having to urinate in the red pot that was passed from hand to hand, possible contagion from the child's scabby head, never stepping on dry land again, never again seeing the faces of family members sitting in the dark somewhere in the middle of two hundred others.

How can researchers study and make sense of these mobile vehicles and shifting, intense emotional landscapes of water and land, freedom and unfreedom and fear and hope that carry people, their histories, their secrets, their families, their sadness, dreams and despair thousands of miles around the globe?

As a geographical location, the boat traverses and abuts many landscapes that are more familiar research territory for geographers and migration studies scholars alike: oceans (Steinberg 2005), borders (Jones 2016), ports (Cowan 2015; Heyman 2004) and thresholds between land and sea (Walters 2008). As William Walters (2016) argues of deportation, and Paglen and Thompson (2006) of rendition flights, the boat is a hidden infrastructure, not necessarily meant to be discovered, hidden in plain sight while traversing crowded oceans, vessels with unmarked flags.

Boats can serve as vehicles to freedom, a means of achieving liberation. But they can also become vehicles of unfreedom, entrapment or exploitation. Processes of data collection on boat migration hold potential to set researchers themselves adrift. Given the intense and shifting forms of confinement, harm, movement and peril expressed by Perara (2016, 30), 'The refugee boat, as an ambiguous artifact of mobility and survival, rides the currents of freedom and unfreedom, life and death, stasis and flow', one must ask: how might researchers navigate this particular kind of geographical site – the boat – ethically, safely, politically and soundly – to conduct research?

While notorious, with much attention in mainstream media paid to boats and the human tragedies they carry and cause, they also prove – notoriously – to be sites where it is difficult to access people or information. Death and disappearance at sea (Weber and Pickering 2011; Williams and Mountz 2016), coercion by authorities and exploitation by smugglers and others en route all render marine travellers highly precarious. In fact, publics often become aware of boats only in the wake of tragedy: through their disappearance, sinking or crashes. Only in death do departed migrants become known, as their plights are mined by authorities, politicians, publics, activists and researchers for blame and accountability, mobilised for politics and social change. The economic and legal status of those on board exacerbates this precarity and leaves researchers with a panoply of traumatic experiences, issues and ethical dilemmas (Maillet et al. 2017).

This chapter outlines methodological challenges associated with and creative endeavours to research migration by boat. I proceed by first contemplating whether there is something distinctive about boats, compared with other vehicles and modes of transit. I then enumerate some of the main challenges to conducting research on boat migration. I then offer several creative ways forward, drawing from and building on research published by a range of scholars working in this area. These suggested methodologies range from access to information requests to mapping projects and interviews designed to access information in times and places that do not render those travelling by boat *more* precarious as a result of research – following the principle of first, do no harm. Finally, I end with conclusions and hopes for future research on boat migration.

ARE BOATS DIFFERENT FROM OTHER VEHICLES USED FOR MIGRATION, AND, IF SO, HOW?

Between 2010 and 2013, I led a research project that examined the use of islands off the coasts of Australia, Italy and the United States of America as sites of detention where people travelling by boat were detained after being intercepted and seeking to make a claim for asylum. While creating a codebook for use in coding the large data set on boat migration, island detention and asylum-seeking, our research team once sat and attempted – non-ironically, and for an embarrassingly lengthy conversation – to define 'boat'. We debated whether to include boats that had once floated but could no longer be counted. We debated whether to include anything that floated, or only those vessels able to carry a minimum number of passengers. We also debated how or whether to include *all* boats, or only those used for purposes of migration across an international border. This is what we came up with:

Boats:

- Physical boats, anything that floats or has floated
- Boats often coded with Contractor, Enforcement, Facilities, Interception, Legality and Jurisdiction, Migration history, Military, Missing people, Transfer
- *Not* Missing People (*code* instead 'With Missing People').

This makes boats just like other kinds of vehicles utilised for human migration and simultaneously distinct from them. Migration by bus or train or on foot, for example, would involve a different set of associated issues and correlating codes.

Building on these similarities and distinctions across vehicles, is there some way in which boat migration necessarily involves different methodological approaches to research than other equally dynamic forms of migration? The answer is 'yes' and 'no'.

Boats are similar to other vehicles in that their mobility, unpredictability and politicisation involves particularly xenophobic and racialised responses to images of people approaching sovereign territory. One need not look farther than histories of boat migration in the Global North (North America, Europe, Australia), and the Global South to see these racialised, classed and xenophobic responses. Take one contemporary example: the Rohingya. The Rohingya are an ethnic and racial minority that have contended with discrimination and violence directed at them for decades. In recent years, as they took flight and were displaced, large groups of Rohingya attempted sea migration. They were denied landing and found themselves adrift at sea with nowhere to land (Schiavenza 2015). Boat migrations such as these play in global and national media as crises, which elicit enforcement-oriented responses, often with dramatic consequences such as exclusion in the form of detention or repatriation (Mountz and Hiemstra 2013). Take Canada as another example. In response to very few boat arrivals in recent decades (in 1999 from China and 2009 and 2010 from Sri Lanka), marine arrivals nonetheless provoked dramatic changes to legislation that affected all refugee claimants in recent years, following each round of arrivals (Ibrahim 2005).

In other ways, too, boats prove similar to other vehicles-in-motion studied for years by geographers and other scholars. William Walters (2016), for example, looks at flights as the infrastructure of most deportation routes. Many scholars have conducted research along the route of *la bestia,* or the beast, the train carrying Central American migrants north through México to the border with the United States (Brigden 2016). And nearly thirty years ago, Ted Conover (1987) crossed the Mexico-US border with undocumented migrants. Ruben Martinez (2002) also followed migrating families in their transnational journeys between Mexico and the United States in the 1990s and early 2000s. Boats are more difficult, if not entirely impossible, to study in these ways. Barriers to this kind of participant observation, for example, and other forms of embeddedness pose risks to researchers themselves and to others (smugglers and people being smuggled, specifically).

In addition to their mobility across time and space, boats – like other vehicles – move across multiple legal jurisdictions. Whereas trains and buses may cross land borders and inter-state lines, boats circulate in the context of the seas. This means that research may involve different environmental and legal landscapes – as discussed in more depth in chapter 3.

Boats present untold ethical challenges to researchers that must be taken into account and enumerated prior to tackling these challenges with creative ways forward.

ENUMERATING THE CHALLENGES TO RESEARCH ON BOAT MIGRATION

Migration studies have only recently begun to specifically research data, methodological and ethical issues in research on migration by boat. In a recent piece, Maillet, Williams and Mountz (2017) discuss challenges associated with research on human migration in locations that are obfuscated, or hidden intentionally from view by authorities. Williams also outlines core challenges associated with data on migration by boat in chapter 3 of this volume. The three sites these authors address are interception at sea, airport waiting zones and island detention centres. Moving across these three sites, they stage a conversation about the practical, ethical and methodological dilemmas of conducting research about human migration and enforcement in and through these areas. People travelling by boat are rendered vulnerable due to the circumstances they find themselves in. They become moving targets of enforcement, due to the illicit nature of unauthorised entry and the need to employ human smugglers, and therefore their association with criminality. Their efforts to evade authorities render them more precarious; invisibility has its own risks in risky settings. Marine travellers also become precarious due to the sometimes abusive and uneven power relations between smugglers and their clients. In this relationship, those being smuggled clearly exercise less control over their own fates and that of the ship than those in charge. Additionally, precarity intensifies due to the lack of identity documents and legal status in the sovereign territories into which the world is carved, on land and at sea, and which they traverse and where they land without travel documents that render them legible or legal to sovereign gatekeepers.

Once intercepted, migrants at sea face the risk of detention and deportation, which may involve family separation and certainly involves losses of freedom and mobility. The stakes of travel are high, and the stakes of any research which might render people more vulnerable or precarious are also high. As Maillet et al. (2017: 3) note: 'Ethical limitations here related to people's vulnerability as asylum seekers and migrants confined in detention. Not only was their mobility restricted, but they were under surveillance and information gathered in these settings could not necessarily be protected or anonymized'. Researchers, too, can be subjected to surveillance and face restricted access and mobility to sites and sources of data on human migration (albeit in much more limited fashion than people whose corporeal freedom is restricted with detention or deportation).

Ultimately, Maillet and co-authors (2017) argue that 'despite its difficulties and complexities, it is extremely important to do this kind of research'. Their commitment is to pursue dialogue among researchers, activists and migrants about these challenges, so that ideas and difficulties are shared, and researchers do not feel alone in these dilemmas. The next section of this chapter explores creative ways forward, building on the ethical and political commitment to not shy away from difficult topics (see also Coddington 2017). Instead, it is important to continuously explore and revisit 'which research methods proved appropriate when states attempted to suppress information. These problems were important because authorities often used migrants as justification for securitization and state-building' (Maillet et al. 2017).

WAYS FORWARD IN RESEARCHING MIGRATION BY BOAT: THINKING CREATIVELY, MOVING WITH BOATS

Given the risks posed by boat travel and the potential damage of revelations of political material gathered about boats and the people who operate and utilise them for purposes of undetected migration, it is essential to think creatively about how to conduct research and gather data about boat migration. There exist few reliable sources of quantitative data on boat migration – though these are uneven across national settings (see chapter 3). Many existing data come from government law enforcement agencies intent on publicising interception and border enforcement. Governments tend to publish data to achieve political objectives, such as framing the 'reality' of boat migration in ways that suit political objectives such as campaigning for office, responding to public outcry, stoking fear and anxiety among members of the public and advancing expensive and exclusionary enforcement-oriented policies and practices such as interception and detention (Mountz and Hiemstra 2013). Meanwhile, people who are travelling by boat are trying to evade authorities, detection and registration – and thereby avoid being rendered data points. All of these contribute to biases associated with existing data and databases.

Maillet, Mountz and Williams (2017) each pursued different methods to address methodological challenges in settings where authorities intentionally worked to hide information. For Maillet and Mountz, this involved ethnographic research. For Williams, creativity involved not the daily ethnographic encounter but the daily encounter with bureaucrats tasked with both policing and releasing information.

In other settings, given the dearth of accurate data, additional and different creative methodologies are needed. While chapter 3 focuses on trying to envision a generalised approach to studying migration by boat, I instead offer ten possible ways forward, gleaned from existing, cutting-edge research on boat migration: (1) conducting participant observation and ethnography research in situ; (2) interviewing before and after the journey; (3) working or volunteering around the edges of crisis; (4) mapping journeys; (5) considering boats as part of larger, transnational landscapes of emotion and affect, haunting and trauma; (6) using mobile methods that connect researchers to people moving among places; (7) assembling databases from media and other data sources; (8) becoming embedded; (9) examining material culture or things that move onto and off boats and (10) exploring visual method.

1. Conducting participant observation and ethnography research in situ. While it is extremely challenging and may not be possible to conduct ethnographic research *aboard* boats, those boats travel to and from places where such work may, in fact, be possible. Sometimes boat arrivals are hidden in plain sight by authorities, and formal permission to conduct interviews with people under state custody and surveillance may not be possible. This was the case on a visit to Lampedusa in summer 2010. A year after substantial boat arrivals *and* increases in enforcement, Sicilians located far from the island of Lampedusa told the author and research assistant Tina Catania that no boats were arriving on Lampedusa in 2010. But they *were* arriving, and news about them was not being released to the public or making it into local news. Once we arrived on Lampedusa, we learnt first instead from local Lampedusan youth spending time on the beach about recent boat arrivals. Similarly, on Christmas Island, locals and employees on the island on short-term contracts revealed things about their work with asylum seekers while they were drinking at local bars that they were otherwise meant to not discuss, after detention centre employees had signed non-disclosure contracts. Ethnographic encounters served us well and provided crucial information in both of these local settings.

2. Interviewing before and after the journey. Scholars have fruitfully pursued the strategy of researching boat migration once people have landed and are therefore in a safer setting from which to speak. Koser (2002) and van Liempt and Doomerink (2006), for example, both interviewed migrants smuggled into Europe about their journeys. Nancy Hiemstra (2013), Susan Coutin (2016) and others have interviewed people after their deportation home – another kind of hidden journey that one can speak about more safely once it has ended (see Hiemstra 2016 for a review of these approaches). Cuttitta also employs this approach in chapter 5 of this volume. They speak, then, with the safety of legal status and the time and space of reflection. In order to conduct this qualitative research on deportation, each scholar conducted research transnationally, relying on contacts in the destination country and building relationships of trust with families and social networks of deported migrants back home. In Hiemstra's (2013) case, for example, the research involved volunteer work with an organisation funded by the Ecuadorian government to advocate on behalf of Ecuadorian migrants to the United States. Hiemstra's volunteer work involved meeting families and searching for loved ones who had gone missing.

Another example of research conducted with the safety of temporal and spatial distance from the act of boat migration can be found in Ko Lin Chin's (2000) book *Smuggled Chinese*. Migration scholars and civil servants responding to human smuggling considered this text a primary source for knowledge of Chinese smuggling tactics and networks when it was published. Chin interviewed people after their journeys, about their journeys. They were thus able to speak from a safer distance, sometimes long after the journey had ended. Still other scholars such as Hamood (2008), de Haas (2007), Collyer (2007) and Mainwaring (2012), for example, also conducted detailed qualitative research – primarily through the use of interviews – with migrants smuggled by boat.

3. Working or volunteering around the edges of crisis. Often in humanitarian, voluntary capacity, working or volunteering around the edges of crisis is also a feasible and ethically sound way to conduct research while also participating in collective action to assist with the problems facing people rendered highly vulnerable through unauthorised migration at sea. Take, for example, *Médecins Sans Frontières* (MSF; known in English as Doctors without Borders) in its work over the years on the island of Lampedusa. In earlier years, MSF served people held inside of the detention facilities. But once the organisation felt compelled to report publicly on the poor conditions that existed in the facility, its employees were no longer allowed to work on the inside. Instead, the organisation worked on the dock in a tent, seeing migrants where they were offloaded. MSF workers explained to me that they would meet up later during the seasonal agricultural migration with people they had originally met and assisted on the dock. This humanitarian action and contact over time helped to build relationships of trust, making MSF workers knowledgeable about conditions facing migrants even when they are not able to board boats or enter facilities alongside government authorities.

During the 2011 crisis on Lampedusa that brought some 55,000 people to the island during the uprisings in North African countries, everyone on the island would come out to help at the docks when large boats arrived, including two of the largest arrivals in the history of boat migration to the island. This provided researchers on the island an opportunity to participate in collective response and action, to witness these moments first-hand, and to get to know workers and migrants.

Other researchers have volunteered on islands and other border transit points where the migration industry assembles during times of crisis and increased arrivals. Juanita Sundberg (2008) and Andrew Burridge (2009), for example, volunteered with organisations providing humanitarian assistance along the corridors into the EU and along the border between México and the United States.

4. Mapping journeys. Because boat migration often involves activities and territory where government officials actively and intentionally try to obfuscate people and information, mapping becomes a powerful tool pursued by activists and researchers alike to locate and reveal. While the need to map boat journeys seems apparent, there exist surprisingly few projects that involve mapping. Existing mapping projects have endeavoured to show the routes and locations of ships, as well as the location of migrant deaths at sea. Still others map the routes of deportation journeys (e.g., Hiemstra 2013). Migreurop (2013) has published an Atlas of Migration that spatially explicates relationships of power involved in migration to Europe. Another very well-known research project was Forensic Oceanography, based at Goldsmiths, University of London, which mapped the journey of a boat carrying migrants who died after the boat floundered in distress was left adrift although authorities were alerted to this distress (*Globe & Mail* 2014). The vessel came to be known as 'the left to die boat', and the multimedia mapping project and film *Liquid Traces* (Heller and Pezzani 2014) reconstructed the final days and whereabouts of those who died aboard the ship as well as the failings of the international community to rescue them.

Still other mapping projects are less expert but no less powerful in their effects and documentation of data. Researchers, such as Noelle Brigden (2016), have undertaken mental mapping exercises, working with migrants to map their own transnational journeys and share the violence they experienced along the way. Brigden's work is instructive and powerful. By asking people to map out their own transnational journeys, Brigden constructs an alternative cartography of migration. Such subaltern knowledge, while highly politicised, protected and criminalised by state authorities, is simply shared knowledge of life when viewed from alternative perspectives. These maps may demonstrate alternative understandings of time and space: periods of limbo spent waiting in migrant shelters, in detention facilities or in cities where one waits to employ the services of a human smuggler; and alternative mapping of sites of safety and danger, passage and protection.

While not *about* boats per se, Brigden's work can be applied to research on boat migration. People travelling by boat similarly pursue routes dedicated to moving away from encounters with authorities and towards points of entry and safe passage. Their recollections may well offer a more direct way of accessing information about maritime journeys than formal data sets assembled by state authorities.

5. Considering boats as part of larger, transnational landscapes of emotion and affect, haunting and trauma. Often, boat migration is but one leg of a much larger, segmented transnational journey that individuals and families undertake over years and across multiple international borders and nation-states (Collyer 2007; de Haas 2007). People travelling by boat often spend prolonged periods of time in confined spaces, whether on the ship, in detention or in limbo somewhere in between points of departure and arrival. These are transnational landscapes of emotion where life unfolds, not only over the course of the journey and the individual's lifetime but also across generations; these are not to be overlooked by researchers. Many geographical locations of the transnational journey – such as time spent in border cities or camps, or life's memories played out over the course of many years and passed on to children – may offer opportunities to study and understand meanings of boat migration without actually boarding or directly observing boats themselves.

I used this approach in one published analysis of findings from the island detention project (Mountz 2017). In particular, I analysed the eruption of trauma in discussions that were recorded and transcribed from interviews and attempted to place these eruptions both historically amid colonial landscapes and spatial among transnational communities, households and families that are deeply affected by boat migration and detention. Kate Coddington (2017) has written about the trauma associated with research with asylum seekers who travelled by boat and its consequences in secondary fashion by researchers. As geographers, we explored recent scholarship in geography, for example, on landscapes of emotion and affect and geographies of trauma. Van Selm (in chapter 6) also applies a similar methodology in understanding the intersection of multi-scalar geopolitics over transnational spaces, and their impacts on migrants themselves.

6. Using mobile methods that connect researchers to people moving among places. Whereas the previous suggestion involved in situ methods among mobile people, another methodological alternative involves mobile methods that connect researchers to people moving among places, like the boats that carry them. Here, researchers may borrow from methods honed in mobility studies (e.g., Cresswell 2006) that offer not only methods to study movement while moving but also conceptual devices to connect people and phenomena in vastly distant and different locales. Cindi Katz's (2001) counter-topography, for example, endeavours to map the operation of capitalism across different locations. Similarly, transnational, multi-sited ethnography offers tools to study communities and families that may be spread and operate across vast territories (Marcus 1995).

7. Assembling databases from media and other data sources. Kira Williams addresses this approach in chapter 3. Williams offers a state of the art approach that works the edges of knowledge dissemination and tests the limits of authorities' ability to hide information about human migration. For Williams, as for others, access to/freedom of information requests proves a key mechanism through which to request information that might otherwise remain hidden from the public. Williams and the author also assembled an earlier database that relied on published media sources to assemble a database of boat losses; their publication includes discussion of the attendant biases and limitations to these data. Another large project conducted by Spijkerboer and co-authors (2015) utilised data gathered in morgues in small jurisdictions across the borderlands of the European Union, in an effort to contend precisely with the shortcomings of research that relies on publicly available data. Campesi (in chapter 4), Cuttitta (in chapter 5), Burroughs (in chapter 7) and Binotto and Bruno (in chapter 8) likewise assemble databases from a variety of data sources to triangulate their findings in this volume.

8. Becoming embedded. Journalists and researchers became embedded with the migrants in their journeys, like Ted Conover (1987) who crossed the Mexico-US border and wrote a book on the subject. Similarly, some years later, Ruben Martinez (2002) followed families in their transnational journeys for his book. And Italian investigative journalist Gotti notoriously hired a smuggler to travel by boat and end up in detention on Lampedusa island in order to report on the location.

Social media and participant documentation with cell phones also offer creative opportunities to document hidden journeys. Consider one recent example. The British Broadcasting Corporation (BBC 2016) recently used a creative approach to film a documentary about boat migration across the Mediterranean Sea. Rather than travel with migrants, journalists provided them with cell phones and encouraged them to record their journeys and report with the cell phones. The result is a harrowing footage that at times transcends the ability of social scientists or authors to write *about* these experiences.

9. Examining material culture or things that move onto and off boats. Thus far, I have focused in this text on people travelling by boat and on how to build knowledge based on their knowledge, memory and migration history. But in my own research, I have also learnt from the ways that authorities themselves study material items in their investigations of boat migration. When conducting ethnographic research on 1999 boat migrations from China to Canada, for example, government authorities had discovered US currency and paper maps and navigational charts on board the ships. The maps and charts and currency proved essential to their investigation because the crew had jettisoned cell phones and other equipment that would provide digital evidence of the boat's cartographic trajectory. The maps and the currency contributed to evidence that travellers on board were headed to the United States with the intention of transiting through Canada.

Similarly, in our research on detention facilities on islands, we learnt from the material goods and infrastructure to transport them. In order to service and sustain mass detention on remote islands, many people and items had to be brought to the islands: food, water, medical supplies, workers and associated infrastructure such as additional flights and ships. Whereas accessing the detention facilities themselves proved difficult, following the material goods and people who moved in and out of the facilities on a daily basis provided another realm of knowledge and data through which to understand detention and the boat journeys through which detainees arrived there.

10. Exploring visual methods. As some of the examples discussed thus far in this chapter demonstrate, an interdisciplinary range of approaches to understanding boat migration prove helpful in more fully demonstrating the meanings of the boat and people's journeys over time. In her book *Ru*, for example, Kim Thúy uses various forms of writing – mixing autobiography, fiction, poetry and essay – to discuss the journey and its meaning over time and across generations. Her medium is writing, its material form the book. Still others have used visual methods such as filming and mapping (e.g., Brigden 2016). Like written texts, filming can be part of social science, something that happens alongside and in conjunction with research, and something that is conducted by travellers themselves, as in the case of the BBC (2016) documentary *Exile*. The film became not only a living record of the journey of several individuals and families but also an artistic form with a life of its own. The film was viewed widely by the general public, used as an organising and fundraising tool in various national contexts.

CONCLUSION

This chapter has considered the myriad challenges to studying boat migration and proposed ten methodological strategies to overcome or work around them. Without doubt, there are countless more. The life-threatening and charged emotional dimensions of migration by boat lend urgency to the project of creative thinking about how to better understand human migration with these vehicles. And yet this chapter represents a mere start, a brief conversation in a much longer dilemma that shows no sign of abating in the near future as levels of displacement rise, and state investments in policing, fencing, interception and detention increase.

While research on boat migration has expanded in recent years, much work remains to be done. Scholars can better put to use the many exciting methodological innovations happening around them, from uses of smartphones to map emotions and emotional landscapes, to participatory mapping methods. Collaboration with activists, migrants and migrant advocacy organisations proves a fruitful and important way forward; volunteering and collaboration offer the possibility of working through the vast power differentials that distinguish between migrants and researchers and their varied access to resources and mobilities. Finally, reliance on visual and textual methods such as the documentary film and novel discussed in this text offers chances to portray meanings of boat journeys that may be more difficult when subjected to some of the limitations of socially scientific research.

BIBLIOGRAPHY

Brigden, Noelle, 'Improvised Transnationalism: Clandestine Migration at the Border of Anthropology and International Relations', *International Studies Quarterly* 60, no. 2 (2016): 343.

British Broadcasting Corporation (BBC), 'Exodus: Our Journey to Europe', 2016, accessed 1 July 2017. http://www.bbc.co.uk/programmes/b07ky6ft

Burridge, Andrew, 'Differential Criminalization under Operation Streamline: Challenges to Freedom of Movement and Humanitarian Aid Provision in the Mexico-US Borderlands', *Refuge* 26, no. 2 (2009): 78.

Coddington, Kate, and Mountz, Alison, 'Countering Isolation with Use of Technology: How Asylum-Seeking Detainees on Islands in the Indian Ocean Use Social Media to Transcend Their Confinement', *Journal of the Indian Ocean Region* 10, no. 1 (2014): 97.

Collyer, Michael, 'In-between Places: Trans-Saharan Transit Migrants in Morocco and the Fragmented Journey to Europe', *Antipode* 39, no. 4 (2007): 668.

Conover, Ted, *Coyotes: A Journey across Borders with America's Illegal Migrants* (New York: Vintage Books, 1987).

Coutin, Susan, *Exiled Home: Salvadoran Transnational Youth in the Aftermath of Violence* (Durham: Duke University Press, 2016).

Cowen, Deborah, *The Deadly Life of Logistics: Mapping Violence in Global Trade* (Minneapolis: University of Minnesota Press, 2014).

Cresswell, Timothy, *On the Move: Mobility in the Western World* (London: Taylor and Francis, 2006).

De Haas, Hein, 'The Myth of Invasion: Irregular Migration from West Africa to the Maghreb and the European Union', International Migration Institute policy paper (2007).

Globe & Mail, 'Report Cites Collective Failure to Aid "Left to Die" Boat', 7 June 2014, A17.

Hamood, Sara, 'EU–Libya Cooperation on Migration: A Raw Deal for Refugees and Migrants?', *Journal of Refugee Studies* 21, no. 1 (2008): 19.

Heller, Charles, and Pezzani, Lorenzo, 'Liquid Traces: The Left-to-Die Boat Case', 2014, accessed 1 July 2017. https://vimeo.com/89790770

Heyman, Josiah, 'Ports of Entry as Nodes in the World System', *Identities: Global Studies in Culture and Power* 11, no. 3 (2004): 303.

Hiemstra, Nancy, 'Deportation and Detention: Interdisciplinary Perspectives, Multi-scalar Approaches, and New Methodological Tools', *Migration Studies* 4, no. 3 (2016): 433.

Hiemstra, Nancy, '"You Don't Even Know Where You Are": Chaotic Geographies of U.S. Migrant Detention and Deportation', in *Carceral Spaces: Mobility and Agency in Imprisonment and Migrant Detention*, edited by Conlon, Deidre, Morgan, Dominique, and Gill, Nick (Farnham, Surrey: Ashgate, 2013).

Jones, Reece. *Violent Borders: Refugees and the Right to Move* (London: Verso, 2016).

Koser, Khalid, 'Asylum Policies, Trafficking and Vulnerability', *International Migration* 38, no. 3 (2000): 91.

Maillet, Pauline, Mountz, Alison, and Williams, Kira, 'Researching Migration and Enforcement in Obscured Places: Practical, Ethical and Methodological Challenges to Fieldwork', *Social and Cultural Geography* 18, no. 7 (2017): 927.

Mainwaring, Cetta, 'Resisting Distalization? Malta and Cyprus' Influence on EU Migration and Asylum Policies', *Refugee Studies Quarterly* 31, no. 4 (2012): 38.

Marcus, George, 'The Emergence of Multi-Sited Ethnography', *Annual Review of Anthropology* 24, no. 1 (1995): 95.

Martinez, Ruben, *Crossing Over: A Mexican Family on the Migrant Trail* (New York: Picador, 2002).

Migreurop, *The Atlas of Migration in Europe: A Critical Geography of Migration Policies*. (Oxford: Internationalist Publications, 2013).

Mountz, Alison, 'Island Detention: Affective Eruption as Trauma's Disruption', *Emotion, Space and Society* 24, no. 1 (2017): 74.

Mountz, Alison, and Hiemstra, Nancy, 'Chaos and Crisis: Dissecting the Spatio-temporal Logics of Contemporary Migrations and State Practices', *Annals of the Association of American Geographers* 104, no. 2 (2013): 382.

Paglen, Trevor, and Thompson, Adam, *Torture Taxi* (Hoboken, NJ: Melville House, 2006).

Perera, Suvendrini, *Survival Media: The Politics and Poetics of Mobility and the War in Sri Lanka* (New York: Palgrave Macmillan, 2016).

Schiavenza, Matt, 'Asia's Looming Refugee Disaster: Hundreds of Burma's Rohingya Muslims Remain Adrift at Sea – and Nobody Wants to Take Them', *The Atlantic*, 17 May 2015, accessed 1 July 2017. https://www.theatlantic.com/international/archive/2015/05/asias-looming-refugee-disaster/393482/

Spijkerboer, Thomas, Last, Tamara, Cuttitta, Paolo, Baird, Theodore, and Ulusoy, Orcun, 'Human Costs of Border Control', 2015, accessed 1 July 2017. http://www.borderdeaths.org/

Steinberg, Phillip, 'Insularity, Sovereignty and Statehood: The Representation of Islands on Portolan Charts and the Construction of the Territorial State', *Geographiska Annaler* 87, no. 4 (2005): 253.

Sundberg, Juanita, 'Trash-Talk and the Production of Quotidian Geopolitical Boundaries in the USA-Mexico Borderlands', *Social & Cultural Geography* 9, no. 8 (2008): 871.

Thúy, Kim, *Ru* (London: Random House, 2012).

Van Liempt, Ilse, and Doomernik, Joroen, 'Migrant's Agency in the Smuggling Process: The Perspectives of Smuggled Migrants in the Netherlands', *International Migration* 44, no. 4 (2006): 165.

Walters, William, "Bordering the Sea: Shipping Industries and the Policing of Stowaways', *Borderlands E-Journal* 7, no. 3 (2008): 1.

Walters, William, 'The Flight of the Deported: Aircraft, Deportation, and Politics', *Geopolitics* 21, no. 2 (2016): 435.

Weber, Leanne, and Pickering, Sharon, *Globalization and Borders: Deaths at the Global Frontier* (London: Palgrave Macmillan, 2011).

Williams, Kira, 'Arriving Somewhere, Not Here: Exploring and Mapping the Relationship between Border Enforcement and Migration by Boat in the Central Mediterranean Sea, 2006 to 2015', PhD thesis, Wilfrid Laurier University, 2018.

Williams, Kira, and Mountz, Alison, 'Rising Tide: Analyzing the Relationship between Externalization and Migrant Deaths and Boat Losses', in *Externalizing Migration Management: Europe, North America and the Spread of Remote Control*, edited by Zaiotti, Ruben (London: Routledge, 2016).

Chapter 3

Review of and Research Proposal for Methodologies Studying Migrant Interdiction at Sea

Kira Williams

INTRODUCTION

In this chapter, I define and describe maritime interdiction operations (MIOs), identify current issues in studying them and propose eleven methodologies to move forward in future research. A typical operation has multiple components, including, but not limited to, sea surveillance, boat interdiction, detention, migrant interviews and inter-agency coordination in data construction and sharing. Examples of key issues in studying these operational components include data availability, different definitions, divergences in recording, power relations, reluctance to self-report and data destruction. Based on current limitations and advantages of different methodologies, I argue that a mixed methodology combining critical, grounded, historical and correlational methodologies is most appropriate for studying migrant interdiction at sea. Scholars would initially use critical theory in order to identify and understand causal mechanisms. Selected actors and processes would then in turn be empirically described and verified by historical and correlational methodologies. While I argue that this approach would directly address most current data issues in studying boat migration, other issues would remain. I therefore advise future researchers to use additional tools to compensate for these specific problems.

The chapter proceeds as follows. First, I form a brief definition and history of MIOs and how these operations relate to international migration governance. I then identify current issues in studying such operations, including how to specify and conceptualise migrants, boats and operations as units of analysis. I continue by exploring and discussing existing appropriate research methodologies to study these objects. Combining some of these methodologies, I finally provide a proposal by which to give general methodological direction to future researchers. I close the chapter by expanding on issues with my proposal.

CONTEXT: MARITIME INTERDICTION OPERATIONS

Here I identify and describe maritime interdiction operations (MIOs) in order to frame potential methodological approaches to describing, explaining and predicting them. MIOs attempt to prevent the entry of undocumented migrants at sea. These operations have become a regular tool of wealthier states in managing migration through a policy of containment. As a whole, operations at sea are an international mobility governance mechanism; however, their multiple activities separately constitute different mechanisms at the same time. For example, sea surveillance and migrant interviews are surveillance mechanisms, as shown in chapter 9. In theory, the governance character of these mechanisms is that they intend to influence migrant behaviour on an international scale (Barnett 2002, 239; Lavenex and Wichmann 2009, 86; Martin 2012, 1047). Demonstrating which mechanisms are governance mechanisms, moreover, would require empirical research beyond the scope of this chapter. The fact that MIOs and transnational migrants at sea pose challenges to governance supports this finding. Two modes by which MIOs oppose broader migration governance are contestation of sovereignty through territory and population management.

Current literature in border studies has yet to examine the origin and development of MIOs. Western European states developed organised maritime interdiction as a strategy to achieve their military objectives by blockading enemy states (Jones 1983, 760; Morabito 1997; Ziegler 1995). They later formalised and implemented international law concerning how interdiction should occur. To avoid war while maintaining their enforcement powers, imperial powers created new interdiction instruments, one of which later evolved into MIOs. In migration studies, modern MIOs attempt to prevent the entry of undocumented migrants into a state at sea, often defined by its territory or jurisdiction (Guilfoyle 2009, 90, 189–90; Palmer 1996, 1565).

MIOs have become a critical part of understanding international migration at sea. The issue of containment at sea first emerged after growing concern over the movement of 'boat people' from Southeast Asia in the 1970s (Gammeltoft-Hansen 2008; Lutterbeck 2006). These concerns were reinforced by the publicity of migrant boat incidents worldwide and the security threats that they posed, as further explored in chapter 6 (Pugh 2004). Since that time, a host of wealthier states, led by Australia, Canada, the European Union (EU) and the United States, have practised regular MIOs to manage migration at sea (Loyd and Mountz forthcoming; Mountz 2010,

128, 136). This evolved in parallel with state and media discourses of 'crisis', as described in chapters 7 and 8. A typical MIO has multiple components, including, but not limited to, sea surveillance, boat interdiction, detention, migrant interviews and inter-agency coordination in data construction and sharing (Ziegler 1995). For example, the EU, through Frontex, its coordinating border agency, featured assets for most of these activities in its Joint Operation Triton (table 3.1) (Frontex 2014b). Decoupling the activities present in a MIO demonstrates two points. First, the components of operations at sea aid in constituting multiple mechanisms affecting migrants. Second, the combination of mechanisms found in operations at sea may in turn become a governance mechanism.

Disaggregated, the activities comprising MIOs fall into multiple categories of mechanisms. Sea surveillance is a surveillance mechanism. It measures and monitors the distinction between those with legal residency status within the EU and undocumented migrants coming from outside (chapter 6). The purpose of producing this spatial distinction is to map the location of migrants, as a population group, relative to the state's jurisdiction (Maillet, Mountz and Williams 2017). Boat interdiction, in turn, is an international mobility mechanism: It attempts to manage migrants as a population group by influencing their movement. When undocumented migrants are detected via surveillance, state navies or coast guards interdict them to prevent freedom of movement.

MIOs matter because state border enforcement authorities frequently use them to detain or interdict migrants for processing and subject them to an expedited immigration process (Williams 2018). During detention, state officials interview the migrants to collect information on their characteristics and routes of travel. This additional surveillance mechanism

Table 3.1. List of Assets Involved in Sample Maritime Interdiction Operation (Joint Operation *Triton*)

Activity	Assets Deployed	Cost per Month (Millions 2014 Euros)
Sea Surveillance	2 Fixed-wing aircraft	1.06
	1 Helicopter	0.3
Boat Interdiction	3 Coastal patrol vessels	1.02
	2 Coastal patrol boats	0.18
Migrant Interviews	7 Debriefing teams	0.21
Inter-Agency Coordination	Staff and core infrastructure	0.04
	Floating storage and offloading	0.01
	Naval HQ office	0.01
Total	–	**2.83**

Source: Frontex (2014b).

helps state bureaucrats plan future tactics. The governance character of these mechanisms is that they intend to influence migrant behaviour. State coordination in surveillance and interdiction operations (e.g., through Frontex) reveals their quest for an international geography. The EU, for example, has signed many bilateral treaties with North African states, funds International Organization for Migration projects in known sending regions and develops its policy from the actions and experiences of states like Australia and the United States (European Commission 2011; Loyd and Mountz forthcoming; Mountz 2010, 121; Ronzitti 2009, 125). It also shares surveillance data with third-party states (Aas 2011, 333; Mathiesen 2004). So while MIOs, as a whole, intend to manage migrant movement and are therefore international mobility mechanisms, their constituent activities are also part of larger governance mechanisms like surveillance.

So far, I have argued for but not demonstrated that MIOs and their activities are part of governance mechanisms. Such a demonstration would require empirical research showing how these social structures affect individual behaviour – which is beyond the scope of this chapter but is partly addressed in chapter 4. From a theoretical perspective, bilateral (or multilateral) operations and transnational migrants at sea pose a number of challenges to establishing governance. One challenge is that states have incentives to compete with each other in trying to manage population movement. As we will see in chapter 5, international and customary law divides the world's seas into a variety of geographies which do not coincide with and are not considered sovereign territory (Coppens 2013; Steinberg 2001, 2009). Many states have laid jurisdictional claims in areas such as search and rescue or resource rights beyond the limits of their territory (Gammeltoft-Hansen 2008). Conflicts emerge where claims overlap and migrant bodies become sites of contestation (Gregory 2006; Mountz 2013). The governments of Italy and Malta, for instance, have been in a protracted battle over the jurisdiction of their humanitarian obligations to assist ships in distress at sea since at least 2006 (Bialasiewicz 2012; di Pascale 2010). This spat has limited cooperation in the Central Mediterranean in forming larger-scale governance mechanisms (see chapter 4). In a similar way, states, nations and territory as social structures may inhibit coordination where their interests clash. MIOs can thus be a means by which states compete in interests over space.

MIOs also matter because states may use them to compete in their population management goals. While these objectives vary, a number of scholars agree that enforcing border policy is critical in maintaining sovereignty via social exclusion (Aas 2011, 333; Basch, Glick-Schiller and Szanton-Blanc 1997, 183–84). Insofar as operations at sea exist and expand, then, they reinforce the nation as sovereign within a given space, even if that space is not that state's territory (Maillet, Mountz and Williams 2018). Stronger states are less likely to make the capacity bargains which typically lead to networks of governance (Geddes and Taylor 2013, 52). States can make use of migrants at sea to achieve these co-opting negative discourses in justifying crises which generate dramatic changes in policy (chapter 7; Mountz 2010). Differing state policies on population management (e.g., supporting emigration) reveal limitations on their ability to control migration through containment (Elden 2009; Samers 2010, 181). Movement itself, thus, can highlight the limits of sovereignty and create social anxiety about global conditions (chapter 5; Appadurai 2001, 36–37). If nations seek to quell this anxiety through reinforcing the state, then the operations at sea made therein pose a challenge to the global migration regime, especially for asylum seekers and refugees.

APPROPRIATE RESEARCH METHODOLOGIES TO STUDY MIGRANT INTERDICTION AT SEA

A core scientific problem of the importance of maritime interdiction is how to approach studying it. Identifying which approaches to do so are most appropriate requires an appraisal of their relative benefits and consequences. This section therefore examines which methodologies are available and describes their potential benefits and consequences. Selecting the most appropriate method requires a specification of what is being studied, identification of key study issues and a list of appropriate methodologies. Six major issues in understanding these objects are data availability, different definitions, divergences in recording, power relations, reluctance to report and data destruction. A review of the literature offers eleven appropriate methodologies to address these issues. A brief description and critique of each methodology follow to understand the advantages and limitations of each methodology in studying migrant boat interdiction at sea.

Specification of and Issues with the Units of Analysis

In order to discuss issues and possibilities in studying migrant interdiction at sea, it is necessary to specify its units of analysis and their associated characteristics. There are three analytical objects. MIOs are first, along with their geographies, timelines, budgets, political structures and participating actors.[1] Second are boats interdicted at sea, including their geographies, numbers of passengers, legal statuses, types and subsequent enforcement responses (see chapter 3).[2] Third are the migrants involved and their characteristics, such as entry numbers, origin, destination, legal status, health status[3] and subsequent enforcement response. I chose these units of analysis due to their relevance to migrant interdiction at sea with respect to international migration; they are the focus of this chapter.

MIOs, boats and migrants as units of analysis have limitations which should be acknowledged. Trying to separate migrants from boats and MIOs can be helpful in understanding international migration; however, it tends not to be, because separation obscures causal mechanisms relating the three through selection bias. This claim calls into question what is meant by 'understanding' and 'helpful'. The philosophy of science employs multiple concepts of understanding, such as truth, falsifiability and verifiability (Lauden 1981, 144; Salmon 1984). From a pragmatic perspective, the analytical use of objects in migration studies is to assist in constructing a logical framework of known social relations in determining migration outcomes using these concepts (Little 1991, 4–5). Relations which connect a series of characteristics, through events, to a given outcome in the world are called 'causal mechanisms' (ibid., 15).[4] Statistical approaches cannot solely establish these mechanisms, because they are limited in isolating the micro-level ways in which social relations affect behaviour (Achen 2002, 443). I therefore argue that models of MIOs, boats and migrants are not instrumental but rather meant to make inductive generalisations about causal mechanisms operating in the real world (Hausman 1992; Sugden 2010, 1). Models are not the migrants but instead serve as heuristics by which to understand, explain and act upon migrants (Ruhs and Anderson 2010, 10, 30).

Framing MIOs, boats and migrants as units of analysis can also create migrant behaviour instead of reflecting it. Which methodologies we select to study them then can have substantial social consequences. This is possible because categorisation is a type of power relation, one which alters migrant agency. State and scholarly attempts to empirically measure and order migration have therefore changed its causal mechanisms (Burawoy 1998, 11–14). This obscures understanding because researchers and policymakers assume these identifications to be true when, in fact, they are artefacts of studying international migration. Mobility scholars, by contrast, have proposed a number of conceptualisations of movement imbued with meaning, power, place and time (Cresswell 2006, 3; Urry 2000, 186). These 'nomadic ontologies' are opposed to what Cresswell (2006, 25) calls 'sedentarism', or the idea that people and places are mostly fixed. Migration theory remains sedentarist, with migrant categories rescaling complex and dynamic social relations into simple, static notions of identity and place. Without critical examination, deployment of these categories in studying migration by boat is not helpful in understanding movement, since their analytical objects and empirical measurements capture only an oversimplified and biased perspective. It is thus necessary to explore the construction and deployment of such objects themselves as a core part of research on migration by boat.

Issues in Studying Migrant Interdiction at Sea

There are a number of issues in studying MIOs, boats and migrants. This subsection identifies the most prevalent problems in the literature in parallel with those in chapter 3. Relevant data are frequently absent or insufficient to describe the phenomena of interest in international migration (Bijak 2010, 16–17; Hennebry and Preibisch 2010, 16; Massey and Zenteno 1999; McLeman 2013, 604–5). Availability varies by region, with many states publishing little to no data on interdiction at sea. Table 3.2 illustrates data availability for the Mediterranean Sea from 2006 to 2015, which has no data for a variety of characteristics. For example, EU authorities have not recorded or publicly reported the types of boats they detect or interdict at sea. Sometimes data do exist, but their method of estimation renders them invalid; that is, they fail to accurately measure what researchers intend them to.

Frontex records undocumented migrant entries at sea in its quarterly reports, but these numbers do not include many of those detected or interdicted at sea before arrival (Frontex 2017).[5] It is also possible that there are valid data on interdictions at sea, but they are incomplete or unreliable. Although major boat and migrant losses, for instance, are commonly reported in the EU media, the coverage is incomplete, and the generating process for those observed remains unclear.[6] Even where data are available and complete, they may be currently inaccessible. There is a record of boats interdicted and detected by Frontex, but it is not publicly available (Williams 2018). Data gaps increase error and bias in estimating descriptive statistics, relationships or interdictions at sea. Sufficiently large gaps may render estimation altogether infeasible (Greene 1993, 275).

Different definitions, divergences in recording, power relations, reluctance to report and data destruction are additional issues in studying MIOs, boats and migrants. Data recorded in different regions often use different definitions for measurement (Bijak 2010, 15; Ellis and Wright 1998, 129–31; Rogers 2008, 276–83). Where definitions cannot be mapped to equivalent

Table 3.2.   Summary of Data Availability Issues in Interdiction at Sea, Mediterranean Sea, 2006–2015

Issue	*Example*	*Source*
There are no data.	Boat types	–
There are data, but they are not valid.	Migrant entry counts	Jandl (2004)
There are data and they are valid, but they are incomplete or unreliable.	Boat and migrant losses	Williams and Mountz (2016)
There are data and they are valid and complete or reliable, but they are currently inaccessible.	Boat detections and interdictions	Frontex (2014)

concepts or such a mapping strips too much information, aggregation of data to achieve a larger sample size or wider geographic scale is biased (Cramer 1964; Greene 1993, 279; Massey and Capoferro 2007, 259–65). The time or frequency at which groups collect data may also vary, rendering direct comparison of traditional sources of information in migration difficult or impossible (Hoffman and Lawrence 1996, 35–42; Ozden et al. 2011, 12).

Power relations alter data definition, collection and storage by influencing research objectives and uses (Burawoy 1998, 23). States may have incentive to falsely measure, collect and report data or lack the capacity to properly do so (Ley 2003, 432–35). Data construction, as a whole, embeds existing social hierarchies through rationalism such as racism, sexism, classicism and sedentarism (Cresswell 2006, 95–107; Silvey and Lawson 1999, 124–26; Urry 2000, 186–88; Walton-Roberts 2004, 362). Undocumented migrants, typical of interdiction at sea, tend not to self-report their legal status on surveys due to fear of penalty (Andersson and Nilsson 2009, 169–70; Heckmann 2004; Massey and Zenteno 1999). Finally, authorities sometimes redefine or even destroy data in order to reduce their potential political effects. In the Central Mediterranean, for example, there previously were no public data on 2010 migrant entries into Italy despite clear reports of boat arrivals (Alison Mountz, personal communication, 25 October 2014).

Appropriate Research Methodologies

An appropriate approach to studying migrant interdiction at sea must address the previously mentioned limitations. The stakes in doing this are high: given the social importance of migrant interdiction at sea, selecting inappropriate methodologies to study them could have far-reaching social consequences. This subsection presents a nearly exhaustive list of potential study methodologies to be used in conjunction with the proposed ways forward in chapter 3.[7] A detailed description of these methodologies, their applications and limitations is beyond the scope of this chapter. Table 3.3, instead, summarises these eleven methodologies and some of their major problems. I chose these methodologies based on a subjective reading of the literature and their applicability to interdictions at sea. We can summarise social science research methodologies as qualitative or quantitative based on their philosophical commitments, often referred to as *positivist* and *post- or antipositivist*, respectively (King, Keohane and Verba 1994, 3–7). Scholars build this division upon the fact-value distinction, or the Humean claim that normative statements cannot be derived from positive ones (Putnam 2002). Method selection may also represent community norms insofar as scholars consider them 'scientific' (Haas 1992, 3–12). Each method features a brief description

Table 3.3. Summary of Appropriate Research Methodologies for Migrant Interdiction at Sea

Type	Method	Description	Scale; Source	Major Problems
Qualitative	Pragmatic	Use best methods available	Micro/Macro; Primary/ Secondary	Insufficient specification
	Ethnographic	Capture social meanings and ordinary activities	Micro; Primary	Biased sampling
	Grounded	Infer research or theory from data collected	Micro/Macro; Secondary	Limitations of induction
	Critical	Understand symbols and communication of meaning	Micro/Macro; Secondary	Theory/Practice Problem
	Historical	Discuss past conditions in context of present	Macro; Secondary	Biased sampling
	Content Analysis	Study and interpret communications	Micro/Macro; Secondary	Data availability and causation
Quantitative	Experimental	Randomly select a group for treatment	Micro; Primary	Infeasible and likely invalid
	Quasi- Experimental	Select two or more different groups for treatment	Micro; Primary	Infeasible and likely invalid
	Natural Experimental	Observe groups naturally subjected to random treatment	Micro/Macro; Primary	Infeasible
	Correlational	Infer relationships from secondary data	Micro/Macro; Secondary	Data availability and causation
	Simulation	Imitate process in a deductive system with empirical elements	Micro/Macro; Primary	Limitations of deduction

Source: Author, as adapted from Denzin and Lincoln (2005), King, Keohane and Verba (1994), Lewis-Beck, Bryman and Liao (2004) and Neuendorf (2002).

of the method as well as its usual scale of analysis and source of data. Source, in this context, refers to whether researchers produce data directly (primary) or collect from another source (secondary). A review of the migration by boat literature suggests that a wide variety of methodologies, scales and sources of data are present in the field. It is from these sources that this chapter will propose a generalised methodology for moving forward.

The ability of these designs to estimate MIOs, boat and migrant statistics has limitations. On the qualitative side, pragmatic and grounded theory approaches suffer from insufficient specification to guide the researcher in studying the analytical object (Pratt 2012, 2). Grounded theory, in addition, is limited by the ability of induction to make valid claims about the world (ibid., 3). Additionally, correlation between social relations and events cannot prove causation; we must test inductive regularities against migration theory (Kuhn 1996; Little 1991, 16). Ethnographic and historical approaches provide detailed context by which to understand causal mechanisms; however, key informants, locations, documents and even time can often only be selected in ways which significantly skew sampling (Freeman 1983; Thies 2002, 355).[8] Critical theory emphasises the importance of philosophical assumptions and commitment in understanding social processes but widely neglects practice (empiricism) in favour of theory (Bohman 2013). Empiricism in social science is important insofar as it directs our attention to human activity itself and not simply its logical relationships (Dewey 1954, 9). Finally, content analysis lends understanding the production of documents, including target audience, policies, politics and financial support, but document availability constrains its use (Sommer and Sommer 1991, 362). It is also not usually effective in sorting out causal mechanisms.

Quantitative methodologies may initially appear more promising in understanding migrant interdiction at sea but experience feasibility and validity issues. Experimental and quasi-experimental designs require selecting among undocumented migrants or state actors who lack incentive to self-report. Studies along these lines would likely be conducted in laboratory settings, where controlled conditions would remove the causal mechanisms most relevant in behaviour and render results invalid (Little 1991, 18). While a natural experiment solves the issue of subject selection, it necessitates an in-depth study of a MIO from start to finish which is simply infeasible at this time. This is possible because states design operations to be covert, making direct observation of all of their activities difficult.

Correlational studies are similar to content analyses in that they are limited by data availability and explanation of causal relationships (Shaughnessy, Zechmeister and Zechmeister 2014). If data were available, however, then a correlational study could explore interdictions at sea in an empirical way mostly previously absent in the literature (Williams and Mountz 2016). Simulation, via agent-based modelling, is an increasingly used approach in the field (An 2012, 25; Kniveton, Smith and Wood 2011, 534). These models are useful in understanding how the individual actions of agents can affect system behaviour and outcomes over time but are problematic to deploy due to the deductive limits of theory (Crooks, Castle and Batty 2008, 422). Scholars have also yet to sufficiently formalise traditional theories of international migration to be used in simulation (Bijak 2010, 47–50).

PROPOSAL: A MIXED METHODOLOGY TO STUDY
MIGRANT INTERDICTION AT SEA

Based on available methodologies and limitations previously noted, I propose that a mixed methodology combining critical, grounded, historical and correlational methodologies is most appropriate for studying migrant interdiction at sea. This approach bases itself upon critical theory which, in turn, is empirically described and verified by historical and correlation methodologies. Findings update understanding of causal mechanisms through a grounded theory method. I identify a number of potential sources of qualitative and quantitative data. The proposed approach directly handles three of the six methodological issues mentioned previously in the 'Appropriate Research Methodologies to Study Migrant Interdiction at Sea' section. Further tools compensate for the remaining three challenges: different definitions, divergences in recording and data destruction.

Design

The analytical objects and limitations in researching them make a mixed methods approach most appropriate for studying migrant interdiction at sea. Though each of the eleven methodologies reviewed may be appropriate for different aspects of MIOs, boats or migrants, the most appropriate overall approach is an integration of critical, grounded, historical and correlational methodologies. This approach uses a critical, theoretical underpinning to study interdiction at sea using available documentation and data on MIOs, boats and migrants. In turn, the collected data allow researchers to update their research as it progresses with the ultimate goal of identification of causal mechanisms and verification of theory (table 3.4). The primary advantage of

Table 3.4. Summary of Mixed Methodology and Its Components

Stage	Methodologies	Purpose	Expected Outcomes
1. Theoretical formulation	Critical Theory	Identify and explore causal mechanisms and actors	Selection of theory List of relevant actors and processes
2. Empirical collection and verification	Correlational Historical	Describe and analyse actions and outcomes of mechanisms	Data collection Data analysis
3. Inference and updating	Grounded Theory	Compare outcomes to expectations; update research	Verification of theory New actors and processes

Source: authors own research.

the approach is to identify and describe causal mechanisms in a valid, empirical way which overcomes the limitations of each method on its own.

The reliability, validity and representativeness of a correlational study are desirable but are limited in practice (Burawoy 1998, 11–13). A theoretical, qualitative approach permits the identification and exploration of the actors relevant to causing migrant interdiction at sea. Critical theory useful for understanding social meaning is integral to this process. This approach would be relatively theory-eclectic, in the sense that a number of traditional migration theories could be used. Researchers would moreover complement theory with a concurrent empirical description and analysis of its characteristics in order to verify its outcomes. Important sources of historical data could include state policy documents and legislation, bilateral agreements and memoranda of understanding between states and archival information on operations from relevant actors. Scholars could enhance these data by interviews with key personnel or migrants.

Examples of correlational data could include MIO characteristics, boat losses and migrant losses. Multiple sources for these data exist, such as media reports, international organisation budgets, scholarly literature, police records, court documents and border agency statistical publications. The international migration literature has generally made poor use of a large number of unconventional data sources (Heckmann 2004; Hoffman and Lawrence 1996, 5–25; Jandl 2004, 146). One example are freedom of information requests, which Hutton (2014) used to generate a complete list of every boat interdicted by the Australian government from 2001 to 2013. Researchers would then conduct statistical analysis to search for relationships in the data to support or fail to support causal mechanisms in the theory. Statistical tools would include but not be limited to descriptive statistics, linear modelling, analysis of variance, time-series analysis and spatial analysis. Scholars could incorporate historical data using, for example, regression discontinuity analysis or differences-in-differences estimation. They would update existence, types and workings of causal mechanisms from these findings to inform additional research, beginning the cycle anew.

Potential Challenges

My proposed mixed methodology approach directly handles three of the six issues in the 'Appropriate Research Methodologies to Study Migrant Interdiction at Sea' section: data availability, incorporation of power relations and reluctance of subjects to self-report. The use of multiple and novel data sources provides sufficient data for the historical and correlational methodologies. A critical theoretical approach analyses power relations and their roles in social behaviour. A reluctance to self-report can be overcome by cross-comparing data for reliability and imputing gaps with least unbiased estimators.

The three outstanding problems are differences in definition, divergences in recording and data destruction. A small amount of literature has emerged in the past twenty years to deal with the first two issues. Methodologists in migration indirectly outline five tools for definition and recording issues: residual estimation, multiplier estimation, survey methods, capture-recapture methods and regularisation estimation (de Beer et al. 2010; Jandl 2004, 143–46; Raymer 2007, 986). While the applicability of these tools is highly contextual, it is likely that at least one will apply for a given MIO. For example, residual estimation allows one to impute the numbers of migrants entering, interdicted or missing at sea. Consider missing migrants as an example. In the Central Mediterranean case, it is possible to impute their count using current data by subtracting the total number of migrants detected during a MIO by the number who arrive or whom authorities interdict. Additional tools may also be applicable, such as proportional hazards modelling. With boat counts and loss rates becoming available in some regions (e.g., Australia), it may be possible to estimate hazard rates and thus interpolate boat and migrant losses.

International migration literature does not cover data destruction. Rarely, a secondary source may republish destroyed data. Even when it is not possible to retrieve data which has been destroyed, it is possible to keep multiple, secure records of data used in a study. There are data management standards in social science describing how nearly any type of data can be stored electronically for later use (DDIA 2014; ICPSR 2011). Bilateral treaties, for instance, can be collected and stored in generic formats (e.g.,. txt,. rtf or. pdf) on private servers for security. Beyond preservation, storing all data used in studying migrant interdiction at sea has two further benefits. Publication of data adds to public knowledge and awareness for interdiction at sea, which the public often poorly understands. Stored data are also reproducible for future researchers or policymakers to verify or expand upon findings. These methodologies compensate for but do not completely solve potential challenges in the mixed methodology. I have employed and tested this approach in my doctoral thesis, which I believe has allowed me to provide the first comprehensive, detailed account of the empirics of maritime interdictions operations (Williams 2018).

CONCLUSION

This chapter proposed that a mixed methodology is most appropriate for studying migrant interdiction at sea. This approach combined elements of critical, ground, historical and correlational methods to understand, empirically describe, analyse and update theory on causal mechanisms. I defined and described maritime interdiction operations to provide research context. After specification of the units of analysis, eleven appropriate methodologies to study migrant interdiction at sea and their limitations were explored. Six key study issues were data availability, different definitions, divergences in recording, power relations, reluctance to self-report and data destruction. Although the mixed methodology did not directly handle different definitions, divergences in recording and data destruction, there were additional potential compensations. These compensations would have further benefits to implementation, making their use preferable in studying migrant interdiction at sea.

NOTES

1. Lists of characteristics are not meant to be exhaustive. They, instead, reflect the information subjectively considered most relevant to the analytical objects.

2. That is, data on how enforcement authorities responded to the boat's detection.

3. That is, data on the health outcomes of migrants on board the ship. For example, how many migrants were injured or killed? How many were taken to hospital? For more specific information, see Weber and Pickering (2011).

4. It is assumed that these causal mechanisms are governed by a set of causal laws. In this case, events are causally related only if these laws move mechanisms from cause to effect (Little 1991: 15).

5. The origin of this discrepancy is complex. In summary, the number of migrants recorded as detected or intercepted in the Central Mediterranean Sea far exceeds the entries counts for the same time periods. Since most interdicted migrants were likely to enter the EU, this suggests that those who entered were purposely left unrecorded. These data, then, do not capture the true value of entries.

6. If the generating process were better understood, then it might be possible to infer the characteristics of the population from available samples.

7. 'Nearly exhaustive' because I exclude a number of methodologies as being irrelevant to the analytical objects. For example, a philosophical approach would not be useful in producing estimates of operations at sea. The list in table 1.3 is also non-exhaustive, since future theories may propose new methodologies and do not consider mixed methods.

8. It should be noted that the representativeness of the sample is not a major concern in some studies. There is a large body of literature reflecting the use of case study selection. For the purposes of generalisability, however, biased sampling poses a problem. For more information, see Liberman (2005) or Geddes (1990).

BIBLIOGRAPHY

Aas, Katja, '"Crimmigrant" Bodies and Bona Fide Travelers: Surveillance, Citizenship, and Global Governance', *Theoretical Criminology* 15, no. 3 (2011): 331.

Achen, Christopher, 'Toward a New Political Methodology: Microfoundations and ART', *Annual Review of Political Science* 5, no. 1 (2002): 423.

An, Li, 'Modeling Human Decisions in Coupled Human and Natural Systems: Review of Agent-Based Models', *Ecological Modelling* 229 (2012): 25.

Andersson, Hans, and Nilsson, Susanna, 'Asylum Seekers and Undocumented Migrants' Increased Social Rights in Sweden', *International Migration* 49, no. 4 (2011): 167.

Appadurai, Arjun, *Fear of Small Numbers: An Essay in the Geography of Fear* (Durham: Duke University Press, 2001).

Barnett, Laura, 'Global Governance and the Evolution of the International Refugee Regime', *International Journal of Refugee Law* 14, no. 2–3 (2002): 238.

Basch, Linda, Glick-Schiller, Nina, and Szanton-Blanc, Christima, *Nations Unbound: Transcolonial Projects, Postcolonial Predicaments, and Deterritorialized Nation-States,* second edition (Amsterdam: Gordon and Breach Publishers, 1997).

Bialasiewicz, Luisa, 'Off-Shoring and Out-Sourcing the Border of Europe: Libya and EU Border Work in the Mediterranean', *Geopolitics* 17, no. 4 (2012): 843.

Bijak, Jakub, *Forecasting International Migration in Europe: A Bayesian View* (London: Springer, 2010).

Bohman, James, 'Critical Theory'. In *The Stanford Encyclopedia of Philosophy* (Palo Alto: Stanford University, 2013). http://plato.stanford.edu/archives/spr2013/entries/critical-theory/

Burawoy, Michael, 'The Extended Case Method', *Sociological Theory* 16, no. 1 (1998): 4.

Coppens, Jasmine, 'The Lampedusa Disaster: How to Prevent Further Loss of Life at Sea?', *TransNav: The International Journal on Marine Navigation and Safety of Sea Transportation* 7, no. 4: 589.

Cramer, Jan, 'Efficient Grouping, Regression, and Correlation in Engle Curve Analysis', *Journal of the American Statistical Association* 54 (1964): 233.

Cresswell, Timothy, *On the Move* (New York: Routledge, 2006).

Crooks, Andrew, Castle, Christian, and Batty, Michael, 'Key Challenges in Agent-Based Modelling for Geo-Spatial Simulation', *Computers, Environment, and Urban Systems* 32, no. 6 (2008): 417.

Data Documentation Initiative Alliance (DDIA), 'DDI Specification'', accessed 1 July 2013. http://www.ddialliance.org/Specification/

de Beer, Joop, Raymer, James, van der Erf, Rob, and van Wissen, Leo, 'Overcoming the Problems of Inconsistent International Migration Data: A New Method Applied to Flows in Europe', *European Journal of Population* 26 (2010): 459.

Denzin, Norman, and Lincoln, Yvonna, ed., *The Sage Handbook of Qualitative Research*, third edition (Thousand Oaks: Sage, 2011).

Dewey, John, *The Public and Its Problems* (Athens: Ohio University Press, 1954).

di Pascale, Alessia, 'Migration Control at Sea: The Italian Case', in *Extraterritorial Immigration Control: Legal Challenges*, edited by Ryan, Bernard, and Mitsilegas, Valsamis (Leiden: Martinus Nijoff Publishers, 2010).

Elden, Stuart, *Terror and Territory: The Spatial Extent of Sovereignty* (Minneapolis: University of Minnesota Press, 2009).

Ellis, Mark, and Wright, Richard, 'When Immigrants Are Not Migrants: Counting Arrivals of the Foreign Born Using the US Census', *International Migration Review* 32, no. 1 (1998): 127.

European Agency for the Management of Operational Cooperation at the External Borders (Frontex), *Operations Division Joint Operations Unit. Concept of Reinforced Joint Operation Tackling the Migratory Flows towards Italy: JO EPN-Triton*. Brussels: European Union, 2014b.

European Agency for the Management of Operational Cooperation at the External Borders (Frontex), 'Publications: Risk Analysis', accessed 1 July 2017. http://frontex.europa.eu/publications/?c=risk-analysis

European Agency for the Management of Operational Cooperation at the External Borders (Frontex), 'Re: Total Migrants and Boats Detected, Intercepted, and Turned Back during JO HERMES, 2007; 2009–2014', accessed 1 July 2014a. http://www.asktheeu.org/en/request/re_total_migrants_and_boats_dete#outgoing-3141

European Union. European Commission, *Communication from the Commission to the European Parliament, the Council, the European Economic and Social Committee and the Committee of the Regions: A Dialogue for Migration, Mobility and Security with the Southern Mediterranean Countries*. Brussels: European Union, 2011. http://eur-lex.europa.eu/LexUriServ/LexUriServ.do?uri=COM:2011:0292:FIN:EN:PDF

Freeman, Derek, *Margaret Mead and Samoa: The Making and Unmaking of an Anthropological Myth* (Cambridge: Cambridge University Press, 1983).

Gammeltoft-Hansen, Thomas, 'The Refugee, the Sovereign and the Sea: EU Interdiction Policies in the Mediterranean', Danish Institute for International Studies working paper (2008): 6. http://www.econstor.eu/bitstream/10419/44650/1/560120990.pdf

Geddes, Andrew, and Taylor, Andrew, 'How EU Capacity Bargains Strength States: Migration and Border Security in South-East Europe', *West European Politics* 36, no. 1 (2013): 51.

Geddes, Barbara, 'How the Cases You Choose Affect the Answers You Get: Selection Bias in Comparative Politics', *Political Analysis* 2, no. 1 (1990): 131.

Greene, William, *Econometric Analysis*, second edition (Englewood Cliffs: Prentice Hall, 1993).

Gregory, Derek, 'The Black Flag: Guantanamo Bay and the Space of Exception', *Geografiska Annaler: Series B, Human Geography* 88, no. 4 (2006): 405.

Guilfoyle, Derek, *Shipping Interdiction and the Law of the Sea* (Cambridge: Cambridge University Press, 2009).

Haas, Peter, 'Introduction: Epistemic Communities and International Policy Coordination', *International Organization* 46, no. 1 (1992): 1.

Hausman, Daniel, *The Inexact and Separate Science of Economics* (New York: Cambridge University Press, 1992).

Heckmann, Friedrich, 'Illegal Migration: What Can We Know and What Can We Explain? The Case of Germany', *International Migration Review* 38, no. 3 (2004): 1103.

Hennebry, Jenna, and Preibisch, Kerry, 'A Model for Managed Migration? Re-examining Best Practices in Canada's Seasonal Agricultural Worker Program', *International Migration* 50, no. s1 (2012).

Hess, Sabine, 'De-naturalising Transit Migration: Theory and Methods of an Ethnographic Regime Analysis', *Population, Space and Place* 18, no. 4 (2012): 428.

Hoffmann, Eivind, and Lawrence, Sophia, *Statistics on International Labour Migration: A Review of Sources and Methodological Issues*. International Labour Organization, 1996.

Hutton, Margaret, 'Database of Asylum Seeker Boats', accessed 1 July 2014. http://sievx.com/dbs/boats/index.php?table_name=Boats

Inter-University Consortium for Political and Social Research (ICPSR), 'Guidelines for Effective Data Management Plans', accessed 1 July 2011. http://www.icpsr.umich.edu/files/datamanagement/DataManagementPlans-All.pdf

Jandl, Michael, 'The Estimation of Illegal Migration in Europe,' *Studi Emigrazione* (2004): 141.

Jones, Thomas, 'The International Law of Maritime Blockade: A Measure of Naval Economic Interdiction', *Howard Law Journal* 26 (1983): 759.

King, Gary, Keohane, Robert, and Verba, Sidney, *Design Social Inquiry: Scientific Inference in Qualitative Research* (Princeton: Princeton University Press, 1994).

Kniveton, Dominic, Christopher Smith, and Wood, Sharon, 'Agent-Based Model Simulations of Future Changes in Migration Flows for Burkina Faso', *Global Environmental Change* 21 (2011): S34.

Kuhn, Thomas, *The Structure of Scientific Revolutions* (Chicago: University of Chicago Press, 1996).

Laudan, Larry, 'A Problem-Solving Approach to Scientific Progress', in *Science and Hypothesis* (London: Springer, 1981).

Lavenex, Sandra, and Wichmann, Nicole, 'The External Governance of EU Internal Security', *European Integration* 31, no. 1 (2009): 83.

Lewis-Beck, Michael, Bryman, Alan, and Futing, Tim, *The Sage Encyclopedia of Social Science Research Methods* (London: Sage Publications, 2004).

Ley, David, 'Seeking Homo Economicus: The Canadian State and the Strange Story of the Business Immigration Program', *Annals of the Association of American Geographers* 93, no. 2 (2003): 426.

Lieberman, Evan, 'Nested Analysis as a Mixed-Method Strategy for Comparative Research', *American Political Science Review* 99, no. 3 (2005): 435.

Little, Daniel, *Varieties of Social Explanation: An Introduction to the Philosophy of Social Science* (Boulder: Westview Press, 1991).

Loyd, Jenna, and Mountz, Alison, *Boats, Borders, and Bases: Race, the Colder War, and the Rise of Migration Detention in the United States* (Los Angeles: University of California Press, forthcoming).

Lutterbeck, Derek, 'Policing Migration in the Mediterranean', *Mediterranean Politics* 11, no. 1 (2006): 59.

Maillet, Pauline, Mountz, Alison, and Williams, Kira, 'Exclusion through Imperio: Entanglements of Law and Geography in the Waiting Zone, Excised Territory and Search and Rescue Region', *Social and Legal Studies* (2018).

Maillet, Pauline, Mountz, Alison, and Williams, Kira, 'Researching Migration and Enforcement in Obscured Places: Practical, Ethical and Methodological Challenges to Fieldwork', *Social and Cultural Geography* 18, no. 7 (2017): 927.

Martin, Susan, 'Environmental Change and Migration: Legal and Political Frameworks', *Environment and Planning C: Government and Policy* 30, no. 6: 1045.

Massey, Douglas, and Capoferro, Chiara, 'Measuring Undocumented Migration', in *Rethinking Migration: New Theoretical and Empirical Perspectives*, edited by Portes, Alejandro, and DeWind, Josh (New York: Berghan Books, 2007).

Massey, Douglas, and Zenteno, Rene, 'The Dynamics of Mass Migration', *Proceedings of the National Academy of Sciences of the United States of America* 96, no. 6 (1999): 5328.

Mathiesen, Thomas, 'The Rise of the Surveillant State in Times of Globalization', in *The Blackwell Companion to Criminology*, edited by Sumner, Colin (New York: Wiley-Blackwell, 2008).

McLeman, Robert, 'Developments in Modelling of Climate Change-Related Migration', *Climatic Change* 117, no. 3: 599.

Morabito, Robert, 'Maritime Interdiction: The Evolution of a Strategy', Department of Operations thesis, Naval War College, US Department of the Navy, 1996.

Mountz, Alison, 'Political Geography: Reconfiguring Geographies of Sovereignty', *Progress in Human Geography* 37, no. 6 (2013): 829.

Mountz, Alison, *Seeking Asylum: Human Smuggling and Bureaucracy at the Border* (Minneapolis: University of Minnesota Press, 2010).

Neuendorf, Kimberly, *The Content Analysis Guidebook* (Thousand Oaks: Sage, 2002).

Ozden, Caglar, Parsons, Christopher, Schiff, Maurice, and Walmsley, Terrie, 'Where on Earth Is Everybody? The Evolution of Global Bilateral Migration, 1960–2000', *World Bank Economic Review* 25, no. 1 (2011): 12.

Palmer, Gary, 'Guarding the Coast: Alien Migration Interdiction Operations at Sea', *Connecticut Law Review* 29 (1996): 1565.

Pratt, Judith, 'The Problem of Grounded Theory', Centre for Institutional Studies, University of East London, 2012. http://www.uel.ac.uk/csjc/documents/Grounded Theory.pdf

Pugh, Michael, 'Drowning Not Waving: Boat People and Humanitarianism at Sea', *Journal of Refugee Studies* 17, no. 1 (2004): 50.

Putnam, Hilary, *The Collapse of the Fact-Value Dichotomy and Other Essays* (Cambridge: Harvard University Press, 2002).

Raymer, James, 'The Estimation of International Migration Flows: A General Technique Focused on the Origin-Destination Association Structure', *Environment and Planning A* 39, no. 4 (2007): 986.

Rogers, Andrei, 'Demographic Modeling of the Geography of Migration and Population: A Multiregional Perspective', *Geographical Analysis* 40, no. 3 (2008): 276.

Ronzitti, Natalino, 'The Treaty on Friendship, Partnership, and Cooperation between Italy and Libya: New Prospects for Cooperation in the Mediterranean?', *Bulletin of Italian Politics* 1, no. 1 (2009): 125.

Ruhs, Martin, and Anderson, Bridget, Who Needs Migrant Workers? *Labour Shortages, Immigration, and Public Policy* (Oxford: Oxford University Press, 2010).

Salmon, Wesley, *Scientific Explanation and the Causal Structure of the World* (Princeton: Princeton University Press, 1984).

Samers, Michael, 'An Emerging Geopolitics of "Illegal" Immigration in the European Union', *European Journal of Migration and Law* 6, no. 1 (2010): 27.

Shaughnessy, John, Zechmeister, Eugene, and Zechmeister, Jeanne, *Research Methods in Psychology*, tenth edition (Toronto: McGraw Hill, 2014).

Silvey, Rachel, and Lawson, Victoria, 'Placing the Migrant', *Annals of the Association of American Geographers* 89, no. 1 (1999): 121.

Sommer, Barbara, and Sommer, Robert, *A Practical Guide to Behavioral Research: Tools and Techniques*, third edition (New York: Oxford University Press, 1993).

Steinberg, Phillip, *The Social Construction of the Ocean* (Cambridge: Cambridge University Press, 2001).

Steinberg, Phillip, 'Sovereignty, Territory, and the Mapping of Mobility: A View from the Outside', *Annals of the American Association of Geographers* 99, no. 3 (2009): 467.

Sugden, Robert, 'Credible Worlds: The Status of Theoretical Models in Economics', *Journal of Economic Methodology* 7, no. 1 (2000): 1.

Thies, Cameron, 'A Pragmatic Guide to Qualitative Analysis in the Study of International Relations', *International Studies Perspectives* 3 (2003): 351.

Urry, John, 'Mobile Sociology', *British Journal of Sociology* 51, no. 1 (2000): 185.

Walton-Roberts, Margaret, 'Transnational Migration Theory in Population Geography: Gendered Practices in Networks Linking Canada and India', *Population, Place, and Space* 10 (2004): 361.

Weber, Leanne, and Pickering, Sharon, *Globalization and Borders: Deaths at the Global Frontier* (London: Palgrave Macmillan, 2011).

Williams, Kira, 'Arriving Somewhere, Not Here: Exploring and Mapping the Relationship between Border Enforcement and Migration by Boat in the Central Mediterranean Sea, 2006 to 2015', PhD thesis, Wilfrid Laurier University, 2018.

Williams, Kira, and Mountz, Alison, 'Rising Tide: Analyzing the Relationship between Externalization and Migrant Deaths and Boat Losses', in *Externalizing Migration Management: Europe, North America and the Spread of Remote Control*, edited by Zaiotti, Ruben (London: Routledge, 2016).

Ziegler, Richard, 'Ubi Sumus? Quo Vadimus?: Charting the Course of Maritime Interception Operations', Thesis for the Department of Advanced Research Thesis, Naval War College, US Department of the Navy, 1996.

Section Two

GEOPOLITICS AND
LEGAL REGIMES

This part of the book explores the geopolitics and legal regimes surrounding contemporary migration by boat. While the previous section introduced us to and showed issues in studying migration by boat, the following three chapters by Giuseppe Campesi, Paolo Cuttitta and Joanne van Selm examine its complex political and social realities. Previous work in the field has often shown us the consequences of governance institutions on the everyday lives on migrants; however, scholars have yet to contribute a nuanced understanding of the legal regimes and geographies of migration by boat, and, in particular, how these play out in international geopolitics. Although a large body of work currently exists which analyses the legal and political status of migration at sea, and, on a more limited level, its related border enforcement, only a small number of scholars have delved into the empirical relationship between legal regimes, geographies and geopolitics with migration by boat. This section therefore brings together three case studies relating these phenomena by leading researchers in the field.

Campesi, Cuttitta and van Selm reveal that the micro-level, corporeal realities of migrants who move by boat are empirically tied to multi-scalar, complex legal and political structures. Campesi relates how the long-term construction of Italy's maritime border control not only frames its geopolitics with the wider European Union (EU) and Libya but also modifies the legal regimes and spaces in which migrants, boats and maritime interdiction operations find themselves. As it turns out, the positionality and lived experiences of migrants become deeply entangled with their physical, legal and political locations and the constructed personhoods which follow therefrom. Cuttitta conceptualises and empirically shows how international governmental organisations, states and even non-governmental organisations work together to build migrant legality via political location. In Italy's maritime border control policies, he finds that such legal regimes impact the lives of migrants, the boats in which they move and enforcement through logics of inclusion and exclusion. Van Selm takes a wider analysis of how the EU's political construction and handling of the 'migrant crisis' since 2014 affected both asylum seekers making their way through the sea and Balkans and individual EU member states. She thereby shows that it is not only migrants who become empirically harmed by ineffective border control policies but also entire populations of states, like Greece, which become the 'frontline' border. Political death could thus happen to migrants, state populations and, Van Selm argues, the entire EU project through the relationships between legality, geography and migration by boat.

By its conclusion, then, this section addresses a number of critical questions in current studies of migration by boat: What are the more specific relationships between legality, geography and migrant outcomes at sea? How do states, migrants or discourse bring them about in practice? How do these practices work in specific regions or locations? Are there broader, empirical connections between these patchworks from which we can learn something new? These chapters therefore contribute to previous scholarship by connecting the analytical and empirical gaps between the legal regimes, geographies and geopolitics with migration by boat.

Chapter 4

Italy and the Militarisation of Euro-Mediterranean Border Control Policies

Giuseppe Campesi

INTRODUCTION

In recent years, many have underlined the increasing role played by the military in migration control policies at the Euro-Mediterranean border (see chapter 5 by Cuttitta; Andersson 2012; Garelli and Tazzioli 2017; Lutterbeck 2006; Vives 2009). Scholars see this as an outcome of the so-called 'securitisation' of migration, which has urged policy makers and public opinion to look at migration as if it were a security threat (Ceyhan and Tsoukal 2002; Huysmans 2006). It could also be regarded as an example of the convergence between internal and external security, and the mixing of police and military functions (Bigo 2000; Easton et al. 2010; Lutterbeck 2005).

When referring to the involvement of the military in border control activities, scholars typically talk about 'border militarisation'. But what exactly is meant with the concept of 'militarisation'? Borders have traditionally played a relevant defensive function, protecting state's security and territorial integrity. This was traditionally the remit of the military (Andreas 2003), and in this sense, it should therefore be nothing surprising today to see the military involved in border control functions. The point is that the role of the military is increasingly called into these matters and is no longer directed to the protection of the external security of the state, and to its defence from traditional military threats, but rather to protect the internal security from non-military threats such as migration, smuggling, organised crime and so on. This function of filtering out the unwanted cross-border movement was traditionally assigned to civil law enforcement agencies. Therefore, in this chapter when I refer to the militarisation of the border, I adapt the definition of 'police militarisation' proposed by Kraska (2007) to refer to the growing influence of military agencies, technologies and operational models in border policing and immigration law enforcement.

The militarisation of border control policies is not a new phenomenon. The growing involvement of the army in the control of the US-Mexico border (Andreas, 2000; Dunn 2001; Palafox 2000) and of the navy in the management of irregular migration through the Caribbean Sea (Legomsky 2006) has indeed been widely described. Whereas the driving force in the US case appeared to be the role that the military had begun to play in the war on drugs, at EU level the involvement of the military appears to be part of the evolution of the concept of Integrated Border Management (Hobbing 2005). In EU official lexicon *integrated* refers to both the facts that border control policies increasingly involve the action of many institutional actors (police, military, EU agencies, countries of origin and/or transit) and that the geopolitics of border control produces a wide frontier zone extending well beyond EU territorial outlines (European Council 2006).

In this chapter, I analyse the leading role played by Italy in the increasing militarisation of border control policies taking place at the EU level. I do this by focusing on the evolution of the Italian maritime border control policies in the past twenty years, and thus describing the process that has led to the creation of a complex and integrated border control apparatus. I start with a preliminary examination of the wider context in which the control of irregular migration by sea takes place in the Mediterranean scenario, focusing then on the description of the Italian border control apparatus. In particular, I will describe the legal basis and the complex institutional framework that shaped maritime border surveillance policies in the past twenty years. These policies will be analysed by describing their evolution up to the latest operational activities launched in the Strait of Sicily with the aim to tackle the refugee crisis. By way of conclusion, some final remarks will offer a key to interpret the main driving forces behind the increasing militarisation of immigration law enforcement at the Euro-Mediterranean border.

SITUATING ITALY IN THE GEOPOLITICS OF THE EURO-MEDITERRANEAN BORDER CONTROL REGIME

Over the past decades the Mediterranean Sea established itself as one of the geographical fault lines where migration pressure is most intense. For EU member-states it presents challenges similar to those which Australia and the United States have faced in the management of their maritime borders (Legomsky 2006; Magner 2004), although the geopolitical picture is even more complex. The EU border is not in fact a national border, but a regional border managed through forms of police cooperation which can be in many respects regarded as post-national (Zaiotti 2011). In analysing the Euro-Mediterranean border control regime, one has thus to take into account not only bilateral relations between bordering countries but also the complex multilateral relations among EU member-states, as well as EU neighbourhood policies. This creates a network of 'supralateral' (Paoletti and Pastore 2010) relations that is much more complex than the web of bilateral relations between nation-states on which maritime border control policies in the United States and Australia rely. The political and diplomatic scenario of the Euro-Mediterranean border control policies is further complicated by the complexity of the legal framework, where national and international law on maritime border controls and asylum, regional human rights law and EU law also apply.

For more than twenty years, Italy has been at the core of the geopolitics of migration control in the Mediterranean, but its role cannot be fully understood without considering the wider EU political framework and its policies for the integrated border management (Hobbing 2005). In the EU, border surveillance is regulated according to regional standards, such as the so-called Schengen Borders Code (regulation [EC] No. 562/2006), requiring member-states to provide appropriate staff and resources to prevent 'illegal' border crossings, as well as close and constant cooperation between national services responsible for border control and between member-states, eventually coordinated by the EU coordinating border agency Frontex (Campesi 2015). The concept to develop a common standard for the integrated management of the EU border has faced the complexity of the Euro-Mediterranean geopolitics, where it is possible to identify a number of 'regional formations' in which bilateral relations between member-states and their respective neighbours are intertwined with the role played by EU policies in building a border region articulated on several local control regimes (Kasparek and Wagner 2012; Mountz and Loyd 2013).

One can single out at least three different strategic areas for maritime border controls in the Euro-Mediterranean region, differing in their geo-morphological characteristics, in the relations between neighbouring countries and in the institutional capacities of the main EU member-states in the region. The first is that of the Atlantic and of the Western Mediterranean, pivoting on Spain and its diplomatic relations with neighbouring countries (especially Morocco, Mauritania, Senegal). The second is that of the Central Mediterranean, where migration control policies are centred on the role of the Italian security forces and have been over the past decade strongly affected by the difficult relations with Libya. The third is finally the Eastern Mediterranean region, which is centred on Greece. The peculiarity of this region lies not only in its geography but also in the complexities of the relation with Turkey, which over the years has proved to be a quite reluctant partner of migration control. The EU integrated border management is therefore entangled in complex geopolitical formations that are constantly redefined by the attempt at controlling migratory movements and by the corresponding resistance of migrants that, in response to increased surveillance, constantly seek new routes displacing the points of 'crisis' as local border control regimes consolidate. The continuous shifting of main migration routes is clear in table 4.1 presented next, showing the number of intercepted migrants along the Euro-Mediterranean border. Italy (where more than 90 per cent of migrants are intercepted along this Central Mediterranean route) has repeatedly found itself under high migratory pressure, a pressure that has become particularly acute over the past two years.

As table 4.2 shows, 153,842 migrants and asylum seekers had reached Italy in 2015. This is a number that, while marking a decrease compared to 2014, represents an increase of 565 per cent when compared to the yearly average of arrivals in the 2003–2013 decade (21,000). Over the years there has also been a profound change in the main disembarkation points on Italian shores. Starting from the early twenty-first century, migratory pressure has indeed focused on Sicily, and particularly on the tiny island of Lampedusa, as the number of migrants landing in Puglia and Calabria went gradually decreasing. This reflects a change in migratory routes, which now have Libya, and to a lesser extent Tunisia, as main starting point, while the Adriatic route has become almost irrelevant (Monzini 2004, 2008).

Data from 2013, 2014 and 2015 signal an increase in the landings outside Sicily, but these should not be misinterpreted. As underlined by the Interior Ministry's reports to the Italian Parliament on police activities, already in 2007 nearly 70 per cent of landings were taking place in the context of

Table 4.1. Migrants Intercepted Trying to Cross Euro-Mediterranean Border between Border Crossing Points (2006–2015)

Year	Western Atlantic and Western Mediterranean Routes	Central Mediterranean Route	Eastern Mediterranean Route
2006	31,600	NA	NA
2007	12,500	NA	NA
2008	17,708	39,800	52,300
2009	8,886	11,043	39,975
2010	5,199	4,450	55,688
2011	8,788	64,261	57,025
2012	6,571	15,151	37,224
2013	7,121	45,298	24,799
2014	8,118	170,664	50,834
2015	10,053	153,946	885,386

Source: Author's elaboration on data retrieved from Frontex (2013, 2014a, 2015).

Table 4.2. Number of Migrants Landing on Italian Shores According to Their Disembarkation Point (1998–2015)

Year	Sicily	Lampedusa	Apulia	Calabria	Sardinia	Other	Total
1998	8,828	NA	28,458	848	NA	NA	38,134
1999	1,973	NA	46,481	1,545	NA	NA	49,999
2000	2,782	NA	18,990	5,045	NA	NA	26,817
2001	5,504	NA	8,546	6,093	NA	NA	20,143
2002	9,699	9,699	3,372	2,122	NA	NA	15,193
2003	8,819	8,819	137	177	NA	NA	9,133
2004	13,594	10,497	18	23	NA	NA	13,635
2005	22,824	15,890	19	88	8	NA	22,939
2006	21,400	18,495	243	282	91	NA	22,016
2007	16,875	12,177	61	1,971	1,548	NA	20,455
2008	34,540	31,252	127	663	1,621	NA	36,951
2009	8,282	2,947	308	499	484	NA	9,573
2010	1,264	459	1,513	1,280	207	NA	4,264
2011	57,181	51,753	3,325	1,944	207	35	62,692
2012	8,488	5,202	2,719	2,056	4	NA	13,267
2013	37,886	14,753	1,030	3,980	29	NA	42,925
2014	120,239	4,194	17,565	22,673	166	9,457	170,100
2015	104,709	21,238	11,190	29,437	5,451	3,055	153,842

Source: Author's elaboration on data retrieved from Ministero dell'Interno (1998, 2000, 2008, 2011, 2013, 2014, 2015).

search and rescue operations having the island of Lampedusa as the main disembarkation point (Ministero dell'Interno 2008, 93). The share has further increased in the following years, when, as we will see, the patrolling in the Strait of Sicily has become even more intense. What most recent data suggest is therefore that the government of Italy finally decided to ease the pressure on the island of Lampedusa, which over the past years was turned into the main border crossing point for migrants intercepted in the Strait of Sicily (see chapter 8 by Binotto and Bruno; Cuttitta 2014).

Parallel to the change in the geography of migration routes was the change in the nationalities of migrants arriving on Italian shores. As the data on the declared nationality in the past fifteen years show (Ministero dell'Interno 2011, 2013, 2014, 2015; see Monzini 2008), the incidence of people coming from conflict areas has increased, while the number of migrants coming from neighbouring countries in the Balkan region or North Africa has dramatically decreased.

This is probably due to two concomitant factors: on the one hand, visa facilitations granted to neighbouring countries in exchange of their cooperation in the control of irregular migration (Cuttitta 2011; Trauner and Kruse 2008); on the other, the growth of political instability which triggered forced migration from the regions surrounding the Mediterranean towards the EU

(Nouran, Monzini and Pastore 2015, 20). The crossing of the Mediterranean is a mobility strategy which is now mainly reserved to refugees and migrants coming from sub-Saharan Africa, the Horn of Africa and Middle East crisis areas, while the citizens of the Western Balkan and North African countries now have different migratory strategies at their disposal, strategies largely levering on the possibility to travel to Europe under a visa-free or visa-facilitation regime. For these reasons, as we shall see, Italy's efforts have moved in the direction of seeking the cooperation of key transit countries in the region and of Libya in particular, which over the past decade has been the focus of the Italian 'migration diplomacy' (Andrijasevic 2010; Paoletti 2011).

THE ITALIAN BORDER CONTROL APPARATUS

Over time, Italy has developed a complex institutional apparatus for the control of irregular migration by sea, further strengthening it with the adoption of the Law No. 189/2002 which is commonly regarded as the anti-immigration manifesto of the then-ruling right-wing coalition. The 2002 reform, however, did little to modify the legal prerogatives and the rules of engagement assigned to border police, which essentially remained as those already provided by the law of the sea and international refugee law (di Pascale 2010). Rather, it redesigned the institutional framework according to which border controls take place by expanding the number of agencies involved.

Italian law explicitly conceives of the control of irregular migration by sea as an 'interagency' task whose strategic leadership is assigned to the Interior Ministry. The latter has the task of promoting coordination between the relevant Italian authorities and EU agencies, as well as, in coordination with the Ministry of Foreign Affairs, promoting agreements with countries of origin and/or transit aimed at fostering the 'cooperation in the fight against illegal immigration'.[1] In 2002, a new Central Direction for Immigration and Border Police (CDIBP) was established at the Ministry of Interior, which was entrusted with the overall coordination of border control policies.

The arrangements for coordination between the different security agencies that, under the leadership of the CDIBP, are entrusted by the law with the task of enforcing controls at maritime borders were further specified in 2003 with the enactment of a Ministry of Interior's decree which identified three main strategic dimensions for the control of irregular migration by sea. The first dimension includes activities carried out in countries of origin and/or transit, eventually under the umbrella of bilateral cooperation agreements.[2] The second dimension includes activities carried out in international waters, where the Italian Navy is called to exercise its prerogatives in the monitoring, surveillance, identification and control of 'naval targets' at sea and in the fight against 'illegal immigration'.[3] The third dimension includes activities carried out in territorial waters and the contiguous zone, where border controls and immigration law enforcement are mainly entrusted to the *Guardia di Finanza*,[4] whereas the Coast Guard is responsible for the coordination of search and rescue.[5]

The Italian border control strategy thus relies on the role played by different actors, operating at different institutional levels and in different operational contexts (see figure 4.1).

The Italian Navy has traditionally been the key actor in the surveillance of the high sea, and since the late 1990s it has been increasingly mobilised for the control of irregular migration. The enactment of the Law No. 189/2002 made its role in the field even more explicit, and since then the Italian Navy has put into place a permanent activity at sea 'aimed at the localization, identification and tracking of vessels suspected of smuggling, through the use of all the available aero-naval equipment' (Ministero per i rapporti con il Parlamento 2004, 112). Since 2004, the Italian Navy is also deployed on a permanent basis for the control of irregular migration in the Strait of Sicily, and occasionally in the lower Adriatic and in the Ionian Sea.

The *Guardia di Finanza* has traditionally played the role of customs police, mainly concerned with economic crimes such as contraband and tax evasion. Over the years its remit has been extended to cover all cross-border challenges, ranging from undocumented migration to trafficking in drugs and arms. The *Guardia di Finanza* is now entrusted with the exclusive responsibility for border controls at sea in the territorial waters and the contiguous zone (Ministero dell'Interno 2000, 176), and its paramilitary apparatus, originally developed for the fight against the smuggling of illicit drugs, has been gradually upgraded and converted to the control of irregular migration by sea. Since 2006, the action of the *Guardia di Finanza* is further supported by the action of the EU agency Frontex, which over the past ten years has launched a number of joint operations focusing mainly on the patrol of the Strait of Sicily (Campesi 2015, 176–85).

The actions of the Italian and other member-states' security forces acting in the framework of Frontex's joint operations build increasingly on the technical and operational cooperation with third countries of origin and/ or transit, according to a model which has been aptly defined as 'external governance' (Lavenex and Wichmann 2009) or 'extra-territorial' (Cremona and Rijpma 2007; Mitsilegas 2010) control of borders. The aim of the cooperation is indeed to anticipate control activities by acting in foreign territorial waters, so as to intercept the movement of vessels carrying migrants even before they can leave the jurisdiction of the country of origin and/or transit (see also chapter 5 by Cuttitta in this volume). In recent years the EU has sought cooperation in the field of migration control within

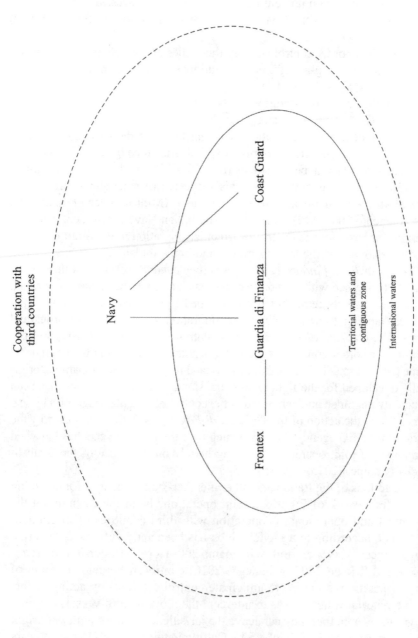

Figure 4.1. The Italian Sea Border Control Apparatus. *Source:* Figure constructed by author.

the diplomatic framework of its wider neighbourhood policies (Jeandesboz 2009; Lavenex 2006). However, in spite of these attempts, bilateral cooperation between member-states and their closest neighbours remains key in the organisation of local border control regimes in the Euro-Mediterranean region.

Italy is a prime example in this regard, given that since the end of the 1990s it signed several cooperation agreements with key countries of origin and/or transit countries in the Central Mediterranean. Cooperation was particularly intense with Albania, Tunisia and Libya, without any doubt the countries from which during the past two decades a higher number of irregular migrants have arrived (Monzini 2004, 45; 2008, 13). As we shall see, under the umbrella of these agreements, Italy launched technical assistance programs for the training of border police, exchanged liaison officers, shared intelligence on cross-border crimes, started the repatriation of irregular migrants and, above all, launched joint border patrols on the high sea or well inside third countries' territorial waters.

THE EVOLUTION OF ITALIAN BORDER CONTROL POLICIES

Italy's border control policies in the past twenty years can be divided into three phases, each characterised by the conditions of the geopolitical context and of the main policy responses. During this period an overall change in main migration routes occurred, with a substantial closing of the route in the Lower Adriatic Sea and a parallel increasing of migration movements in the Ionian Sea and then in the Strait of Sicily, which is a much wider stretch of sea when compared with the Strait of Otranto (Monzini 2004, 45). Border control policies adapted to the changing political geography of irregular migration by sea and saw an overall change in their institutional framework due to the evolution of the Italian and EU strategies for the integrated border management. This led to an increase in the number of relevant actors. The three phases correspond to three distinct stages of (a) development, (b) consolidation and (c) crisis of the Italian border control policies.

The Development of a Border Control Strategy (1997–2002)

The first phase of the development of an Italian border strategy took place between 1997 and 2002, at the end of which Apulia ceased to be the main destination point for irregular migration movements. This period was marked by the first authentic 'migration crisis' experienced by Italy due to the geopolitical instability in the Western Balkans. In response of this, the country developed its integrated border control model through a number of institutional adjustments that would have finally been consolidated with the enactment of the Law No. 189/2002, which officially authorised the Italian Navy to perform immigration law enforcement duties along with border police.

From the beginning, however, Italy sought the involvement of the Albanian authorities, in order to protect its border control capacity beyond the high sea and well inside Albanian territorial waters. It was as a result of the agreements reached with the government of Albania in August 1997 that Italy launched an Interagency Police Mission whose aim was to provide training, support and technical assistance in view of the reform and overall reorganisation of the Albanian Police (Ministero dell'Interno 2001, 13). The Mission relied on the 28th Naval Group of the Italian Navy and other equipment made available by the *Guardia di Finanza* for the joint patrolling of Albanian territorial waters (Ministero dell'Interno 2003, 11; Ministero per i rapporti con il Parlamento 2003, 87).

According to data provided by the Italian government, between 1997 and 2000 more than 1,000 boats have been intercepted in Albanian territorial waters during the 'training missions' run by Italian security forces. This led to the diversion of more than 25,000 potential irregular migrants. At the same time, territorial delegations had intercepted on Albanian territory more than 4,000 people heading towards their potential points of embarkation to Italy (Ministero dell'Interno 2001, 25). Paola Monzini, citing Italian intelligence sources, claimed that in 2000 only a quarter of the boats departing from Albania were able to reach the Italian waters, while more than half were intercepted before leaving the Albanian contiguous zone (Monzini 2004, 57).

Due to the agreements reached with Albania, Italy expanded its ability to control migration flows in the lower Adriatic well inside the Albanian territorial waters. This was concretely done by deploying patrol vessels of the navy and of the *Guardia di Finanza* carrying Albanian border police officers on board in order to provide legal coverage for the exercise of executive powers on foreign territory. This led to a rapid decline in the irregular migration movements recorded in the region, calling for an overall revision of the terms of the cooperation between Italy and Albania. A new and less operational stage thus started in 2002, when a new Permanent Interagency Italian Liaison Office was opened in Tirana (Ministero dell'Interno 2003, 11).

The Italian strategy for the extra-territorial control of its borders already showed many of the tensions between humanitarian needs and securitarian drives that would characterise border control policies in the years to come. Cooperation with Albania on border control was launched in years of severe humanitarian crisis fuelled by the political instability that plagued the Western Balkans, culminating in the exodus of the Kosovars in 1999. At the time, Italy faced a typical mixed migration flow, where refugees fleeing war and persecution mingled with the Albanian citizens who were migrating mainly for economic reasons.[6] The policy response was in some ways contradictory: while on the one hand the government granted temporary protection measures to those who had reached Italy fleeing political and economic instability in Albania in 1997 and the Kosovo crisis in 1999, on the other hand, the cooperation with Albania on border control aimed essentially at stemming the flow of migrants before it could even reach the Italian territory (Pugh 2000, 36).

Such a strategy clearly put tension on refugee law, as it allowed Italy to circumvent its humanitarian obligations by invoking the jurisdiction of the country of origin/transit, in the territory of which the patrol boats of the Italian Navy and of the *Guardia di Finanza* were carrying out controls. This was done according to a border control strategy that would have become a paradigm for the control of irregular migration by sea, a strategy that allowed to project control capabilities beyond the domestic jurisdiction of the destination country, while at the same time avoiding any extension of jurisdiction arising from the exercise of sovereign prerogatives (Basaran 2008).

The Consolidation of the Italian Border Control Strategy (2003–2013)

The second phase covered almost a decade and was interrupted by the eruption of the Arab Spring in 2011, causing the geopolitical landscape in the Mediterranean region to dramatically change. This long season marked the Strait of Sicily becoming the main transit area for irregular migrations by sea and Libya the privileged transit country for North African, Sub-Saharan, Middle-Eastern and Asian migrants (Monzini 2004, 58–59; 2008, 15–16). In response to the change in migratory routes, the government of Italy and Frontex intensified patrols in the Strait of Sicily.

In 2004, the Italian Navy launched a mission called *Constant Vigilance*, under the umbrella of which there was a patrol boat in permanent migration control service on the high sea, plus maritime patrol aircraft and other naval units ready for rapid intervention (Ministero per i rapporti con il Parlamento 2010, 124). This multinational action was also intensified in parallel with the launch of the first joint operations coordinated by Frontex. The first that was launched in the central Mediterranean region was *Nautilus*, which remained active for only a few years because of disagreements between Italy and Malta over who should bear the burden of the reception of migrants rescued at sea. *Nautilus* was later replaced by *Hermes*, which had until then covered the route leading from Algeria to Sardinia, and *Aeneas* whose operational activities were focused on the Ionian Sea (Campesi 2015, 176–85).

In response to the increased migration flows in the Strait of Sicily, Italy also attempted a 'policy transfer' (Monzini 2004, 69), which tried to replicate with Northern African countries the integrated border control strategy successfully experimented with Albania. If, on the one hand, cooperation with Tunisia had already begun in 1998 and was then further strengthened in 2003 (Cuttitta 2008, 52; 2011, 32), then, on the other, the displacement of the main points of departure towards Libya led Italy to seek the cooperation of the Gaddafi regime, with which the country had already signed a memorandum of understanding on police cooperation by 2003 (Andrijasevic 2010; Hamood 2008; Klepp 2010). Nevertheless, the real breakthrough in the cooperation with Libya came only with the signing of the Treaty of Friendship on 30 August 2008, with which the agreement on the joint patrol of the Strait of Sicily signed in 2007 was put into effect (Bialasiewicz 2012). Under the umbrella of these agreements, a number of push-back operations were carried out that led to the condemnation of Italy before the European Court of Human Rights in the well-known *Hirsi Jamaa and Others v. Italy* (2012) judgement.

Police cooperation with Libya apparently led to immediate results, with a rapid decrease of landings in Sicily in 2009 and then in 2010. Italy hailed the joint patrolling of the Strait of Sicily as a great achievement of its diplomacy (Ministero dell'Interno 2011, 45), while Frontex pointed to the availability of Libya to 'accept the repatriation of illegal migrants' as one of the factors that more than others had strengthened 'the deterrent effect of joint operations' in the region (Frontex 2010, 18). This was said in spite of the violent controversies that the cooperation with Gaddafi had sparked (European Parliament 2010; Human Rights Watch 2009), which would have finally led to an overall revision of the rules of engagement regulating patrolling operations at sea borders. In spite of the fact that not all member-states were convinced of the need for a reform of the Schengen Borders Code, fearing a weakening of the fight against irregular migration (Carrera and Den Hertog 2015), the EU Council finally enacted the Decision 2010/252/EU, which established that 'no person shall be disembarked in, or otherwise handed over to the authorities of a country in contravention of the principle of non-refoulement, or from which there is a risk of expulsion or return to another country in contravention of that principle'.[7]

The Decision, which the EU replaced with Regulation (EU) No. 656/2014, applied only to Frontex's operations and this allowed Italy to continue to divert migrants intercepted in international waters to neighbouring countries' authorities, as evidenced by most recent reports on police activities released by the Ministry of the Interior. According to these reports, between 2012 and 2013 Italy returned to Tunisian and Libyan authorities, respectively, 968 and 3,918 migrants intercepted during operations carried out under the umbrella of the cooperation agreements that the country had reached in 2011 and 2012 with the provisional authorities that had replaced Ben Ali and Gaddafi (Ministero dell'Interno 2013, 9; 2014, 1601).

The government of Italy reached initial informal agreements for cooperation on border control with the Tunisian transitional government by April 2011, which they later consolidated in March 2012 with the signing of a memorandum of understanding. The aims of these agreements were the repatriation of the Tunisians arriving on Italian soil and the rapid recovery of police cooperation, with the providing of technical equipment and training to the Tunisian National Guard (Ministero dell'Interno 2013, 26–27; 2014, 1619).

Much more complex were relations with post-Gaddafi Libya. Since 2012, Italy sought understandings with the National Transitional Council, by sending a technical mission charged with the task of assessing the state of the patrol boats (forty-seven vessels) delivered to the country on the basis of previous agreements, as well as the status of the detention facilities built with Italian money (facilities in Tripoli, Benghazi, Sebha, Garabulli and Homs). Following these initial contacts, in April 2012 the respective interior ministers signed a memorandum of understanding which provided for the exchange of liaison officers, a readmission agreement, training activities for the Libyan police and the recovery of detention centres (Ministero dell'Interno 2013, 27). The year after, they also reached agreements on joint patrols with the support of the *Guardia di Finanza*'s equipment (Ministero dell'Interno 2014, 1618). In the meanwhile, Italy had launched a civilian mission under the lead of the Ministry of Defence for the reform of Libya's security sector and also called for the EU to step in. This eventually happened with the enactment of the Decision 2013/233/CFSP, which gave off the EUBAM (EU Border Assistance Mission) in Libya for the assistance of Libyan security forces in developing an integrated border management strategy.

The Crisis of the Italian Border Control Strategy

In spite of the attempts at restoring the integrated border management strategy built during the decade 2003–2013, the Arab Spring changed the geopolitical scenario in the Mediterranean region by opening a phase in border control policies whose essential traits are still evolving. In addition to fuelling political instability in some countries, leading to significant population movements fleeing civil unrest (Tunisians in 2011) and conflict (Syrians from 2012), the season that opened in 2011 saw Libya plunge into a spiral of violence which ultimately prompted both Italy and the EU to halt all forms of cooperation pending the stabilisation of the country (Ministero dell'Interno 2015, 26). In this context, the role of Libya as a regional hub for international migration heading to the EU further consolidated, with a progressive increase in the number of migrants who set sail from its shores from 2013 (Nouran, Monzini and Pastore 2015, 30).

The response to the increase in migratory movements crossing the Strait of Sicily mainly focused on strengthening surveillance, with the deployment of increasingly sophisticated and expensive technologies such as EUROSUR (European Border Surveillance System), the information platform launched with the enactment of the Regulation (EU) No. 1052/2013 which integrated all national surveillance systems along the southern EU border. The system, launched at the end of 2013, was designed to enhance the capabilities of maritime border control, offering to security agencies a detailed information framework for monitoring, tracking and intercepting unauthorised crossings (Rijpma and Vermeulen 2015). In parallel to the development of the surveillance technologies, a number of operational activities were launched that have made the Strait of Sicily one of the most patrolled straits of sea in the world (see chapter 5 by Cuttitta). In this scenario, the role of the military has further increased.

The first initiative was launched by the government of Italy in the aftermath of the boat-sinking tragedy of 3 October 2013, in which over 350 people lost their life. The tragedy, which deeply impacted upon public opinion, also moved the EU to launch a Mediterranean Task Force with the aim of finding a solution to the problem of migration by sea. It seemed to open a season in which the humanitarian implications of the phenomenon were finally taking over security concerns, which had dominated the political agenda in previous years. The Italian response was to launch a unilateral navy operation called *Mare Nostrum*, which effectively increased the navy presence in the Strait of Sicily covering a wide area of the Central Mediterranean (70,000 sq. km). The government of Italy presented *Mare Nostrum*, whose budget was unprecedented in the history of the Euro-Mediterranean border control activities, as an operation whose main objective was to ensure 'the presence of security forces on the high sea for the safety of life at sea and humanitarian assistance' (Ministero per i rapporti con il Parlamento 2015, 89). So dominant was the humanitarian framing that many NGOs saw the steps undertaken by the Italian government as the opening of a de facto humanitarian corridor in the Strait of Sicily (Amnesty International 2014, 25). *Mare Nostrum* ended in December 2014, when a new navy operation called *Dispositivo di sorveglianza e sicurezza marittima* took over the patrolling tasks on the high sea, although acting on a reduced operational area (Ministero per i rapporti con il Parlamento 2015, 91).

The attitude of EU institutions with respect to the steps undertaken by the Italian government was ambivalent. Initially hailed as an operation born in the wake of the strategic lines drawn by the Mediterranean Task Force established in the aftermath of the tragedy of Lampedusa, *Mare Nostrum* then began to raise concern with its EU partners as its rules of engagement were becoming a powerful pull factor for 'illegal' migrants (Carrera and den Hertog 2015, 4). Italy, looking for an exit strategy for the commitment it undertook with the launch of this costly operation, repeatedly called for EU intervention, and this stimulated a broad discussion on the kind of support that Frontex could offer, possibly by enhancing its joint operations in the region. *Hermes* and *Aeneas* however had a much lower budget and were employing means which were not suitable to carry out the extensive search and rescue efforts on the high sea the Italian Navy was capable of. It was clear that Frontex was not able to replicate an operation similar to *Mare Nostrum*, but it was not just a matter of the means to be deployed.

Frontex expressed all concerns of Italy's EU partners with its usual bureaucratic coldness, culminating in the draft operational plan for the future *Triton*, which was supposed to replace both Frontex-led operations and *Mare Nostrum*. The Plan suggested that the presence of the Italian Navy near Libyan coast may have 'encouraged' potential migrants to attempt a crossing with poorly equipped boats on the assumption that they would be rescued and disembarked on the Italian soil (Frontex 2014b, 4). Other member-states demonstrated a certain reluctance to participate in the new operation in the fear that it might end up working as a pull factor for illegal migrants, offering them a comfortable 'taxi service'. *Triton* was approved only on a condition that its operational area was strictly confined to the margins of Italian territorial waters and would be strictly limited to border surveillance, and not to the rescue at sea in international waters (Carrera and den Hertog 2015, 10).

It was only in April 2015, when more than 800 migrants lost their life in yet another shipwreck in the Strait of Sicily, the mandate of *Triton* was extended and its budget tripled in order to provide it with the means for conducting rescue actions similar to those undertaken by the Italian Navy with *Mare Nostrum* (Frontex 2015). The redefinition of *Triton*'s operational plan took place in a political context still somewhat dominated by a humanitarian inspiration; nevertheless, the document by which the Council gave mandate to the Commission to increase Frontex's 'presence at sea' stated that the stepping up of the agency's search and rescue capacity was to take place 'within the framework of its mandate' (European Council 2015), which still remained that of an agency aimed at border surveillance.

This sharp clarification not only condensed all the controversy of the past few months, but it also foreshadowed an overall change of strategy in the management of the Euro-Mediterranean border, with the intensification of security concerns that the outbreak of the refugee 'crisis' in the following months (see chapter 8 by Binotto and Bruno). Since the early stages of elaboration of the new EU agenda on migration (European Commission 2015), the humanitarian rhetoric has indeed suffered a decisive twist, being progressively incorporated into the discursive frame of the fight against smuggling. Migrants were still seen as victims to be rescued, but the danger was no longer just represented by the crossing of the Mediterranean with unseawor-thy boats, as it was mainly represented by the criminal organisations on which they relied for their attempts at crossing the EU border.

The new framing stimulated the EU to abandon the approach focused on search and rescue and to develop a border control strategy inspired by mili-tary operations against piracy, which under the umbrella of an UN mandate were also operating on the territory of foreign countries. The European Coun-cil of 23 April 2015 thus envisioned the launch of a CSDP (Common Security and Defence Policy) operation whose aims were radically different from the predominantly humanitarian mission assigned to *Mare Nostrum* and the bor-der surveillance tasks assigned to *Triton*. The new operation should 'disrupt trafficking networks, bring the perpetrators to justice and seize their assets', but in doing this it should also 'undertake systematic efforts to identify, capture and destroy vessels *before* they are used by traffickers' (European Council 2015). This clearly implied the possibility to carry out raids on the territory of the third countries concerned, and in particular of Libya, in which any cooperation on migration control was suspended.

The launch of the new military crisis management operation called EUNAVFOR Med, and then renamed *Sophia*, was finally approved with the enactment of the Council Decision (CFSP) 2015/778, which entrusted to the Italian Navy the responsibility to conduct the operations. The mission's operational plan envisaged three sequential phases:

(a) A first phase which aimed at the patrolling of the high sea and the gather-ing of information on migration networks;
(b) A second phase during which military units may conduct boarding, search, seizure and diversion on the high seas of vessels suspected of being used for human smuggling or trafficking. These activities should as a rule take place in international waters, with the possibility of acting in the territorial and internal waters of a third country, 'in accordance with any applicable UN Security Council Resolution or consent by the coastal State concerned';[8]
(c) A third phase during which military units will, 'in accordance with any applicable UN Security Council Resolution or consent by the coastal State concerned, take all necessary measures against a vessel and related assets, including through disposing of them or rendering them inoperable, which are suspected of being used for human smuggling or trafficking, in the territory of that State, under the conditions set out in that Resolution or consent'.[9]

EUNAVFOR Med *Sophia* was officially launched in June 2015, with the involvement of twenty-two member-states. During its early stages, it operated in an area which went from *Triton*'s operating margin up close to Libyan and Tunisian territorial waters. The transition to the second phase took place in October 2015, when the UN enacted the Security Council's resolution No. 2240/2015, which granted participating member-states the power to 'dispose' of the vessels intercepted in international waters, destroying them. As repeatedly underlined by Federica Mogherini, the resolution represented in some way an affirmative vote from the international community to the steps undertaken by the EU in the Mediterranean (EU External Action 2015a), this notwithstanding its offering a rather weak legal justification to EUNAVFOR Med *Sophia*'s operative actions. In particular, the Resolution did not provide EUNAVFOR Med *Sophia* with the international mandate necessary to act in Libyan territorial waters as envisaged by the original operational plan. This limited its operational area to international waters, thus essentially reducing the mission to the running of search and rescue activities which were in all respects similar to those carried out by *Mare Nostrum* (see also chapter 5 by Cuttitta in this volume).

This scenario changed in March 2016, when in Libya the Government of National Accord, led by Fayez Al-Serraj, took office. Immediately after this, the EU launched talks in order to obtain its consent to the extension of EUNAVFOR Med *Sophia*'s action to Libyan territory, as well as the resumption of technical assistance missions that in 2013 were put on stand-by. Italy strongly supported such diplomatic efforts with the clear aim of signing a cooperation agreement with Libya similar to the one agreed with Turkey (Rettman 2016). In this context, the emphasis was put on the need to create the conditions necessary to act in Libya with the cooperation of the new government's security forces. It thus expanded EUNAVFOR Med *Sophia*'s mandate with the enactment of the Council Decision (CFSP) 2016/993, and the mission consequently reshaped into a technical assistance mission tasked, among other things, with the duty to train the Libyan Coast Guard and Navy.

CONCLUSION: MAKING SENSE OF THE INCREASING MILITARISATION

As we have seen, Italy has been a crucial actor in the militarisation of border control in the Euro-Mediterranean region. In recent years the country has launched the most expensive sea border patrol military operation and subsequently stimulated the EU to launch a CSDP mission to disrupt trafficking networks in the Strait of Sicily. But already in the late 1990s, the control of irregular immigration in the Adriatic Sea was based on the stable presence of the Italian Navy, along with the *Guardia di Finanza*, in Albania.

This undoubtedly reflected a deeper change in the role of the armed forces in contemporary world, with their increased involvement in the management of humanitarian crises or in civil law enforcement activities (Andreas and Price 2001; Edmundus 2006). For these reasons any reference to the concept of warfare is particularly out of place (Garelli and Tazzioli 2017), as the role of the armed forces in the management of borders is more inspired by the logic of civil law enforcement and should be regarded as an example of the process that some have defined as 'costabularisation' (Campbell and Campbell 2009; Easton et al. 2010), and others as 'policiaricisation' (Bigo 2001; Kraska 2007) of the military. These practices have multiple implications for migrants, as they are criminalised, mistreated, confined and, of course, many losing their lives taking risks to reach Italian shores.

By describing the evolution of border control policies in the long run, this chapter also put the militarisation of border controls in perspective. The militarisation of border controls has indeed found its roots in the effort to extra-territorialise immigration law enforcement, a policy that in the past decade has been taken over by the EU, with the development of the so-called external governance of internal security (Lavenex and Wichmann 2009) but whose early manifestations date back to late 1990s, with the launch of technical assistance programs aimed at security sector reform in crisis areas, which at that time had Western Balkans as privileged destination (Dursun-Ozkanca and Vandemoortele 2012). The EU neighbourhood policies have further fuelled the complementarities between the external dimension of the internal security policies and the technical assistance programs launched under the CSDP (Monar 2012), offering a further exemplification of the intermingling of internal and external security which is generally credited for the increasing involvement of the military in law enforcement activities.

Italy is the EU country that more than others has stimulated the involvement of the military in immigration law enforcement in the Euro-Mediterranean region. This was probably due to both the role that paramilitary forces, such as the *Guardia di Finanza* and the role it has traditionally played in border control policies (Lutterbeck 2004), and to the country's geographical proximity to regions that have fallen in situations of deep civil and political disorder. From the analysis I have done, it became clear that such involvement was due not so much to the humanitarian need to provide greater search and rescue capacity on the high sea, as to the political will to strengthen the external governance of internal security by using the fight against smuggling and trafficking in human beings as a cover for legitimising an increased presence of EU security forces in crisis contexts. Such a strategy was recently clearly stated in the Italian 'non-paper' on the evolution of EU immigration policies, where 'a constant European law enforcement presence in the Saharan belt' was envisaged. This is done with the stated objective 'of formally training, equipping, assisting and cooperating on security with countries in the region (border control, joint patrolling, irregular migration and trafficking, terrorism, drugs, organised crime, etc.), while informally improving our early warning and prevention mechanisms' (Presidenza del Consiglio dei Ministri 2016, 3). In sum, the Italian strategy for the extra-territorialisation of border controls appears, mutatis mutandis, is an attempt at replicating the approach adopted in the late 1990s to control irregular migration arriving from Albania, albeit in the wider diplomatic context now offered by the EU neighbourhood policy and CSDP.

NOTES

1. Art. 11(1-bis), Legislative Decree No. 286/1998.
2. Art. 2(1), Ministry of Interior, Decree of 14 July 2003.
3. Art. 3(2), Ministry of Interior, Decree of 14 July 2003.
4. Art. 3(1), Ministry of Interior, Decree of 14 July 2003.
5. Art. 2(2), Ministry of Interior, Decree of 14 July 2003.
6. Of the 46,000 migrants landing on Apulian shores in 1999, over 22,000 were from Kosovo and 7,400 Roma (Monzini 2004, 44).
7. General principle No. 1.2, Decision 2010/252/EU.
8. Art. 2(2)(b)(ii), Council Decision (CFSP) 2015/778.
9. Art. 2(2)(c), Council Decision (CFSP) 2015/778.

BIBLIOGRAPHY

Amnesty International, *Lives Adrift. Refugees and Migrants in Peril in the Central Mediterranean* (London: Peter Benenson House, 2014).

Andersson, Ruben, 'A Game of Risk: Boat Migration and the Business of Bordering Europe', *Anthropology Today* 28, no. 6 (2012): 7.

Andreas, Peter, *Border Games. Policing the US.-Mexico Divide* (New York: Cornell University Press, 2000).

Andreas, Peter, 'Redrawing the Line: Borders and Security in the Twenty-first Century', *International Security* 28, no. 2 (2003): 78.

Andreas, Peter, and Price, Richard, 'From War Fighting to Crime Fighting: Transforming the American National Security State', *International Studies Review* 3, no. 3 (2001): 31.

Andrijasevic, Rutvica, 'DEPORTED: The Right to Asylum at EU's External Border of Italy and Libya', *International Migration* 48, no. 1 (2010): 148.

Basaran, Tugba, 'Security, Law, Borders: Spaces of Exclusion', *International Political Sociology* 2, no. 1 (2008): 339.

Bialasiewicz, Luiza, 'Off-shoring and Out-sourcing the Borders of Europe: Libya and EU Border Work in the Mediterranean', *Geopolitics* 17, no. 4 (2012): 843.

Bigo, Didier, 'The Möbius Ribbon of Internal and External Security(ies)', in *Identities, Borders, Orders: Nudging International Relations Theory in a New Direction*, edited by Albert, Mathias, Jacobson, David, and Lapid, Yosef (Minneapolis: University of Minnesota Press, 2001).

Bigo, Didier, 'When Two Become One: Internal and External Securitisations in Europe', in *International Relations Theory and The Politics of European Integration. Power, Security and Community*, edited by Kelstrup, Morten, and Williams, Michael (London: Routledge, 2006).

Campbell, Donald, and Campbell, Kathleen, 'Soldiers as Police Officers/Police Officers as Soldiers: Role Evolution and Revolution in the United States', *Armed Forces & Society* 36, no. 2 (2010): 327.

Campesi, Giuseppe, *Polizia della frontiera. Frontex e la produzione dello spazio europeo* (Rome: Deriveapprodi, 2015).

Carrera, Sergio, and den Hertog, Leonhard, 'Whose Mare? Rule of Law Challenges in the Field of European Border Surveillance in the Mediterranean', Brussels: CEPS paper in Liberty and Security in Europe No. 79/201, 2015.

Ceyhan, Ayse, and Tsoukal, Anastassia, 'The Securitization of Migration in Western Societies: Ambivalent Discourses and Policies', *Alternatives* 27, no. 1 (2002): 21.

Cremona, Marise, and Rijpma, Jorrit, 'The Extra-Territorialisation of EU Migration Policies and the Rule of Law', EUI working papers: LAW 2007/01, 2007.

Cuttitta, Paolo, ' "Borderizing" the Island Setting and Narratives of the Lampedusa "Border Play" ', *ACME: An International E-Journal for Critical Geographies* 13, no. 2 (2014): 196.

Cuttitta, Paolo, 'The Case of the Italian Southern Sea Borders: Cooperation across the Mediterranean?', in *Immigration Flows and the Management of the EU's Southern Maritime Borders*, edited by Pinyol, Gemma (Barcelona: CIDOB Migraciones, 2008).

Cuttitta Paolo, 'Readmission in the Relations between Italy and North African Mediterranean Countries', in *Unbalanced Reciprocities: Cooperation on Readmission in the Euro-Mediterranean Area*, edited by Cassarino, Jean-Pierre (London: Middle East Institute, 2011).

di Pascale, Alessia, 'Migration Control at Sea: The Italian Case', in *Extraterritorial Immigration Control. Legal Challenges*, edited by Ryan, Bernard, and Mitsilegas, Valsamis (Leiden: Martinus Nijhoff Publishers, 2010).

Dunn, Timothy, 'Border Militarization via Drug and Immigration Enforcement: Human Rights Implications', *Social Justice* 28, no. 2 (2001): 7–30.

Dursun-Ozkanca, Oya, and Vandemoortele, Antoine, 'The European Union and Security Sector Reform: Current Practices and Challenges of Implementation', *European Security* 21, no. 2 (2012): 139.

Easton, Marleen, den Boer, Monica, Janssens, Jelle, Moelker, Rene, and Vander Beken, Tom (ed.), *Blurring Military and Police Roles* (The Hague: Eleven International Publishing, 2010).

Edmundus, Timothy, 'What Are Armed Forces for? The Changing Nature of Military Roles in Europe', *International Affairs* 82, no. 6 (2006): 1059.

European Union. European Commission, *A European Agenda on Migration*. COM (2015)240, Brussels, 13 May 2015.

European Union. European Council, *Council Conclusions on Integrated Border Management*. JHA Council, 4–5 December 2006.

European Union. European Council. 'Special Meeting of the European Council, 23 April 2015 – Statement', accessed 8 August 2016. http://www.consilium.europa.eu/en/press/press-releases/2015/04/23-special-euco-statement/>

European Union. European Parliament, *European Parliament Resolution on Executions in Libya*. Strasbourg, 17 June 2010.

European Union. Frontex, *Annual Risk Analysis* (Warsaw: Frontex, 2010).

European Union. Frontex, *Annual Risk Analysis* (Warsaw: Frontex, 2013).

European Union. Frontex, *Annual Risk Analysis* (Warsaw: Frontex, 2014a).

European Union. Frontex, *Annual Risk Analysis* (Warsaw: Frontex, 2015).

European Union. Frontex, *Concept of Reinforced Joint Operation Tackling the Migratory Flows towards Italy: JO EPN-Triton* (Warsaw: Frontex, 2014b).

Frontex, 'Frontex Expands Its Joint Operation Triton', accessed 8 August 2016. http://frontex.europa.eu/news/frontex-expands-its-joint-operation-triton-udpbHP

Garelli Glenda, and Tazzioli, Martina, 'The Biopolitical Warfare on Migrants: EUNAVFOR and NATO Operations of Migration Government in the Mediterranean', *Critical Military Studies* (forthcoming).

Government of Italy. Ministero della Difesa, *Fine 2014: Terminano le operazioni del Dispositivo Navale di Sorveglianza e Sicurezza Marittima (DNSSM)*, fact sheet, accessed 8 January 2017. http://www.marina.difesa.it/cosa-facciamo/operazioni-concluse/Pagine/dnssmm_2.aspx

Government of Italy. Ministero della Difesa, *Mare Nostrum*, fact sheet, accessed 8 January 2017. http://www.marina.difesa.it/cosa-facciamo/operazioni-concluse/Pagine/mare-nostrum.aspx

Government of Italy. Ministero dell'Interno, *Relazione sull'attività delle forze di polizia e sullo stato dell'ordine e della sicurezza pubblica nel territorio nazionale (anno 1997)* (Rome: Senato della Repubblica, Camera dei Deputati, 1998).

Government of Italy. Ministero dell'Interno, *Relazione sull'attività delle forze di polizia e sullo stato dell'ordine e della sicurezza pubblica nel territorio nazionale (anno 1999)* (Rome: Senato della Repubblica, Camera dei Deputati, 2000).

Government of Italy. Ministero dell'Interno, *Relazione sulla realizzazione degli obiettivi fissati, sui risultati raggiunti e sulla efficacia degli interventi effettuati a sostegno delle Forze di polizia albanesi (anno 2000)* (Rome: Senato della Repubblica, Camera dei Deputati, 2001).

Government of Italy. Ministero dell'Interno, *Relazione sulla realizzazione degli obiettivi fissati, sui risultati raggiunti e sulla efficacia degli interventi effettuati a sostegno delle Forze di polizia albanesi (anno 2002)* (Rome: Senato della Repubblica, Camera dei Deputati, 2003).

Government of Italy. Ministero dell'Interno, *Relazione sull'attività delle Forze di polizia e sullo stato dell'ordine e della sicurezza pubblica e sulla criminalità organizzata (anno 2007)* (Rome: Senato della Repubblica, Camera dei Deputati, 2008).

Government of Italy. Ministero dell'Interno, *Relazione sull'attività delle Forze di polizia e sullo stato dell'ordine e della sicurezza pubblica e sulla criminalità organizzata (anno 2009)* (Rome: Senato della Repubblica, Camera dei Deputati, 2011).

Government of Italy. Ministero dell'Interno, *Relazione sull'attività delle Forze di polizia, sullo stato dell'ordine e della sicurezza pubblica e sulla criminalità organizzata (anno 2012)* (Rome: Senato della Repubblica, Camera dei Deputati, 2013).

Government of Italy. Ministero per i rapporti con il Parlamento, *Relazione sullo stato della disciplina militare e dell'organizzazione delle Forze armate (anno 2001)* (Rome: Senato della Repubblica, Camera dei Deputati, 2003).

Government of Italy. Ministero per i rapporti con il Parlamento, *Relazione sullo stato della disciplina militare e dell'organizzazione delle Forze armate (anno 2003)* (Rome: Senato della Repubblica, Camera dei Deputati, 2004).

Government of Italy. Ministero per i rapporti con il Parlamento, *Relazioni sullo stato della disciplina militare e sullo stato dell'organizzazione delle Forze armate (anno 2008)* (Rome: Senato della Repubblica, Camera dei Deputati, 2008).

Government of Italy. Ministero per i rapporti con il Parlamento, *Relazioni sullo stato della disciplina militare e sullo stato dell'organizzazione delle Forze armate (anno 2014)* (Rome: Senato della Repubblica, Camera dei Deputati, 2015).

Government of Italy. Presidenza del Consiglio dei Ministri, *Italian Non-paper. Migration Compact: Contribution to an EU Strategy for External Action on Migration*, Rome, 15 April 2016, accessed 8 August 2016. http://www.governo.it/sites/governo.it/files/immigrazione_0.pdf

Hamood, Sara, 'EU-Libya Cooperation on Migration: A Raw Deal for Refugees and Migrants?', *Journal of Refugee Studies* 21, no. 1 (2008): 19.

Hobbing, Peter, 'Integrated Border Management at the EU Level', CEPS working document No. 227/August 2005.

Human Rights Watch, *Italy's Forced Return of Boat Migrants and Asylum Seekers, Libya's Mistreatment of Migrants and Asylum Seekers* (New York: Human Rights Watch, 2009).

Huysmans, Jeffrey, *The Politics of Insecurity: Fear, Migration and Asylum in the EU* (London: Routledge, 2006).

Jeandesboz, Jean, 'The Genesis of the European Neighbourhood Policy: Alternative Narratives, Bureaucratic Competitions', in *The Frontiers of Governance: Understanding the External Dimension of EU Justice and Home Affairs*, edited by Balzacq, Thierry (New York: Palgrave Macmillan, 2009).

Kasparek, Bernd, and Wagner, Fabian, 'Local Border Regimes or a Homogeneous External Border? The Case of the European Union's Border Agency Frontex', in *The New Politics of International Mobility Migration Management and Its Discontents*, edited by Geiger, Martin, and Pécoud, Antoine (Osnabrück: Institut für Migrationsforschung und Interkulturelle Studien, 2012).

Kraska, Peter, 'Militarization and Policing – Its Relevance to 21st Century Police'. *Policing* 1 (4): 501–13.

Lavenex, Sandra, 2006. 'Shifting Up and Out: The Foreign Policy of European Immigration Control', *West European Politics* 29, no. 2 (2007): 329.

Lavenex, Sandra, and Wichmann, Nicole, 'The External Governance of EU Internal Security', *Journal of European Integration* 31, no. 1 (2009): 83.

Legomsky, Stephen, 'The USA and the Caribbean Interdiction Program', *International Journal of Refugee Law* 18, no. 3–4 (2006): 677.

Lutterbeck, Derek, 'Between Police and Military: The New Security Agenda and the Rise of Gendarmeries' *Cooperation and Conflict* 39, no. 1 (2004): 45.

Lutterbeck, Derek, 'Blurring the Dividing Line: The Convergence of Internal and External Security in Western Europe', *European Security* 14, no. 2 (2005): 231.

Lutterbeck, Derek, 'Policing Migration in the Mediterranean', *Mediterranean Politics* 11, no. 1 (2006): 59.

Magner, Tara, 'A Less than Pacific Solution for Asylum Seekers in Australia', *International Journal of Refugee Law* 16, no. 1 (2004): 53.

Mitsilegas, Valsimis, 'Extraterritorial Immigration Control in the 21st Century: The Individual and the State Transformed', in *Extraterritorial Immigration Control. Legal Challenges*, edited by Ryan, Bernard, and Mitsilegas, Valsamis (Leiden: Martinus Nijhoff Publishers, 2010).

Monar, Jörg, *The External Dimension of the EU's Area of Freedom, Security and Justice: Progress, Potential and Limitations after the Treaty of Lisbon* (Stockholm: Swedish Institute for European Policy Studies, 2012).

Monzini, Paola, *Il traffico di migranti per mare verso l'Italia. Sviluppi recenti (2004–2008)* (Rome: Centro Studi di Politica Internazionale, 2008).

Monzini, Paola, 'Il traffico di Migranti per via marittima: il caso dell'Italia', in *L'Italia promessa. Geopolitica e dinamiche organizzative del traffico di migranti verso l'Italia*, edited by Monzini, Paola, Pastore, Ferruccio, and Schiortino, Giuseppe (Rome: Centro Studi di Politica Internazionale, 2004).

Mountz, Alison, and Loyd, Jenna, 'Constructing the Mediterranean Region: Obscuring Violence in the Bordering of Europe's Migration "Crises"', *ACME: An International E-Journal for Critical Geographies* 13, no. 2 (2013): 173.

Nouran, Abdel Aziz, Paola Monzini, and Pastore, Ferruccio, *The Changing Dynamics of Cross-Border Human Smuggling and Trafficking in the Mediterranean* (Rome: Istituto Affari Internazionali, 2015).

Palafox, Jose, 'Opening Up Borderland Studies: A Review of U.S.–Mexico Militarization Discourse', *Social Justice* 27, no. 3 (2000): 56.

Paoletti, Emanuela, 'Power Relations and International Migration: The Case of Italy and Libya', *Political Studies* 59, no. 2 (2011): 269.

Paoletti, Emanuela, and Pastore, Ferruccio, 'Sharing the Dirty Job on the Southern Front?', IMI working papers, 2010.

Pugh, Michael, *Europe's Boat People: Maritime Cooperation in the Mediterranean* (London: Institute for Security Studies, Western European Union, 2000).

Rettman, Andrew, 'EU Navies Prepare to Start Work in Libyan Waters', *euobserver*, 19 April 2016, accessed 8 August 2016. https://euobserver.com/foreign/133115

Rijpma, Jorrit, and Vermeulen, Mathias, 'EUROSUR: Saving Lives or Building Borders?', *European Security* 24, no. 3 (2015): 454.

Trauner, Florian, and Kruse, Imke, 'EC Visa Facilitation and Readmission Agreements: A New Standard EU Foreign Policy Tool?', *European Journal of Migration and Law* 10, no. 4 (2008): 411.

Vives, Luna, 'Over the Fence: The Militarization of the Senegalese-Spanish Sea Border', *African Geographical Review* 28, no. 1 (2009): 5.

Zaiotti, Ruben, *Cultures of Border Control: Schengen and the Evolution of European Frontiers* (Chicago: University of Chicago Press, 2011).

Chapter 5

Inclusion and Exclusion in the Fragmented Space of the Sea Actors, Territories and Legal Regimes between Libya and Italy

Paolo Cuttitta

INTRODUCTION

This chapter looks at the Central Mediterranean migration route between Libya and Italy, which accounts for the overwhelming majority of the irregularised migrants arriving to Italy by sea,[1] to analyse its maritime space. By unpacking the interaction between the different actors, logics, territories and legal regimes at play, it shows what kind of a space takes shape in this maritime region, and also the consequences there are for people trying to cross from North Africa to Europe.[2]

If we adopt the perspective of people setting off on unauthorised journeys, we can see the Strait of Sicily as a uniform space. Arguably, indeed, the shores from which migrants leave Libya are to a large extent perceived by migrants as a much more important border than legal partitions such as those between national and international waters. The time and place of embarkation is the border between the previous steps of their migratory experience and what is supposed to be the last step, the one that will end on EU soil. It is the sea which they must cross, which separates them from their goal. At sea, different factors contribute to determine whether this goal can be reached; whether the prevailing logic will be that of exclusion or that of inclusion.

Indeed, if we look at sea-crossings from the northern shore of the Mediterranean, we can see that sea journeys are – if rather randomly – governed by these two logics: the logic of inclusion, allowing for migrants to physically enter Europe, and the logic of exclusion, preventing people from arriving on EU soil. These seemingly opposed logics coexist at EU borders, and in particular they unfold in an unpredictable way in the space of the sea. The latter, indeed, is less uniform than it may appear. It is, rather, a highly fragmented space.

Formal (legal) geographical partitions, such as national waters, contiguous zones, international waters, search and rescue (SAR) regions, along with the relevant legal regimes resulting from different (and sometimes overlapping) laws, are the first factors determining such fragmentation, as shown in chapter 6 of this edited book by van Selm. They can play a crucial role in determining the outcome of a sea-crossing. Further factors, which can be even more important than legal partitions, are the policies and practices developed by the different state and non-state actors: deals made between different state and supra-state (e.g., EU, Italian and Libyan) authorities, their patrolling activities and SAR practices, the decisions made by their judiciaries, the practices of smugglers and merchant ships, and the SAR activities of humanitarian non-governmental organisations (NGOs). All these factors contribute to producing the space of the sea, by rippling its surface and turning it from a uniform and smooth space to a rough and jagged space.

The next section introduces the concepts of 'space of the sea', 'inclusion' and 'exclusion'. The following sections analyse two territories (Libyan and Maltese SAR regions, Libyan and international waters) and key actors at play (EU and Italian authorities, also including the maritime operations *Triton* and *Sophia*; Libyan authorities; commercial vessels; SAR NGOs), to show how the interaction between these elements contributes to shaping the fragmented space of the sea and to serving the logics of inclusion and exclusion. See chapter 3 by Williams and chapter 4 by Campesi for more information on maritime operations.

INCLUSION AND EXCLUSION
IN THE SPACE OF THE SEA

We can best grasp the different fragmentations characterising the Strait of Sicily, as well as the dynamics and logics underlying them, by regarding the sea as a space of its own. By first looking at the sea as a uniform space and then unpacking the highly complex and unpredictable logics and dynamics which are at play there, it becomes easier to understand how uneven such space in fact is.

If we look at the larger picture of the region, including North Africa and Italy, from the perspective of EU destination countries, we can see the sea as one of three different spaces. The first is the North African space, consisting of the land territories of countries of origin and/or transit of migrants. The second is the EU space, represented by the Italian land territory, which is their destination (with the *caveat* that Italy is only seen as a transit destination towards other EU countries by most of those crossing the sea). The third is the space in-between: the space of the sea, where the journey from the first to the second space takes place.

In these three spaces, two logics play: (1) exclusion, aimed at keeping bodies where they are, at preventing them from reaching Europe and at returning them to North Africa; and (2) inclusion, resulting in people arriving to Europe (Cuttitta 2017b). By logic of inclusion I mean the logic guiding any policy and practice (also including protection principles or legal obligations such as the prohibition of *refoulement*)[3] eventually allowing for irregularised sea-crossers to reach European soil, and possibly also remain there. In other words, what is meant by inclusion here is the merely physical (and often only temporary) inclusion into European territory. In the same vein, exclusion is meant as the merely physical exclusion from European territory: it comprises of all policies and practices which are aimed at or end up preventing people from attempting or completing the sea journey.[4]

In the three different spaces, the balance between these two logics differs. The North African space is primarily one of exclusion, in which the aim of delocalised EU migration and border policies, supported by non-state actors as well as by the state authorities of the relevant countries of transit or origin, is to prevent people from setting off for the EU. Inclusion, meaning the transfer of people to EU space, happens only within the framework of occasional and minor relocation schemes.[5] In sum, the logic of inclusion is either absent from the North African space, or it is clearly subordinated to the logic of exclusion.

In the other two spaces, instead, the logic of inclusion has a place of its own and operates in a more balanced relationship with the logic of exclusion. In destination countries, for example, at their internalised borders, such as hotspots (Martin and Tazzioli 2016), the logic of inclusion operates to select those who deserve protection and thus resident status, whereas the logic of exclusion is translated into the logic of forced removal, whose aim is to return the others, the illegalised.

Similarly, in the space of the sea, the logic of exclusion goes along with that of inclusion. There, the logic of inclusion mainly takes shape in rescue operations carried out by both state and non-state actors. These include vessels and aircraft of Italian and EU authorities, as well as commercial ships and the rescue vessels of several humanitarian NGOs. Relevant activities include the first assistance and aid granted to the migrants found at sea, as well as the transfer of the rescued to an Italian port. Thus, these people are brought from the space of the sea to EU space.

The logic of exclusion, instead, manifests itself in at least three ways. First, the intelligence and policing activities carried out by state (Italian) and suprastate (EU) authorities of destination countries in international waters. Such activities aim at collecting information, arresting smugglers and destroying vessels, in order to disrupt criminal networks and thus prevent people from embarking on sea-crossings (see chapter 4 by Campesi; Cuttitta 2017b; Garelli and Tazzioli 2016; Tazzioli forthcoming; chapter 3 by Williams). Second, the activities carried out by the Libyan state authorities (IOM 2017; *Libya Herald* 2016, 2017), returning to the place of embarkation those migrants who are intercepted or rescued before they are found by European authorities or non-state SAR actors. Third, the death of many people (Last et al. 2017) resulting from the interaction of the agency of migrants and smugglers with restrictive migration and border policies and practices, whereby the latter sometimes also include insufficient SAR efforts (Heller and Pezzani 2016). Despite the differences, the logics of inclusion and exclusion feed into each other; inclusion and exclusion operate jointly to design and implement externalised EU border policies (Cuttitta 2017b).

Importantly, the double logic of the sea unfolds in a multiform, irregular and uneven space, in which not only are there different sovereignties and territorial partitions, but these sovereignties and territorialities are also subject to crises and negotiations, as well as twists of fate, resulting in a high degree of uncertainty about the outcomes of actions occurring in a given maritime territory. Furthermore, a plurality of state and non-state actors are involved. The fact that such actors have different motivations, tasks and modi operandi increases the complexity of the interaction between uncertain spatialities, on the one hand, and the seemingly opposed logics of inclusion and exclusion, on the other hand, thus making the outcomes of such interaction highly unpredictable.

TERRITORIES AND ACTORS

According to the 1982 United Nations Convention on the Law of the Sea, the sea is divided into territorial seas (also known as national or territorial waters) and high seas (also known as international waters). Territorial waters are part of the national territories, and therefore fall under the sovereignty of coastal states.[6] International waters also include contiguous zones. Contiguous zones are adjacent to territorial waters and may not extend beyond 24 nautical miles from the coastline. International law allows for state authorities to exercise control in their contiguous zones in order to punish (or prevent) infringements of their immigration laws and regulations from being committed within their territories or territorial waters.

Furthermore, the 1979 International Convention on Maritime Search and Rescue (SAR Convention) divides international waters (also including the contiguous zones) into SAR regions, each one falling under the responsibility of a different coastal state.[7] In each SAR region, the relevant state must provide SAR services under the coordination of a Maritime Rescue Coordination Centre (MRCC). Once it is informed of a distress case, the MRCC identifies the vessel(s) to be involved in the SAR operation (based primarily on the proximity and speed of nearby vessels, and secondarily on additional criteria, such as the kind of vessel and its degree of appropriateness for SAR operations), and informs the rescue ship about where the rescued should be disembarked.

On their way to Italy, migrants may cross the territorial waters, contiguous zones and SAR regions of Libya, Malta, Tunisia and Italy, whereby the applicable legal framework also changes accordingly.

The actors operating across these territorial partitions are manifold: as of June 2017, besides smugglers and migrants, there are the MRCCs, the coast guards and the navies of the coastal countries, the Operation *Triton* of the EU border agency Frontex (Tazzioli 2016), the EU Common Security and Defence Policy mission EUNAVFOR Med *Sophia* (Garelli and Tazzioli forthcoming), the humanitarian operation *Pontus* of the Irish Navy (*Naval Today* 2017), commercial vessels accidentally involved (Heller and Pezzani 2016), as well as humanitarian NGOs voluntarily participating in SAR operations (Cusumano 2017; Cuttitta 2017a; Stierl 2017). The Italian Navy carries out autonomous patrolling activities only within the small operation *Mare Sicuro*. Previously, it managed the large-scale military-humanitarian operation *Mare Nostrum*, which it launched in October 2013 and ended in December 2014. Frontex has coordinated joint operations in the Strait of Sicily for over a decade, and the current *Triton* mission started in November 2014. The Irish operation *Pontus* (consisting of just one navy ship) started in May 2015, while *Sophia* was launched in June that year.

The number of SAR vessels deployed by NGOs changes depending on the plans of the different organisations, as well as on the resources available to them. The first NGO rescue vessel was set up by the Migrant Offshore Aid Station (MOAS) in 2014. MSF (Médecins Sans Frontières) and Sea-Watch followed in 2015 and further NGOs (Jugend Rettet, SOS Méditerranée, Sea Eye, Proactiva Open Arms, Boat Refugee Foundation, Save the Children, CADUS/Lifeboat) in 2016 (Cusumano 2017; Cuttitta 2017a; Stierl 2017). In late 2016, thirteen NGO vessels were carrying out SAR activities off Libyan coasts.

THE LIBYAN AND MALTESE SAR REGIONS

Libya never declared its SAR region nor established its MRCC, and its coast guard authorities are not adequately equipped or trained to carry out and coordinate SAR effectively. Therefore, the Italian MRCC, which is managed by the Italian Coast Guard, has *de facto* taken over SAR responsibilities in that area. SAR coordination by the Italian MRCC in the would-be Libyan SAR region has been happening on a regular basis since the end of 2013. After over 600 people lost their lives in two shipwrecks that occurred in the Strait of Sicily in October 2013,[8] the government of Italy launched its military-humanitarian operation *Mare Nostrum*, whose assets were deployed close to Libyan waters, in order to intercept migrant boats before they would go adrift or capsize. 'Mostly, the Libyan authorities don't even answer if we call them to inform them about distress cases, so we are obliged to intervene', the Italian Coast Guard told me in September 2015.[9] At that time, the Italian Operation *Mare Nostrum* had been stopped, but vessels of both the Frontex *Triton* and the *Sophia*, as well as NGOs' rescue vessels, were patrolling next to Libyan waters under the SAR coordination of the Italian MRCC.

Malta lies in the middle of the Strait of Sicily, on route between Libya and Italy. Although migrants typically aim to reach Italy, rather than Malta, thousands of them happened to land on the island state since the early 2000s. Until 2013, almost all those who managed to reach EU territory from Libya had to cross the Maltese SAR region before either being intercepted and brought to Italy or autonomously landing there. While the Maltese SAR region is disproportionately large, the SAR capacity of the Maltese authorities is very limited, as is their willingness to accept the disembarkation of migrants on Maltese territory. Indeed, the small size of Malta and the fact that migrants irregularly landing there and travelling further to other EU countries can be returned to the island state under EU law, regardless of whether they are illegalised migrants or 'dublinised' asylum seekers,[10] explain why 'the issue of irregular immigration . . . emerged as a major, if not *the* major, policy challenge in Malta' (Lutterbeck 2009, 121) during the past decade. This resulted in Maltese authorities often ignoring distress cases, resulting in tragic consequences, or refusing to authorise the disembarkation of people rescued by commercial vessels in the Maltese SAR region (Klepp 2011). Significantly, Malta refused to sign the 2004 amendments to the 1974 International Convention for the Safety of Life at Sea (SOLAS Convention), which placed on the countries coordinating SAR the burden to organise the disembarkation (Coppens 2013).

Things changed after the two shipwrecks of October 2013. Since then, only few hundred people a year have arrived in Malta (and some were just people in urgent need of medical care who were transferred with helicopters from the vessels that had rescued them). This was a result of the deployment of patrol boats in what is supposed to be the Libyan SAR region, and their involvement in SAR under the coordination of the Italian MRCC, first with *Mare Nostrum*, then with *Sophia* and *Triton*, as well as with national navy and NGO vessels (Cusumano 2017; Cuttitta 2017a, b; Garelli and Tazzioli forthcoming; Tazzioli 2016). This caused the *de facto* exclusion of the Maltese SAR region from the Libyan-Italian route, because migrants have been intercepted long before they enter the Maltese SAR region since then. As foreseen by the operational plans of both EU operations *Triton* and *Sophia*, all migrants apprehended are handed over to the Italian authorities and disembarked in Italy.[11]

The deployment of military and civil vessels of both state and non-state actors in the Libyan SAR region arguably supports the logic of inclusion, at least in the short term. First, because some of the rescued people might otherwise have been left to die by the lacking SAR capacities and willingness of Libyan and Maltese authorities. Second, because the prohibition of *refoulement* (and, under circumstances, the prohibition of collective removal) results in the obligation to transfer to Italy the people rescued in the Libyan SAR region under the coordination of the Italian MRCC. Indeed, according to the principle of the port of safety, people rescued at sea should not be disembarked in territories where their 'lives and freedoms . . . would be threatened' (IMO 2004), and the 2012 judgement of the European Court of Human Rights in the case *Hirsi Jamaa and Others v. Italy* confirmed that 'the notion of "place of safety" should not be restricted solely to the physical protection of people, but necessarily also entails respect for their fundamental rights'. Therefore, European authorities cannot, in principle, return people to any North African country. Given the unavailability of Malta, Italy remains the only viable option.

In the long term, however, the deployment of military vessels serves the logic of exclusion in the first place, insofar as it is aimed at enhancing police cooperation with the Libyan authorities in order to combat smugglers and prevent migrants from attempting the sea-crossing.

The cases of the Maltese and Libyan SAR regions show that the role of specific policies and practices can be at least as important as that of legal partitions and formal responsibilities in determining the outcome of sea journeys across international waters. This is also the case for national waters, as the next section demonstrates.

LIBYAN VERSUS INTERNATIONAL WATERS

If a boat in distress is spotted while still in Libyan territorial waters, that is, within 12 nautical miles from the coast, the sovereignty principle requires that Libyan authorities are informed in the first place. The Libyan authorities are then supposed to intervene in their national waters to rescue the migrants and to return them to a Libyan port. Interestingly, the following cases reveal that these principles and customs may occasionally be subverted.

On 29 April 2016, the MRCC Rome received a distress call from a dinghy that was still in Libyan territorial waters, seven nautical miles off Sabratha (*la Repubblica* 2016). The Italian Coast Guard contacted first their Libyan counterpart, then the nearest commercial vessel (an Italian cargo). The latter soon reached the drifting dinghy, which was now only four nautical miles off Libyan coast. An estimated eighty to ninety people were missing, while twenty-six were rescued by the cargo, brought to international waters and handed over to the Italian authorities, who were awaiting them there and eventually transferred them to Lampedusa. In the absence of official humanitarian corridors from Libya, an unofficial one was created. In this case, the logic of inclusion prevailed over that of exclusion, despite territorial sovereignty principles. On other occasions, after contacting the Libyan Coast Guard and receiving no answer, or being told that they were unable to intervene, the Italian MRCC sent the nearest NGO ship to rescue migrants in Libyan waters.[12] MSF alone intervened five times in Libyan waters, with the permission of the Libyan authorities, in 2016 (MSF 2017). The rescued were then transferred to Italy, either by the MSF rescue ship itself or by another vessel under the coordination of the Italian MRCC. On 15 August 2015, MOAS carried out a rescue operation in Libyan waters not only with the permission but also with the practical cooperation of the Libyan Coast Guard. MOAS's ship then transferred the 201 rescued to Sicily (Xchange 2015).

The contrary was the case on 7 June 2016, when Libyan authorities were alerted by the Italian Coast Guard about a vessel which was heading northwards but was still in Libyan waters. The Italian Coast Guard also alerted a nearby NGO ship, which was patrolling in international waters. Different vessels converged from north and south towards the migrant boat, which continued its journey and left Libyan territorial waters. Eventually, the first to intercept it in international waters, in the Libyan SAR region normally managed by the Italian MRCC, were the Libyan authorities, who took the migrants on board and returned them to Libya.[13] Thus, the logic of exclusion prevailed over that of inclusion. If the alarm had been sent out only few minutes later, the migrants would have been rescued by the NGO vessel and brought to Sicily instead.

Importantly, these incidents show that the outcome of sea journeys, and therefore the prevalence of either inclusionary or exclusionary logics, are often left to the randomness of fate (e.g., which rescue boat arrives first), as well as to the arbitrariness of administrative decisions (e.g., whether the Libyan Coast Guard takes the rescued back to Libya or lets the rescue vessel transfer them to Italy).

EXCLUSION THROUGH DEATH

Commercial ships were increasingly involved by the Italian authorities in SAR operations during *Mare Nostrum*, and even more after its end which left the area adjacent to Libyan waters unattended (Pezzani and Heller 2015). While their involvement was later reduced, they are still often required to intervene when they are close to a boat in distress (Italian Coast Guard Headquarters 2017). Because, however, they are not equipped, and their crews are not trained, for SAR, commercial vessels sometimes turn, inadvertently, from actors of inclusion through rescue to actors of exclusion through 'death by rescue' (Heller and Pezzani 2016). Many people, indeed, have lost their lives during rescue operations carried out by cargo ships. Furthermore, rescue interventions result in heavy economic losses for shipowners. Some of them therefore prefer to switch off the automatic identification system, which allows the Coast Guard to find the vessel closest to a boat in distress, of their vessels (IIHL 2016), or simply to take longer routes,[14] rather than risking to be involved in SAR operations. This seems to have been the case after the involvement of commercial vessels in SAR reached its peak in 2015. Indeed, the share of people rescued by the shipping industry sank from 32.98 per cent in the first five months of 2015 to only 1.29 per cent in the period from June to December,[15] which cannot be explained only by the higher number of assets deployed by state and supra-state authorities, as well as by NGOs, in the summer of that year. In sum, the immanent violence of the border regime ends up reproducing itself, transforming potential actors of inclusion through rescue into eventual actors of exclusion through death.

The border regime has a similar impact on the smugglers as well: enhanced policing activities have pushed them to use vessels that are increasingly unseaworthy and overcrowded. Since *Sophia* started seizing and destroying wooden boats, thus preventing smugglers from reusing them, migrants have been increasingly embarked on rubber dinghies (Parlamento Italiano 2016), which are more likely to sink only a few miles after departure. Like merchant ships, smugglers thus turned into actors of exclusion through death.

BETWEEN INCLUSION AND EXCLUSION: SAR NGOs

SAR NGOs are basically expressions of the logic of inclusion, but they can also serve the logic of exclusion. Some of them not only have a humanitarian but also a political aim (Cuttitta 2017a; Stierl 2017), namely to denounce the current restrictive border regime, to campaign for safe passage to the EU, to monitor the situation and to play the watchdogs of state and supra-state authorities, for example, by setting up a reconnaissance airplane (Sea-Watch 2016b). Others, instead, do not mind also following the logic of exclusion by supporting state authorities in their intelligence activities against smugglers.

The case of MOAS is telling with this regard. In May 2015, while disembarking 369 people at a Sicilian port, they allowed the Italian police to identify and arrest two purported smugglers, by providing them with pictures taken by their drones during the SAR operation. Other NGOs, instead, refused to share sensitive information with Italian authorities. A legal obligation for them to do so would only arise from an official request from judicial authorities.

MOAS also flies its drones over Libyan waters, with an authorisation from the Libyan authorities (MOAS 2016). This raises the question of what happens to boats spotted by a MOAS drone while still in Libyan waters. Arguably, the NGO should contact either the Libyan authorities directly, or the Italian MRCC, which then would have to alert their Libyan counterpart. If able and willing to do so, the Libyan authorities would then intervene by 'rescuing' the migrants and returning them to a Libyan port, not only in the cases in which they are in immediate risk of life but also in the cases in which they would still be able to reach international waters and be assisted by other vessels, which would eventually bring them to Italy. This derives from the extensive interpretation of the term 'distress' adopted by the Italian MRCC, as well as by the NGOs working under its coordination. Indeed, the condition of 'distress' is what makes a rescue intervention obligatory under international law. While the legal definition of the term 'distress' is vague (see chapter 6; Coppens 2013; Klepp 2011; Moreno-Lax 2011), its extensive interpretation assumes that any unseaworthy or overcrowded vessel is *ipso facto* in distress. Other state authorities, such as the Maltese, adopt a more restrictive interpretation. Since MOAS adopts, like the Italian MRCC, the extensive interpretation, it can be presumed that any case of a migrant boat spotted by its drones in Libyan waters will be reported to the Libyan authorities, either directly or via the Italian MRCC.

In sum, a humanitarian concern (considering all migrant vessels to be in distress is clearly aimed at reducing the risk of casualties), in combination with territorial sovereignty constraints, might turn a rescue intervention into a forced return, thus serving the logic of exclusion.

Finally, the drones deployed by MOAS might be used for purposes of police cooperation (e.g., exchange of information about smuggling activities) between the NGO and Libyan authorities. This seems plausible in light of the fact that MOAS also hosted Libyan Navy officials on board its rescue vessels (Süddeutsche Zeitung 2016).[16] Flying MOAS drones over Libyan waters could also enhance cooperation with Italian and European authorities involved in security operations mandated to protect Italian and EU borders (the operations run by the Italian Navy and *Guardia di Finanza*;

Frontex's Operation *Triton*) and to disrupt smuggling networks (Operation *Sophia*).

BETWEEN INCLUSION AND EXCLUSION: OPERATIONS *SOPHIA* AND *TRITON*

In spite of their security mandates, EU vessels must also carry out SAR if necessary. Furthermore, their reconnaissance aircraft also contribute to spotting boats in distress. Whether and in how far EU operations serve the logics of inclusion, however, depends to a large extent on where their assets are deployed. Frontex was criticised when its *Triton* mission was launched simultaneously with the end of *Mare Nostrum*: While the assets of the Italian mission were constantly operating next to Libyan national waters, the EU agency limited *Triton*'s operational area to thirty nautical miles south of Sicily. This resulted in more deaths (Heller and Pezzani 2016), until the EU eventually decided to expand the geographical scope of the operation following the death of an estimated 700 people in another shipwreck occurred on 18 April 2015.

Even after the extension of the operational area, however, the degree of actual involvement of Frontex assets in rescue operations kept fluctuating across time depending on two variables: the number of vessels deployed and the place where they are deployed within the enlarged operational area.

As regards *Sophia*, other variables also play a role. As long as the naval operation does not go beyond its phase 2 A, which allows it to operate only in international waters, it will mainly serve the logic of inclusion, since activities on the high seas consist to a large extent of SAR interventions, and people rescued there must be brought to Italy (Parliament of the United Kingdom 2016). Things would change in the following phases, which would allow EU assets to operate in Libyan waters (phase 2 B) and Libyan land territory (phase 3), and thus to better tackle smuggling activities, including by arresting smugglers, also in cooperation with Libyan authorities. Entering these phases, however, requires an invitation from the Libyan government, as well as a resolution of the UN Security Council (Wikileaks 2016). A further necessary step is to agree on which country would be responsible for prosecuting the suspected smugglers apprehended on Libyan land or sea territory. As regards the destiny of migrants apprehended on Libyan land or sea territory in the next phases of *Sophia*, the naval mission holds that migrants would surely not be transferred to Italy and would thus remain in Libyan territory.[17] It could, however, be argued that, based either on the principle of effective control (Gammeltoft-Hansen 2011, 109–10) or on that of indirect responsibility for outsourcing or contracting out obligations (Moreno-Lax

2011, 200), in combination with either the principle of *non-refoulement*, which 'binds the action of states even when they de-territorialize the control of their borders' (Trevisanut 2014, 673), or with the right to leave any country, enshrined in article 12 of the United Nations International Covenant on Civil and Political Rights (Markard 2016), EU authorities could be held responsible for the destiny of the people apprehended in Libyan waters or land territory. Consequently, they would be obliged not to hand them over to the Libyan authorities.

Negotiations, as well as legal interpretations, about territoriality and sovereignty with regard to Operation *Sophia* may profoundly change the balance between the logic of inclusion and the logic of exclusion in the space of the sea.

BETWEEN INCLUSION AND EXCLUSION: LIBYAN, ITALIAN AND EU AUTHORITIES

In the meantime, however, the degree to which European assets serve the logic of inclusion has been substantially reduced. The main aim for EU and Italian authorities is for Libya to increase its capacity to prevent migrants from embarking, as well as its capacity to intercept those who manage to embark and to return them to a Libyan port, before the EU or NGO vessels rescue and bring them to Italy (European Union 2017). Therefore, in early 2016, while supporting the establishment of a Libyan Government of National Accord (GNA), the EU asked the GNA to cooperate in this direction. The GNA demonstrated its willingness to cooperate, and the number of people 'rescued' at sea and returned to a Libyan port by the local coast guard and navy authorities reached a record 18,904 in 2016 (IOM 2017). Most of them were intercepted in Libyan waters, but some returns were carried out from the high seas. People intercepted at sea generally face widespread abuses and violence from the Libyan authorities upon their return to Libyan soil (Amnesty International 2016), but often they are subjected to similar treatment (e.g., being confiscated of all their belongings or being shot dead by Libyan officials) while still at sea, before or during the return operations (UNSMIL-OHCHR 2016).

In August 2015, an inflatable vessel with 125 passengers set off from Zuwara, Libya, close to the Tunisian border. Soon, the engine broke, and, while going adrift in international waters, the dinghy was intercepted by a patrol boat of the Libyan Coast Guard. Instead of rescuing the migrants, however, the Libyan officials stole their on-board equipment and abandoned them there. 'They told us in Arabic that the weather would change very soon, and within four hours we would be dead. They didn't do or say anything else', two of the survivors told me.[18] After that, one of the migrants went insane and threw himself into the water. The others were eventually rescued by the Tunisian Navy and brought to Tunisia. Not only does this case provide another example of the violence to which migrants are exposed at sea, but it also demonstrates how unpredictable the final outcome of their journeys can be. Indeed, in 2015 alone, 931 people who had embarked from Libya ended their journey in Tunisia[19] rather than reaching Italy or being returned to Libya.

Ironically, Libyan authorities also serve the logic of inclusion, insofar as some representatives of the Libyan Coast Guard are directly involved in smuggling activities and cooperate with criminal organisations (United Nations 2017). However, given the growing number of people prevented from embarking, as well as forced returns carried out from both territorial and international waters, their function is increasingly one of exclusion. In order to facilitate the intervention of Libyan authorities on the high seas, *Triton* and *Sophia* vessels gradually left the area close to Libyan waters in the summer of 2016. In October, the EU also started training the Libyan Coast Guard and Navy, while Italy started the delivery of ten patrol boats to Libyan authorities in April 2017, after signing an agreement with the GNA in February.

Clearly, the persistent SAR activities of NGO vessels next to Libyan waters were an obstacle for Libyan authorities, which therefore launched a dissuasion campaign. In April 2016, they boarded and searched the Sea-Watch vessel 'Sea-Watch 2';[20] on 17 August Libyan officials shot at, boarded and searched the MSF's 'Bourbon Argos' (*Guardian* 2016); on 9 September, they went as far as to detain two volunteers of the German NGO Sea Eye and seize their speedboat (Sea Eye 2016). In October 2016, Libyan officials boarded a dinghy that was being rescued by the Sea-Watch 2, causing its deflation and the drowning of dozens of people (Sea-Watch 2016a). On 10 May 2017, the Libyan Coast Guard interrupted a rescue operation by Sea-Watch and returned nearly 500 people from international waters to Libya (Reuters 2017). This time the Libyan intervention was coordinated by the Italian MRCC, which instructed the NGO vessel to let the Libyan boat take the lead of the SAR operation. This incident marked a turning point, with the Italian MRCC turning from an actor of inclusion to one of exclusion. Importantly, this happened at a time when the Italian judiciary had also taken first steps in the same direction, by opening up investigations against SAR NGOs regarding facilitation of illegal immigration. The indictment of the relevant NGOs and the seizure of their boats would reduce SAR capacities and discourage humanitarian actors, thus serving the logic of exclusion.

Returns from international waters and even from Libyan waters may not exclude an indirect responsibility of Italy or the EU (Giuffré 2012; Markard 2016). On the one hand, Libyan authorities can legally intercept and return boats even in their contiguous zone within border control operations. On the other hand, legal responsibilities might arise also for indirect action,[21] since the interventions of Libyan authorities returning intercepted migrants to the coast are carried out upon request, in the interest and with the technical support of Italian and European authorities. However, the increasing humanitarian rhetoric deployed by Italian and EU (Cuttitta 2017b; Musarò 2017; Tazzioli 2016) as well as Libyan (*Libya Herald* 2016, 2017) authorities about sea operations has ended up blurring any distinction between rescue operations and interceptions. All interventions at sea, regardless of whether they are carried out by state or non-state actors, and, in the former case, by European or non-European authorities, are now labelled as rescue operations. As a consequence, it is questionable whether they can be considered as outsourced push-backs and Italy and the EU be held responsible for indirect action. The obligation to provide assistance to people in distress, indeed, must prevail over any other consideration. However, as long as no Libyan SAR region is established and SAR operations are carried out under the coordination of the Italian MRCC, it could be argued that the principle of the port of safety should always apply, even if people are first assisted by Libyan authorities. Again, different interpretations of legal obligations could radically change the relationship between inclusion and exclusion in the space of the sea.

CONCLUSION

This chapter has analysed the sea as a space of its own. This allows for the emergence of some clarity in relation to the fragmentation of such a space, as well as recognising the fluctuating and unpredictable relationship between inclusion and exclusion, emerge more clearly. After introducing the space of the sea, as well as the concepts of inclusion and exclusion, the chapter has analysed the different state and non-state actors (EU, Italian and Libyan authorities; NGOs; commercial vessels), as well as their activities and motivations. Furthermore, it has examined the different territorial partitions (national and international waters, contiguous zones and SAR regions) of which the space of the sea is composed, as well as the relevant legal regimes. In doing this, it has tried to highlight the relationship between these elements and the logics of inclusion and exclusion.

Different factors and dynamics are at play in determining the destiny of migrants attempting the sea-crossing to Italy. Arriving to Italy undetected (thus circumventing the hotspot system, as well as the resulting 'dublinisation' or illegalisation) has become almost impossible, because of the increased number of vessels and aircraft patrolling the Strait of Sicily and because of the estimated mortality rates remaining high despite border control and SAR operations (Heller and Pezzani 2017; Williams and Mountz 2016).

Depending on whether, where and by whom they are 'rescued' (which, in turn, depends on many variables), some people will be returned to North Africa, while the others will either die or eventually reach Italian territory. Much is left to the fate, or to the arbitrariness of the administrative decisions of Libyan, Italian and EU authorities (e.g., about where to deploy vessels, or whether to give on-scene command of a SAR operation to a Libyan or to an NGO vessel) – whereby, clearly, what may appear to be 'fate' is always a by-product of the framework created by (arbitrary) policies and practices. If the space of the sea is no longer a legal and political 'outside' of the EU (Buckel and Wissel 2010), it is not an 'inside' space either, and its fragmentation and ambiguity result in an ever-changing, unpredictable (un)balance between the logic of inclusion and that of exclusion.

NOTES

1. The share of the people arriving from Libya on the total number of those arrived to Italy by sea was 83.1 per cent in 2014, 90.75 per cent in 2015 and 91.2 per cent in 2016 (Italian Coast Guard Headquarters 2017).

2. This work was carried out as part of the research project 'Border Policies and Sovereignty: Human Rights and the Right to Life of Irregular Migrants', led by Thomas Spijkerboer and funded by the Nederlandse Organisatie voor Wetenschappelijk Onderzoek (Netherlands Organisation for Scientific Research; NWO) through a Vici grant (number 453–12–004). Since 2013, within this project, the author has been monitoring the Central Mediterranean route through both desk research (document analysis, press review) and fieldwork (interviews with relevant actors) in Italy, Malta, Tunisia and Egypt.

3. Based on the principle of *non-refoulement*, state authorities shall not return anyone to a territory where they fear persecution, also including torture or inhuman or degrading treatment.

4. Clearly, mere physical inclusion can be followed by physical exclusion (e.g., deportation) at some point, and inclusion is not homogeneous as regards the sets of rights, entitlements and opportunities enjoyed by migrants (De Genova 2013; Mezzadra and Neilson 2013). Furthermore, (physical) exclusion can result from fields of relation emerging across borders through policies and practices of migration regulation and control, which can be seen by themselves as forms of (relational) inclusion (Mezzadra and Neilson 2012; Rigo 2007). This chapter, however, does not refer to inclusion and exclusion in this sense, nor in the sense attributed to these terms by Agamben (1995, 2003) in exploring the zones of indistinction between the one and the other.

5. By opening two so-called humanitarian corridors, the Italian Government has allowed for the relocation of 1,500 people from Lebanon and Ethiopia in two years between 2016 and 2018 (Governo Italiano 2017), thus addressing populations that could potentially take the North African and then the Central Mediterranean route.

The only two minor relocations from North Africa to Italy were carried out from Libya in 2007 and 2011 (Cuttitta 2017b).

6. However, the sovereignty of states over their territorial waters is subject to limitations. The most important limitation is the right of 'innocent passage': foreign vessels have the right to transit the national waters of a coastal state so long as the passage 'is not prejudicial to the peace, good order or security of the coastal State' (article 19 of the United Nations Convention on the Law of the Sea).

7. However, there are also exceptions, with SAR regions partially overlapping, resulting in overlapping responsibilities of two different countries. This is the case of Italy and Malta (Coppens 2013).

8. The first occurred only half a mile off the Italian island of Lampedusa on 3 October, and caused the death of 366 people. At least 268 people died during the second shipwreck, which took place in international waters, in the Maltese SAR zone, on 11 October.

9. Interview with Italian Coast Guard spokesperson, Rome, 16 September 2015.

10. 'Dublinisation' refers to the effects of the EU Council Regulation 343/2003 of 18 February 2003 establishing the criteria and mechanisms for determining the member-state responsible for examining an asylum application lodged in one of the member-states by a third-country national. The regulation is called 'Dublin regulation' because it replaces, while translating its principles into EU law, an international convention signed in Dublin in 1990. According to the Dublin regulation, the member-state responsible for examining the application of an asylum seeker is the member-state whose territory the asylum seeker enters first. Those who travel further to other EU countries and file an asylum application can therefore be returned to the country they entered first. 'Dublinised' are all those whose freedom of movement and choice is limited under the Dublin regulation. Similarly, the country of first irregular entry is obliged under EU law to read-mit into its territory any non-EU national irregularly staying in another member-state.

11. Reportedly, an informal agreement was also made by Italy and Malta, according to which Italy would take all the people rescued at sea, regardless of the SAR region (*il Giornale* 2015).

12. Under international law, the duty to render assistance (Article 98 of the United Nations Convention on the Law of the Sea) always prevails. Furthermore, no permission is required for 'innocent passage' (see note 6). Therefore, a SAR intervention is always lawful, regardless of where and by whom it is carried out.

13. Telephone interview with a representative of a SAR NGO, 8 June 2016.

14. Interview with an Italian armed forces officer, 17 September 2015; interview with a representative of a SAR NGO, 26 October 2015.

15. Own calculation based on the following sources: ECSA (2015); Italian Coast Guard Headquarters (2017).

16. Reportedly, this was both a diplomatic move, aimed at preventing the problems occurred to other SAR NGOs (between inclusion and exclusion: operations sophia and triton), and a way to allow the officials to test the drones on behalf of the Libyan ministry of interior.

17. Interview with the EUNAVFOR Med spokesperson, Rome, 21 April 2016.

18. Interview carried out in Tunis, 24 January 2016.

19. Source: Tunisian Red Crescent.
20. Telephone interview with an NGO representative, 8 June 2016.
21. Based on Article 16 of the ILC (International Law Commission) Codification.

BIBLIOGRAPHY

Agamben, Giorgio, *Homo sacer. Il potere sovrano e la nuda vita* (Turin: Einaudi, 1995).

Agamben, Giorgio, *Stato di eccezione* (Turin: Bollati Boringhieri, 2003).

Amnesty International, 'EU Risks Fuelling Horrific Abuse of Refugees and Migrants in Libya', accessed 14 June 2016. https://www.amnesty.org/en/latest/news/2016/06/eu-risks-fuelling-horrific-abuse-of-refugees-and-migrants-in-libya/

Buckel, Sonja, and Wissel, Jens, 'State Project Europe: The Transformation of the European Border Regime and the Production of Bare Life', *International Political Sociology* 4, no. 1 (2010): 33.

Coppens, Jasmine, 'The Lampedusa Disaster: How to Prevent Further Loss of Life at Sea?', *The International Journal on Marine Navigation and Safety at Sea Transportation* 7, no. 4 (2013): 589.

Cusumano, Eugenio, 'Emptying the Sea with a Spoon? Non-governmental Providers of Migrants Search and Rescue in the Mediterranean', *Marine Policy* 75 (2017): 91–98.

Cuttitta, Paolo, 'Delocalization, Humanitarianism, and Human Rights: The Mediterranean Border between Exclusion and Inclusion', *Antipode* (2017b). doi: 10.1111/anti.12337.

Cuttitta, Paolo, 'Repoliticization through Search and Rescue? NGOs and Humanitarian Migration Management in the Central Mediterranean', *Geopolitics* (2017a). doi: 10.1080/14650045.2017.1344834.

de Genova, Nicholas, 'Spectacles of Migrant "Illegality": The Scene of Exclusion, the Obscene of Inclusion', *Ethnic and Racial Studies* 36, no. 7 (2013): 1180.

ECSA (European Community Shipowners' Associations), 'Shipping-Related Challenges in the Mediterranean due to Migratory Flows', Frontex EPN General Meeting, Bergen. 24 June 2015. http://www.ecsa.eu/images/NEW_Presentations_and_Speeches/2015-06-24%20Frontex%20Bergen%20Verhoeven%20ECSA.pdf

European Union. European Council, 'Malta Declaration by the members of the European Council on the External Aspects of Migration: Addressing the Central Mediterranean Route', Press Release 43/17, 2 February 2017.

Gammeltoft-Hansen, Thomas, *Access to Asylum: International Refugee Law and the Globalisation of Migration Control* (Cambridge: Cambridge University Press, 2011).

Garelli, Glenda, and Tazzioli, Martina, 'The Humanitarian War against Migrant Smuggling at Sea', *Antipode* (forthcoming).

Giuffré, Mariagiulia, 'State Responsibility Beyond Borders: What Legal Basis for Italy's Push-Backs to Libya?', *International Journal of Refugee Law* 24, no. 4 (2012): 692.

Governo Italiano. Ministero dell'Interno, 'Firmato protocollo corridoi umanitari', 12 January 2017, accessed 1 July 2017. http://www.libertaciviliimmigrazione.dlci. interno.gov.it/it/notizie/firmato-protocollo-corridoi-umanitari

The Guardian, 'Libya Navy Admits Confrontation with Charity's Rescue Boat', 28 August 2016, accessed 1 July 2017. https://www.theguardian.com/world/2016/ aug/28/libyan-navy-admits-confrontation-charity-rescue-boat-msf

Heller, Charles, and Pezzani, Lorenzo, 'Death by Rescue: Main Narrative', 2016, accessed 1 July 2017. https://deathbyrescue.org/report/narrative/

Heller, Charles, and Pezzani, Lorenzo, 'Blaming the Rescuers. Criminalising Solidarity, Re-enforcing Deterrence', 2017, accessed 1 July 2017. https://blamingtheres cuers.org.

IIHL (International Institute of Humanitarian Law), 'Final Report of the Workshop on "Search and Rescue of Refugees and Migrants in the Mediterranean: Practitioners' Perspectives"', 2016, accessed 1 July 2017. http://www.iihl.org/ rescue-of-refugees-and-migrants-in-the-mediterranean-practitioners-perspectives/

il Giornale, 'Adesso l'Italia si prende anche i profughi che Malta non vuole', 17 September 2015, accessed 1 July 2017. http://www.ilgiornale.it/news/politica/adesso-litalia-si-prende-anche-i-profughi-che-malta-non-vuol-1172070.html

IMO (International Maritime Organization), 'Resolution MSC.167/78. Guidelines on the Treatment of Persons Rescued at Sea', 20 May 2004, accessed 1 July 2017. http://www.imo.org/en/OurWork/Facilitation/personsrescued/Docu ments/MSC.167(78).pdf

IOM (International Organization for Migration), 'Maritime Incidents Libyan Coast 7 January–18 January', 2017, accessed 1 July 2017. https://www.iom.int/sites/ default/files/country/docs/tanzania/Libya-Maritime-Incidents-Libyan-Coast-7-18-January-2017.pdf

Italian Coast Guard Headquarters, 'Search and Rescue Activity and Migratory Flows in Central Mediterranean Sea. Year 2016', 2017, accessed 1 July 2017. http:// www.guardiacostiera.gov.it/en/Documents/search-and-rescue-activity/search-and-rescue-activity-and-migratory-flows-in-central-mediterranean-sea.pdf

Klepp, Silja, 'A Double Bind. Malta and the Rescue of Unwanted Migrants at Sea, a Legal Anthropological Perspective on the Humanitarian Law of the Sea', *International Journal of Refugee Law* 23, no. 3 (2011): 538.

la Repubblica, 'Migranti, naufragio al largo Libia: si temono più di ottanta dispersi', 29 April 2016, accessed 1 July 2017. http://www.repubblica.it/esteri/2016/04/29/ news/migranti_naufragio_al_largo_libia_si_temono_decine_dispersi-138756034/

Last, Tamara, Mirto, Giorgia, Ulusoy, Orçun, Urquijo, Ignacio, Harte, Joke, Bami, Nefeli, Perez, Marta, et al., 'Deaths at the Borders Database: Evidence of Deceased Migrants' Bodies Found along the Southern External Borders of the European Union', *Journal of Ethnic and Migration Studies* (2017). doi: 10.1080/1369183X.2016.1276825.

Libya Herald, 'Coastguard Rescues over 500 off Sabratha and Garabulli', 17 May 2016b, accessed 1 July 2017. https://www.libyaherald.com/2017/05/18/coastguard-rescues-over-500-off-sabratha-and-garabulli/

Libya Herald, 'Over 1000 Migrants Rescued off Coast in Four Days Says Libyan Navy', 20 March 2016a, accessed 1 July 2017. https://www.libyaherald.com/2016/03/20/over-1000-migrants-rescued-off-coast-in-four-days-says-libyan-navy/

Lutterbeck, Derek, 'Small Frontier Island: Malta and the Challenge of Irregular Immigration', *Mediterranean Quarterly* 20, no. 1 (2009): 119.

Markard, Nora, 'The Right to Leave by Sea: Legal Limits on EU Migration Control by Third Countries', *The European Journal of International Law* 27, no. 3 (2016): 591.

Martin, Lauren, and Tazzioli, Martina (ed.), *Governing Mobility through the European Union's 'Hotspot' Centres. A Forum* (Society & Space, 2016). http://societyandspace.org/2016/11/08/governing-mobility-through-the-european-unions-hotspot-centres-a-forum/.

Mezzadra, Sandro, and Neilson, Brett, 'Between Inclusion and Exclusion: On the Topology of Global Space and Borders', *Theory, Culture & Society* 29, no. 4–5 (2012): 58.

Mezzadra, Sandro, and Neilson, Brett. *Border as Method, or, the Multiplication of Labor* (Durham/London: Duke University Press, 2013).

MOAS (Migrant Offshore Aid Station Foundation), 'MOAS Launch 2016 Mediterranean Mission with Two Ships, Two Drones Patrolling the "dead zone"', 31 May 2016, accessed 1 July 2017. https://www.moas.eu/moas-launch-2016-mediterranean-mission-two-ships-two-drones-patrolling-dead-zone/

Moreno Lax, Violeta, 'Seeking Asylum in the Mediterranean: Against a Fragmentary Reading of EU Member States' Obligations Accruing at Sea', *International Journal of Refugee Law* 23, no. 2 (2011): 174.

MSF (Medécins Sans Frontières), 'Le domande più frequenti sulle nostre operazioni di ricerca e soccorso nel Mediterraneo', 11 May 2017, accessed 1 July 2017. http://www.medicisenzafrontiere.it/notizie/news/le-10-domande-più-frequenti-sulle-nostre-operazioni-di-ricerca-e-soccorso-nel

Musarò, Pierluigi, 'Mare Nostrum: The Visual Politics of a Military-Humanitarian Operation in the Mediterranean Sea', *Media, Culture, and Society* 39, no. 1 (2017): 11.

Naval Today, 'Irish Navy Patrol Vessel Deploys to Mediterranean Sea', 23 May 2017, accessed 1 July 2017. http://navaltoday.com/2017/05/23/irish-navy-patrol-vessel-deploys-to-mediterranean-sea/

Parlamento Italiano. Senato della Repubblica, 'Audizione dell'ammiraglio di divisione Enrico Credendino, operation commander della missione Eunavfor Med – Operazione Sophia', 4 February 2016, accessed 1 July 2017. https://www.senato.it/service/PDF/PDFServer/DF/319912.pdf.

Parliament of the United Kingdom. House of Lords, 'Operation Sophia, the EU's naval mission in the Mediterranean: An -Impossible Challenge', 13 May 2016, accessed 1 July 2017. http://www.publications.parliament.uk/pa/ld201516/ldselect/ldeucom/144/144.pdf

Pezzani, Lorenzo, and Heller, Charles, ' "Sharing the Burden of Rescue": Illegalised Boat Migration, the Shipping Industry and the Costs of Rescue in the Central Mediterranean', 2 November 2015, accessed 1 July 2017. https://www.law.

ox.ac.uk/research-subject-groups/centre-criminology/centreborder-criminologies/
blog/2015/10/sharing-burden

Reuters, 'Libyan Coastguard Turns Back Nearly 500 Migrants after Altercation with
NGO Ship', 10 May 2017. http://mobile.reuters.com/article/idUSKBN1862Q2

Rigo, Enrica. *Europa di confine. Trasformazioni della cittadinanza nell'Unione allar-
gata* (Rome: Meltemi, 2007).

Sea Eye, 'What Happened to the "Speedy?"', 2016, accessed 1 July 2017. http://sea-
eye.org/en/was-geschah-mit-der-speedy/

Sea-Watch, 'First Test Flight of Sea-Air Watch Becomes a Success', 29 June 2016b,
accessed 1 July 2017. http://sea-watch.org/en/first-test-flight-of-sea-air-watch-
becomes-a-success/

Sea-Watch, 'Sea-Watch Newsletter', 25 October 2016a.

Stierl, Maurice, ,Border Humanitarians', *Antipode* (2017). doi: 10.1111/anti.12320.

Süddeutsche Zeitung, 'Libyens Küstenwache gefährdet Flüchtlinge und Helfer', 16
September 2016, accessed 1 July 2017. http://www.sueddeutsche.de/politik/2.220/
mittelmeer-libyens-kuestenwache-gefaehrdet-fluechtlinge-und-helfer-1.3250197.

Tazzioli, Martina, 'Border Displacements: Challenging the Politics of Rescue
between Mare Nostrum and Triton', *Migration Studies* 4, no. 1 (2016): 1.

Trevisanut, Seline, 'The Principle of Non-Refoulement and the De-Territorialization
of Border Control at Sea', *Leiden Journal of International Law* 27, no. 3 (2014): 661.

United Nations, 'Final Report of the Panel of Experts on Libya Established Pursuant
to Resolution 1973 (2011)', 1 June 2017, accessed 1 July 2017. http://reliefweb.int/
sites/reliefweb.int/files/resources/N1711623.pdf

UNSMIL-OHCHR (United Nations Support Mission in Libya-Office of the United
Nations High Commissioner for Human Rights), '"Detained and Dehumanised": Report on Human Rights Abuses against Migrants in Libya', 13 December 2016, accessed 1 July 2017. http://www.ohchr.org/Documents/Countries/LY/
DetainedAndDehumanised_en.pdf

Wikileaks, 'Eunavfor Med Operation Sophia. Six Monthly Report: June 22nd to
December 31st 2015', accessed 1 July 2017. https://wikileaks.org/eu-military-
refugees/EEAS/EEAS-2016-126.pdf

Williams, Kira, and Mountz, Alison, 'Rising Tide: Analyzing the Relationship
between Externalization and Migrant Deaths and Boat Losses', in *Externalizing
Migration Management: Europe, North America and the Spread of 'Remote Control' Practices*, edited by Zaiotti, Ruben (London/New York: Routledge, 2016).

Xchange, 'Libyan Coast Guard Assists MOAS during Rescue', 15 August 2015,
accessed 1 July 2017. http://xchange.org/libyan-coastguard-assists-moas-during-
rescue/

Chapter 6

On Choppy Waters: The Shifting Borders of Protection in Europe

Joanne van Selm

INTRODUCTION

People have long made the journey across the Mediterranean to seek safety and a new life. Between 2000 and 2008 the numbers varied each year – with a peak of 53,079 in 2008 (de Bruycker et al. 2013, 15). It was predictable that every year, as the weather and sea conditions improved in spring, the boats would start arriving – or were shipwrecked. Most travelled from North Africa to Malta or Italy, in particular the island of Lampedusa, and some to Spain. After the 2008 peak, as Italy stepped up its 'push back' efforts and cooperation with Libya, numbers dropped to around 5,000 per year in the following two years but surged in 2011 to 59,000, the year of the Arab Spring (Garlick and van Selm, 2012).

It was therefore nothing new to Europeans in the 2010s that migrant boats would cross the Mediterranean Sea or that some would not succeed. The fact that almost a million people would take to boats over the course of 2015 was not only new but was also a significant turning point for the European Union (EU) in terms of its immigration and refugee policies and one of its own core principles: the freedom of movement across internal borders. Scenes of boat migrants arriving in Greece (primarily) as well as trekking across the continent to reach places they expected to be safe, and in some cases were indeed warmly welcomed, overwhelmed the conscience of some and sorely tested the patience of many others. Yet even that reaction was not unprecedented: in many ways it mirrored the reaction to the exodus from Kosovo in 1999, as shown by Campesi in chapter 4 of this volume.

The central theme of this chapter is that EU asylum policy, and more broadly the EU's immigration and refugee policies (to the extent that the EU has a developing refugee policy),[1] are at least partly to blame both for the 'crisis' of a mass influx, examples of which chapters 7 and 8 describe. They are also partly responsible for the fact that migrants have often been forced to take the riskiest routes (by sea) in the riskiest ways (often trusting smugglers). With the sea as effectively the final migration frontier, EU member-states have been forced to see the humanitarian consequences of desperate migration and displacement acts. At sea, humanitarianism emerges in the form of rescue (see chapter 5 by Cuttitta); on land, at least EU territory, security and political concerns re-engage, throwing into doubt the willingness of some states to participate in protection. The EU project itself requires collective action on mobility, and thus on new entrants to any part of the EU territory, but acting together to protect refugees has, thus far, remained elusive. While member-states focus on border enforcement about migrants at sea, they give far reduced, public attention to dry land.

The layering of complexities surrounding this increase of maritime migration makes solutions more difficult to grasp and maintain. The list seems endless, including the conflict at the heart of the major displacement (Syria), the threats of extremism and terrorism linked to Syria and ISIS but also going well beyond, the existential threats to the EU project caused by the handling of the numbers of migrants in 2015 as well as the 2016 Brexit decision in the United Kingdom, the domestic concerns in many European states about economic well-being and rising populism and xenophobia and the sense of a global power vacuum with an apparently weakened government of the United States and the rising powers of Russia and China. Indeed, Europe is largely left as the only developed region playing any role, however reluctantly and with whatever level of resistance, in attempting to assist refugees or those developing countries on the front line of the world's humanitarian crises. The United States under the Trump administration has moved to close down much of its refugee admissions programme, particularly for Muslim refugees. China continues to reject any role in refugee protection in spite of its increasing political and economic weight in the world and the fact that it has signed up to universal refugee laws (Surana 2017). Meanwhile, Russia is involved in some of the displacement-inducing crises (e.g., Syria) and charged by some with inciting xenophobia in European populations through targeted false stories on social media (Human Rights First, 2017). These all make what is anyway a difficult conundrum in itself, managing maritime migration, seemingly intractable.

Yet, the refugee regime emerged from, and has been changed by, past confluences of complex circumstances. As the world struggles to engage with and emerge from all these complexities, the boundaries of European (and global) refugee protection shift. This chapter will tentatively indicate the geopolitical directions those shifts could take.

If the future EU geopolitics remain pointed towards ever more exclusion and restriction (as well as reluctance to use any potentially inclusive or positive policy approaches developed), then the next large influx, whatever its cause, route or target destination, will only result in another 'crisis' and further erosion of the global refugee protection regime at a point in time at which a working regime is most needed. The EU must change its geopolitical direction with respect to not only non-member-states but also member-states within itself; it must act like a collective body of states, not twenty-eight entities acting on their own.

This chapter will therefore posit that it is not only routes that shift but also that policies and laws have been tightened, changing the landscape of both migration and protection. The physical and metaphorical frontier to be crossed to request asylum has, for many EU states, also shifted (and the EU is not alone in this, as explained by Mountz in chapter 2). The EU has enacted a range of regulations to deal with (and limit) arrivals by land and by air – but the sea and lengthy shorelines in the Mediterranean bring a different context to migration and border controls. As such, the boundaries of protection have changed, and are continuing to change; however, asylum and refugee policies remain territorially focused, adding to the problems of matching people in need of protection with a state willing to provide it, rather than contributing to solutions. Both relocation and resettlement have been put forward as measures to demonstrate solidarity and some degree of EU and international 'burden-sharing'. Yet neither has been impactful enough to quantitatively change either on the front line EU states (Greece and Italy in particular) or on the *real* front line states (Lebanon, Jordan and Turkey). Indeed, the 2016 EU-Turkey deal has rather been seen as a low blow to the international refugee protection regime and Europe's role as a humanitarian actor. The 'migrant crisis' thus, I will argue, forces a re-consideration of the meaning of protection.

The chapter proceeds as follows. First, I examine the relationship between increasing migration and crisis to show that such 'crises' have occurred in the EU before. Second, I consider how states try to balance protection, security and humanitarianism at sea, with an emphasis of showing which limitations need to be addressed. Last, I consider how the EU's current policies of engaging in state-based and not collective action deeply weaken its ability to implement a better system of protection for migrants.

PERSPECTIVE ON FACTS AND IMPACTS: AN UNPRECEDENTED MOVEMENT – OR HISTORY REPEATING ITSELF?

A large influx of migrants towards the EU provoked a policy response of 'crisis' from 2014 to 2016. In 2014, 276,000 unauthorised migrants arrived in the

EU, more than 220,000 of them by sea. During 2014, about 3,000 would-be migrants lost their lives crossing the Mediterranean (European Commission, 2016). During 2015 almost one million unauthorised maritime migrants[2] arrived on Europe's shores (IOM 2015); in 2016 more than 387,739 people made and survived the hazardous journey (IOM 2017). During that same two-year period more than 8,000 had perished while attempting to make the crossing – with more than 5,000 of those dying in 2016 (IOM 2017). In the first three months of 2017 some 27,850 people had arrived in the EU after crossing the Mediterranean, and 655 deaths had been reported (IOM 2017). As outlined in chapter 2 by Mountz and chapter 3 by Williams, data limitations in these measurements themselves likely imply that the true numbers of migrants moving and lost were even higher.

The routes these migrants (and their smugglers) are taking across the Mediterranean have shifted, with Italy taking over from Greece as the prime target. This is partly a consequence of not only the EU-Turkey pact of March 2016 (on which more later in the chapter) but also of the fact that states increasingly force migrants to take longer, riskier journeys to get to the EU (see chapter 5 by Cuttitta; Williams and Mountz 2016). The flows are mixed – including people with different motives for migration, taking the same route, perhaps headed to the same destinations, and who will have different outcomes to their migration choices.

These increases in unauthorised maritime arrivals have changed the landscape of refugee protection, asylum and migration management in the EU, as did other significant large-scale arrivals in the past. The largest previous forced displacement in Europe, for example, was that resulting from World War II and its aftermath, which forged the current global refugee protection regime. This current one in itself is surely a test to that regime and the EU policy building upon it and one which might reshape the rules themselves, or at least the way states and international organisations interpret and implement them.

When resettlement for Indo-China 'boat people' ended in the 1980s, EU member-states ended or severely cut back most of their resettlement, and asylum became the main entry channel for people seeking refugee status in the EU. Mass influxes from the Balkans in the 1990s brought the development of temporary protection policies, first in individual EU member-states for Bosnians and later an EU Directive on Temporary Protection, born out of the humanitarian evacuation programme for Kosovars in 1999 (see chapter 4 by Campesi; van Selm 1998, 2000). That was not a resettlement programme, as EU states did not do much resettlement at the time. Resettlement instead re-emerged between 2005 and 2015, and some resettlement has been made available to some Syrians, although temporary protection has not been used, in spite of the EU Temporary Protection Directive, devised for a collective approach to mass influx situations (see van Selm 2015). As such, the protection picture has been fluid for several decades – and the waves generated by the latest 'migrant crisis' are, in the short term, adding to the fluidity. The main question is whether in the long term, a more robust EU refugee protection regime and a migration management approach could emerge.

One of the most impactful aspects of the level of unauthorised maritime arrivals in 2015 – and actually more so in 2016 – was the number of those would-be migrants who in fact did not arrive, whom enforcement authorities often fail to record in their data (see chapter 3 by Williams). Of course, tragedies occur when people attempt to migrate overland or by air too. People die crossing inhospitable terrain such as deserts, for example, and many of those who perish are never found; the known deaths of plane stowaways are visible in terms of media attention (e.g., de Haas 2007; Hamood 2008; *Telegraph*, 2015). As individual deaths, these inspire great mourning, but the scale of a shipwreck often has more impact, as empirically shown by Bruno and Binotto in chapter 8 in this volume. Unauthorised maritime arrivals grab attention but: those which fail attract even more attention, especially given the multiple casualties in any single incident. Headlines about just a few people being rescued from an overcrowded boat can draw attention away from the deaths: those vessels that simply sink without trace sometimes get no attention and potentially bring many more uncounted individual tragedies (see chapter 7 by Burroughs).

A second impactful aspect of the unauthorised maritime migration of 2015 was the long, large marches across Europe, with migrants walking for weeks, sometimes diverted as EU states erected barriers, or transported by bus across countries to reach the suddenly very present frontiers of those member-states which would in fact give them access to asylum procedures. Chapter 7 by Burroughs explores media attention given to such incidents.

A third impactful factor has been the severe conditions endured by those migrants effectively trapped in Greece during the winter of 2015–2016. As the 'mandatory' relocation programme showed poor results, migrants remained in 'tents' on Greek islands, with rain, snow and other elements making conditions appalling and illness rife (e.g., *New York Times* 2017).

The manner of arrivals, the attention drawn to the journeys and the numbers of people moving, the conditions for migrants while on the move and awaiting a solution, all of these make this a striking 'humanitarian crisis' of our current time. But as migration and refugee flows, this is arguably not totally unprecedented – those of the past had their strong impacts and shocking features of scale and humanity too. Those of the past also brought changes to the way states and international organisations managed refugee protection – the question is thus, how will that protection be dealt with now, and how will it change as a result of this latest influx?

PROTECTION, SECURITY AND HUMANITARIANISM IN AN ERA OF MIGRATION BY SEA: HOW DID WE GET HERE AND WHERE DO WE GO FROM HERE?

Protecting refugees who have decided to wait for either a return journey to their country of origin or to be resettled to a third state may not be a realistic short-term prospect during protracted periods of violence which reflect modern displacement. Protecting those whose situation in a first country of asylum has become untenable as a way of life with no prospect of full integration or real protection therefore becomes an international concern.

The international protection regime, grounded in the 1951 Geneva Convention Relating to the Status of Refugees and its 1967 New York Protocol, as well as the mandate of the United Nations High Commissioner for Refugees, is under severe strain. It may seem to be outdated – yet the essential documents have been reaffirmed, for example, in the 2001 Global Consultations and again through the process of the New York Declaration for Refugees and Migrants and the Global Compact for Refugees (UNHCR 2016), and no state has put forward concrete and realistic amendments that would be more appropriate to current needs. It may be that the problems lie in the numbers of displaced persons and complexities of the situations they are fleeing. The numbers are genuinely high, and the situations are complex – but neither necessarily proportionally more so than at previous points in the refugee regime's history and its origin. It still may be that the wealthier countries of the world are weary of receiving people and that the fact that non-refugees travel in 'mixed flows' alongside refugees makes it impossible to be purely compassionate and welcoming; however, it has long been the case that some 90 per cent to 95 per cent of the world's refugees are in developing countries, and discussion of mixed flows goes back to at least the 1990s. What is more, xenophobia and intolerance are at seemingly high levels in industrialised countries, with populist candidates in elections doing comparatively well.

While global displacement and migration remain complicated no matter how we look at them, the fact that in a global system of states, every individual needs the protection of a state and that when the individual-state relationship goes wrong, another state needs to step in is a fairly straightforward process. It is often just that states purposely make the request for protection difficult for migrants, and they typically prioritise admitting and hearing out only those whom they are confident need protection according to their own standards (e.g., Maillet, Mountz and Williams 2018).

The EU illustrates this problem. The erection of overland and aerial barriers to EU entry has pushed increasing numbers of people to take the only route left – the sea – suggesting that people will have to want to literally risk their lives to make it there. The sea presents its own natural barriers, in terms of the risks involved, particularly when travelling in less than optimally sea-worthy vessels. Newland (2016) describes the double irregularity of people seeking to enter a territory without legal entry papers and arrive on a vessel that has not been authorised to enter. Chapter 7 (Burroughs), chapter 8 (Binotto and Bruno) and chapter 9 (Dickson) in this volume demonstrate how powerful and fearful state responses to migration by boat can be.

Although the Universal Declaration of Human Rights 'guarantees' us all the right to 'seek and enjoy asylum in countries other than [our] own' (Article 14), we need to arrive in a country other than our own in order to ask for that protection. We also need to fit the understanding of the universal definition of a refugee as applied by that country's government, which can highly vary from state to state. Chapter 2 (Mountz) summarises and chapter 4 (Campesi) and chapter 5 (Cuttitta) reflect that EU member-states have collectively made it harder to arrive and claim asylum in the EU since the end of the Cold War. Arrivals by air have been blocked by visa restrictions, carrier sanctions and stronger departure controls. Arrivals over land have been effectively hampered by the use of 'safe third country' policies applying this 'safe' definition to states neighbouring the EU, as well as stronger controls by those states with land borders. For many of the earliest EU member-states, overland arrivals have also been effectively diminished because the member-states between them and non-EU countries are required under the EU's Dublin System to take responsibility for any asylum seekers who first arrive in their country.

Until 2014 most 'unauthorised' arrivals in the EU happened to do so by land or by air, in spite of all these restrictions. With the massive increase in such arrivals in 2015, the land routes from Lebanon, Jordan, Turkey and Syria were already blocked in one way or another for most Syrians. As Syrians started to take the boat route in increasing numbers, so did other asylum seekers and unauthorised migrants from further away (e.g., Pakistan, Afghanistan, the Middle East and Sub-Saharan Africa), swelling the numbers to over a million, which provoked the EU to treat these movements as a 'crisis'.

Jendesboz and Pallister-Wilkins (2016) have argued that the 'migrant crisis' resulting from the spectre of massive unauthorised maritime arrivals is in reality no 'crisis' – merely a situation that would clearly result from the no-entry policies of the past two decades. Mountz (2010) and Burroughs in chapter 7 in this volume show how states and media can manufacture crisis for their own political ends. This is particularly the case when those approaches coincide with increased pressures to move, such as the Syrian Civil War and other examples of physical, social and economic insecurity in the Middle East and North Africa. People could still try to move by land or air, but their way is most often blocked, either literally, on land, or bureaucratically when attempting to travel by air. As such, if there is any crisis, it is one of ineffective, or at least unrealistic, EU migration and refugee policy.

Only German Chancellor Angela Merkel's action to permit access to protection, status (where recognised, of course) and assistance in Germany defused this EU-level crisis, at the risk of loss of political domestic support. The German Federal Election of 2017, in which Merkel's CDU/CSU lost sixty-five seats, manifested this potential loss. While the Chancellor's actions to relieve pressure on frontline EU member-states were a gamble, she retains political authority in Germany.

It is plausible that politicians and officials in charge of migration policy might have presumed that rational migrants would not move at sea given its risks. The reality of so many people still migrating by that perilous mode suggests that either there are plenty of irrational people, or, more likely, that the circumstances in which they find themselves are so perilous that the chance they might lose their lives travelling on a rickety craft across the Mediterranean is worth taking.

While the maritime interdiction operations established by the EU (see chapter 4 by Campesi and chapter 5 by Buttitta) recognise that lives should not be lost in trying to reach its borders, at the same time it also believes they should not be trying to get there in the first place. This is where the significant contradiction comes into play (e.g., Christodoulou et al. 2016, 324). States establish a double humanitarian standard when they act to protect life at sea but are unwilling to give the same lives validation and quality on land. This apparent contradiction is all the greater given that the EU had a policy approach ready-made for a migrant influx which could have been employed to manage arrivals through an evacuation process. The Temporary Protection Directive emerged from the Kosovo crisis and the overburdening of FYR Macedonia. The EU designed it to assist EU member-states in the position of Greece in 2015, for example, when influxes were arriving from Lebanon, Jordan and Turkey in the face of long-term stays by Syrians with no hope for return (see van Selm 2015); however, the political decision was taken not to bring it into effect – and the boundaries of EU protection in a policy sense thus changed.

The issue of 'migration management' is often cast as one of opposing discourses of *securitisation* and *humanitarianism*, with the 'irregular' migrant caught between the two: as a threat to Europe but also a life to be saved, but elsewhere, not in the EU (see Vaughn-Williams 2015). Securitisation of migration, particularly arrivals by boat, has been viewed as the opposite of a humanitarian view of migration (Pugh 2004, 51). In the security discourse, migrants arriving by sea are cast as a 'threat' (see chapter 7 by Burroughs and chapter 9 by Dickson) – challenging not only borders but also the traditions of sea-faring and the solidarity of sailors, given that migrants, and more particularly their smugglers, have little or no regard for the safety either of those on the vessels intent on reaching prosperous or safe shores or for people on other ships whose safety might be brought into jeopardy either in accidents or during rescue attempts. Thus, although in general terms the 'securitisation' of migration was cast in the early 2000s as being primarily about the arrival of irregular migrants as recipients of social services, as well as a challenging presence in destination countries, in the case of migration by sea, there is another level of 'security' challenge (see Pugh 2004). What is more, the challenge to humanitarianism lies not only in the sense of refugee protection but also in other international legal regimes, such as the Law of the Sea, Search and Rescue Convention and the Safety of Life at Sea Convention.

These two discourses and practices, however, of security and humanitarian action have been brought into alignment in more recent years. Andersson (2012) describes how border security agencies have taken on the rationale of saving lives (based in humanitarianism) to intercept every boat heading towards the Spanish coast as a potential shipwreck. As Andersson notes, 'humanitarianism enables a "migration of sovereignty" . . . away from European shores by dissolving the patchwork of maritime boundaries'. Meanwhile Perkowski (2015, 332–33) discusses the co-existence of not only the securitisation and humanitarian discourses but also a human rights discourse, as security actors have co-opted the language of human rights and humanitarianism to define their role in intercepting and rescuing migrants at sea. As she notes, this combination of role definitions does not mean that border patrol actors and agencies have moved away from their security focus; rather, it indicates that they are continuing their security practices but under the guise of their newer role of saving lives at sea (Perkowski 2015, 333).

Similarly, Carrera and den Hertog (2015) describe Italy's Operation *Mare Nostrum*'s objective as having always been cast as two-sided, serving both security and humanitarian purposes. Campesi further reveals this 'two-sided' split in chapter 4. Indeed, the Italian Navy's role in implementing the operation was discussed as 'fulfilling humanitarian purposes with military means' (see chapter 4 by Campesi).

By taking on this humanitarian mantle, state border agencies have become colleagues in action of humanitarian and human rights organisations, at least insofar as the rescue element is concerned. Indeed, national border patrol agencies and Frontex (the EU's border coordination agency) have even been joined on the Mediterranean by boats operated by non-governmental organisations such as Medécins Sans Frontières (MSF) and MOAS (see chapter 5 by Cuttitta).

The decision for an organisation such as MSF to participate actively and directly in search and rescue operations was not easy (see del Valle 2016). The humanitarian aspect of the morality and legality of rescue at sea was not so problematic as the practical and political aspects. In previous situations, an NGO vessel (e.g., the German NGO Cap Anamur in the Mediterranean in 2006, which del Valle described, as well as the merchant vessel *Tampa* in Australian waters in 2001 as referenced by Pugh) had found themselves 'stuck' with a boatload of rescued migrants and states rejecting requests for disembarkation. In addition, MSF had to consider whether the operation coincided with its mandate focused on health, and how to avoid both being co-opted by states and becoming a magnet for human smuggling, by aiding in the successful arrival of people who would otherwise have been likely to drown. In the four months from May to August 2015, MSF rescued 15,700 people in the Central Mediterranean, provided medical and humanitarian assistance and disembarked all in Italy (del Valle 2016, 36). Having decided to undertake humanitarian operations at sea in the Mediterranean, MSF was forced, largely by the situation as it evolved, to cooperate with EU state efforts to rescue and transfer migrants. The organisation saved lives in a context in which it had previously not been operational but was forced both to cooperate with states in a way in which it would not have done in a land-based operation and to defend itself against charges of assisting smugglers.

The decision to undertake operations at sea was a difficult response to an obvious dilemma – it was also a response that brought the humanitarian 'sphere' closer to the security approach. The question is how the rapprochement of issues and actors on saving life at sea might translate when it comes to protecting life on land.

All are involved in managing what states and media cast as a humanitarian crisis – but the nature of the solution the different actors seek remains disparate. For states, the goal remains to police the frontiers, and where deemed necessary deny entry to the EU; for NGOs, the goal remains to expand access to protection in the EU and/or to improve conditions in the countries of origin of the asylum seekers and irregular migrants. Indeed, Carrera and den Hertog (2015) describe the long, difficult journey which resulted in Frontex taking over Italy's *Mare Nostrum* operation at the end of 2014, in the form of the Joint Operation *Triton*. *Triton* was more limited in scope than *Mare Nostrum*, it had fewer financial resources and faced a lengthy process of deciding the precise mandate and the operation regulations and laws under which it would act. The need to be met was that of continuing to rescue people who would otherwise drown at sea, while avoiding developing into the 'pull factor' that *Mare Nostrum* had seemingly become. Frontex (2014) argues that if smugglers know that their 'cargo' will be rescued, they are likely to skimp on fuel, water, food, life jackets and so on, putting the already vulnerable migrants at even greater risk, while also potentially charging increasingly high sums with the 'guarantee' of reaching the destination (on board a rescue vessel).

Migrants who arrive on the shores or the vessels of a destination country (whether it be their intended target or not) legally have, by virtue of their physical presence, rights to apply for status, residency and long-term stay. In particular, they have a clear right to apply for asylum or refugee status and to enter procedures to determine the basis for their claim. Those who do not arrive but are intercepted and/or rescued at sea do not necessarily have the same territorial basis to stake their claim. This was most vividly captured by the US policy towards Cuban migrants 'wet-foot/dry-foot' over the period 1995–2016. Those Cubans who were picked up at sea were returned to Cuba or sent to a third country (if a protection need was found). Those Cubans who landed on US territory were granted one year of parole status and then asylum, followed by a long-term residency. From 1966 to 1995 the approach had been that Cubans picked up in US territorial waters were also taken to the United States and granted status (see Rosenblum and Hipsman 2015). Differences in interpretation of rights at sea thus highly depend upon state interpretation and enforcement (Guilfoyle 2009).

The minimal protection that refugees arriving in a state should be afforded, according to the 1951 Convention, is simply non-return, or *non-refoulement* (CRSR51, art. 33). There is moreover an exception clause in the Convention:

> (2) The benefit of the present provision ['Prohibition of Expulsion or Return ("Refoulement")'] may not, however, be claimed by a refugee whom there are reasonable grounds for regarding as a danger to the security of the country in which he is, or who, having been convicted by a final judgment of a particularly serious crime, constitutes a danger to the community of that country.

As Leiserson (2017, 9), however, has thoroughly argued, this clause cannot be used as a blanket approach by states pursuing a *non-entré* strategy, as appears to be the case for EU and other governments with regard to Syrian asylum seekers and refugees in particular. I would argue that the concept that some Muslims have committed terrorist acts and therefore no Muslim refugees should be permitted to enter as they might do the same is not (morally) tenable.

In the case of *attempted* arrivals at sea, the moment of contact between a (would-be) refugee or asylum seeker and the authorities of the destination, or closest safe state, might well come before arrival on land: either through interception of vessels at sea or in a rescue situation at sea. Unlike arrivals over land, or by plane, a ship or boat might, through accident or being turned away, not touch the shore. The question becomes whether being in territorial waters, or being on board, for example, a naval vessel belonging to a particular country, constitutes presence. If it does, then non-consideration of a claim to protection could be *refoulement*. Cuttitta (in chapter 5) discusses further nuances of these distinctions, especially with respect to search and rescue.

The moment and location, at which 'protection' begins, is objectively different in the case of maritime migration, compared to movements over land or by air (Guilfoyle 2009). It could be argued that the fact that a humanitarian act of rescue at sea is so often (ethically, legally) required already alters the relationship between individual and state. When a person's body and political status is under the interdicting state's power, does the request for refugee protection then become immediately relevant? Does the enforcement of such power automatically impart state jurisdiction? If a non-state actor conducts the rescue and takes the victims to port in a given state, is that state responsible? What does this possibility mean for reactions to the rescuers – and can landing be denied? There are legal rules surrounding these issues – but open political and ethical questions need themselves to be resolved in order for the 'crisis' to be resolved. In the meantime, one of the biggest issues delaying resolution is the fact that European states, although attempting to harmonise asylum policies and 'collaborating' on these issues for more than twenty years, still have starkly differing approaches and responses.

EU SOLIDARITY IN REFUGEE PROTECTION – UNITY OR EVERY STATE FOR ITSELF?

Greece was already viewed by other member-states as a country on the fringe of the EU – geographically, socially, politically and economically (Christodoulou et al. 2016, 323). Effectively, Greece is being further weakened by its frontline status on the migrant issue, while still hit hard economically. Indeed, Christodoulou et al. go so far as to write of a 'weakening' of Greek sovereignty.

If an EU member-state has ever been in need of 'solidarity', or as it has previously been called 'burden sharing' or 'responsibility sharing', it was Greece in 2015. The underlying notion of such sharing is that no state should stand alone, particularly while participating in collective membership. In crises past, there has often been 'solidarity' in the form either of financial assistance or, more tangibly and impactful, in moving refugees from the front line state to others. Examples would include the way Hungarians were resettled in 1956 from Austria and Yugoslavia to other European states, the United States, Canada, Australia and New Zealand. The Comprehensive Plan of Action for Indo-Chinese Refugees in the 1980s is another example, as Vietnamese 'boat people' were resettled from Malaysia and Thailand. More recently, the Humanitarian Evacuation Programme for Kosovars saw 54,000 people moved to European countries, the United States, Canada, Austria and New Zealand for either resettlement or short-term protection.

In the case of Greece, 'solidarity' from other EU member-states might have seemed natural. It could be cast as a recognition of the fact that the migrants entering Greek territory by boat were actually seeking to reach 'Europe' or 'safety' almost as concepts rather than countries, or to get to a specific other member-state where they had a connection through relatives or friends, or one, such as Germany or Sweden, where they understood they might stand a chance of making a new life. Such 'solidarity', however, was not forthcoming. Germany accepted to take in however many asylum seekers arriving on its territory and process their cases – but those arrivals were made over land, with difficult journeys on foot, or in some cases by bus, through other member-states and Balkan countries which themselves were adamantly closed to the asylum seekers. This suggests that the EU had to impose solidarity – it did not come naturally.

EU policy mandated member-states to participate in an 'obligatory' relocation programme. Relocating refugees (or migrants or asylum seekers) from one member-state to another means providing for their onward transportation, having determined which of the people involved should be moved, and establishing the conditions for their reception, status determination (if not already granted) and integration path. About 160,000 refugees were to be relocated from Greece and Italy to other member-states during 2016 according to the European Commission's mandatory quota system. Despite this, by the middle of September only 4,900 people had moved.

The very disparate approaches to the migrants landing in Greece, and later Italy, exposed the absolute absence of a unified EU approach to asylum and refugee protection, in spite of two decades of work to harmonise national policies in this area. What is more, and more fundamentally serious for the EU, is that it brought into question the vary basis of a core pillar of the EU project. If each member-state has a different way of dealing with asylum policy, not just on paper but very practically in dealing with a major influx, then the EU has a crisis of identity. This was strongly suggested by the fact that the Schengen Agreement had to be suspended in 2015; the Dublin Agreement was likewise suspended, and so the EU acted as twenty-eight states, not as one.

The only way in which the EU member-states managed to act in unity was in developing an agreement with Turkey in an effort to stem the flow. The EU-Turkey deal of March 2016 put in place a system for encouraging Turkey to assist Syrians, and a one-for-one system whereby Turkey would readmit unauthorised maritime arrivals in Greece, and in exchange for each re-admission, one Syrian refugee would be resettled from Turkey to the EU. Predictably, the number of arrivals in Greece dropped – equally predictably, the Central Mediterranean route now became the more utilised route (Mountz and Williams 2016). The apparent 'success' of the Turkey deal is stimulating the EU to seek more such agreements with countries in regions of origin and to support them in keeping refugees there. I question the extent to which such deals can not only diminish migrant movements but also effectively protect refugees, integrating them in local communities and meaning that their life-choices are such that staying is more attractive than using smugglers to seek something better elsewhere. The notion of 'protection in the region' has been tried in various forms by the EU collectively and separately for many years, and has borne very limited fruits, as this latest surge in migration shows.

The EU has also been looking at more resettlement over the past decade, and several states have implemented resettlement programmes for Syrians at a level not seen in Europe since the Vietnamese resettlements of the 1970s and 1980s. Suggestions that the promise of resettlement could discourage people from using smugglers and making these treacherous journeys might seem promising; however, the current scale of resettlement activities by EU member-states is insufficient for achieving these goals (see van Selm 2016).

Resettlement programmes and other forms of humanitarian admission, on a large scale, would show solidarity with states in the region of origin, in the same way that relocations would or could demonstrate solidarity between EU member-states. The fact that both remain at a low level seems to demonstrate that there is little compassion (with the region) or trust (between member-states), or political room to manoeuvre in balancing domestic needs and fears with international understanding.

CONCLUSION

The major issue being faced in the EU is that 'managing migration' is two-sided – managing the perceived popular opposition to it domestically and managing the actual inflow. Doing the latter would allow developing an EU-wide plan, including strong programmes of assistance in countries and regions of origin, resettlement, and low- and high-skilled migration. Doing the former, however, states have to remain national in approach, and therefore more restrictive. It is possible that the most fundamental problem is that it is all about managing populations instead of protecting people. Perhaps the key is that EU populations need to better understand the pressures on people like them in other countries, who do not seek to take things from Europeans but to have what they have – freedom (to stay, to work, to choose, to move, etc.).

The complex mixture of issues as listed earlier in this chapter makes a quick resolution of any aspect of this movement impossible due to its scale and scope. Yet the impetus remains: shipwrecks, drowning and the consequent humanitarian need for rescue at sea. So long as displacements and pressures continue, translating Merkel's pressure-relieving measure of allowing entry into an EU-wide approach to acknowledging humanity and offering protection to those who need it is the logical approach in my opinion, but it may not be a politically palatable one for most governments.

The EU, as well as its approach to refugee protection, is on choppy waters – but at the same time, it seems to be Europe's lot to try to fix the world's displacement problems, perhaps together with Canada, as others (in particular the United States, China and Russia) to either turn their backs, refuse to engage or add to the problems. How governments and EU institutions lead to reduce boat departures while honouring refugee protection commitments will be vital in calming this metaphorical sea and saving countless lives.

NOTES

1. In 'refugee policy' I include resettlement and funding and activities to assist and support the protection of refugees in regions of origin, alongside an asylum system (see van Selm 2005).

2. Newland (2016, 2) explains the Migration Policy Institute's preference for 'unauthorised' over 'irregular' – with which I agree. Newland therefore uses the term 'unauthorised maritime migration' in place of the more prevalent 'irregular maritime migration'. That same term is used here, with 'arrivals' substituted for 'migration' where it is useful to make the point about disembarkation as opposed to presumed stay.

BIBLIOGRAPHY

Andersson, Ruben, 'A Game of Risk: Boat Migration and the Business of Bordering Europe', *Anthropology Today* 28, no. 6 (2012): 7.

Christodoulou, Yannis, Papada, Evie, Papoutsi, Anna, and Vradis, Antonis, 'Crisis of Zemblanity? Viewing the "Migration Crisis" through a Greek Lens', *Mediterranean Politics* 21, no. 2 (2016): 321.

de Bruycker, Philippe, di Bartolomeo, Anna, and Fargues, Philippe, 'Migrants Smuggled by Sea to the EU: Facts, Laws and Policy Options', Migration Policy Centre, 2013, accessed 1 July 2017. http://www.migrationpolicycentre.eu/docs/MPC-RR-2013-009.pdf

del Valle, Hernan, 'Search and Rescue in the Mediterranean Sea: Negotiating Political Differences', *Refugee Survey Quarterly* 35, no. 2 (2016): 22.

European Commission, 'Irregular Migration and Return', 2016. https://ec.europa.eu/home-affairs/what-we-do/policies/irregular-migration-return-policy_en

European Union. European Agency for the Management of Operational Cooperation at the External Borders (Frontex), *Operations Division Joint Operations Unit. Concept of Reinforced Joint Operation Tackling the Migratory Flows Towards Italy: JO EPN-Triton*. Brussels: European Union, 2014.

European Union. European Commission, 'Questions and Answers: Smuggling of Migrants in Europe and the EU response', 13 January 2015, accessed 1 July 2017. http://europa.eu/rapid/press-release_MEMO-15-3261_en.htm

Garlick, Madeline, and van Selm, Joanne, 'From Commitment to Practice: The EU Response', *Forced Migration Review* 39 (2012): 20.

Guilfoyle, Derek, *Shipping Interdiction and the Law of the Sea* (Cambridge: Cambridge University Press, 2009).

de Haas, Hein, 'The Myth of Invasion: Irregular Migration from West Africa to the Maghreb and the European Union', International Migration Institute, 2007.

Hamood, Sara, 'EU-Libya Cooperation on Migration: A Raw Deal for Refugees and Migrants?', *Journal of Refugee Studies* 21, no. 1 (2008): 19.

Human Rights First, 'Russian Influence in Europe', 11 January 2017, accessed 18 January 2018. https://www.humanrightsfirst.org/resource/russian-influence-europe

International Organization for Migration (IOM), 'IOM Counts 3,771 Migrant Fatalities in Mediterranean in 2015', accessed 1 July 2017a. https://www.iom.int/news/iom-counts-3771-migrant-fatalities-mediterranean-2015

International Organization for Migration (IOM), 'Irregular Migrant, Refugee Arrivals in Europe Top One Million in 2015: IOM', accessed 1 July 2017b. https://www.iom.int/news/irregular-migrant-refugee-arrivals-europe-top-one-million-2015-iom

International Organization for Migration (IOM), 'Migration Flows: Europe', accessed 15 March 2017c. http://migration.iom.int/europe/

Jeandesboz, Julien, and Pallister-Wilkins, Polly, 'Crisis, Routine, Consolidation: The Politics of the Mediterranean Migration Crisis', *Mediterranean Politics* 21, no. 2 (2016): 21.

Leiserson, Elizabeth, 'Securing the Borders against Syrian Refugees: When Non-Admission Means Return', *Yale Journal of International Law* 42 (2017): 185.

Maillet, Pauline, Mountz, Alison, and Williams, Kira, 'Exclusion through Imperio: Entanglements of Law and Geography in the Waiting Zone, Excised Territory and Search and Rescue Region', *Social and Legal Studies* (2018).

Mountz, Alison, *Seeking Asylum: Human Smuggling and Bureaucracy at the Border* (Minneapolis: University of Minnesota Press, 2010).

Newland, Kathleen, *All at Sea: The Policy Challenges of Rescue, Interception and Long-Term Response to Maritime Migration* (Washington: Migration Policy Institute, 2016).

The New York Times, 'Wintry Blast in Greece Imperils Refugees in Crowded Camps', 11 January 2017, accessed 1 July 2017. https://www.nytimes.com/2017/01/11/world/europe/greece-refugees-crisis-winter-storms.html?_r=0

Perkowski, Nina, 'Deaths, Interventions, Humanitarianism and Human Rights in the Mediterranean "Migration Crisis"', *Mediterranean Politics* 21, no. 2 (2016): 331.

Pugh, Michael, 'Drowning Not Waving: Boat People and Humanitarianism at Sea', *Journal of Refugee Studies* 17, no. 1 (2014): 50.

Reuters, 'Nearly 150 Migrants Feared Dead after Boat Sinks, Sole Survivor Says', 29 March 2017, accessed 1 July 2017. http://www.reuters.com/article/us-europe-migrants-rescue-idUSKBN17021E

Rosenblum, Marc, and Hipsman, Faye, 'Normalizaiton of Relations with Cuba May Portend Changes to U.S. Immigration Policy', *Migration Policy Institute*, 13 January 2015, accessed 1 July 2017. http://www.migrationpolicy.org/article/normalization-relations-cuba-may-portend-changes-us-immigration-policy

Surana, Kavitha, *Why Do Some Countries Get Away with Taking Fewer Refugees?*, *Foreign Policy*, 12 September 2017, accessed 18 January 2017. http://foreignpolicy.com/2017/09/12/why-do-some-countries-get-away-with-taking-fewer-refugees-united-states-china/

The Telegraph, 'Plane Stowaway Falls to His Death from British Airways Flight as Another Survives', 19 June 2015, accessed 1 July 2017. http://www.telegraph.co.uk/news/aviation/11685531/Plane-stowaways-body-found-on-roof-as-another-survives-fall.html

United Nations, 'Convention Relating to the Status of Refugees, July 28, 1951, 189 U.N.T.S. 150 [Refugee Convention]', accessed 1 July 2017. http://hrlibrary.umn.edu/instree/v1crs.htm

United Nations. United Nations High Commissioner for Refugees (UNHCR), 'Refugees and Migrants Face Heightened Risks while Trying to Reach Europe', 27 February 2017, accessed 1 July 2017. http://www.unhcr.org/news/press/2017/2/58b458654/refugees-migrants-face-heightened-risks-trying-reach-europe-unhcr-report.html

United Nations High Commissioner for Refugees (UNHCR), 'The New York Declaration: FAQs', accessed 18 January 2018. http://www.unhcr.org/584689257.pdf

van Selm, Joanne, 'Are Asylum and Immigration Really a European Union Issue?', *Forced Migration Review* 51 (2016): 60.

van Selm, Joanne, 'European Refugee Policy: Is There Such a Thing?', UNHCR New Issues working paper No. 115 (2005), accessed 1 July 2017. http://www.unhcr.org/en-us/research/working/42943ce02/european-refugee-policy-thing-joanne-van-selm.html

van Selm, Joanne, *Refugee Protection in Europe: Lessons of the Yugoslav Crisis* (The Hague: Kluwer Law International, 1998).

van Selm, Joanne, 'Temporary Protection: EU Had Plan for Migrant Influx', *euobserver*, 14 October 2015, accessed 1 July 2017. https://euobserver.com/opinion/130678

van Selm, Joanne (ed.), *Kosovo's Refugees in the EU* (London: Continuum, 2000).

Vaughan-Williams, Nicholas, *Europe's Border Crisis: Biopolitical Security and Beyond* (Oxford: Oxford University Press, 2015).

Williams, Kira, and Mountz, Alison, 'Rising Tide: Analyzing the Relationship between Externalization and Migrant Deaths and Boat Losses', in *Externalizing Migration Management: Europe, North America and the Spread of Remote Control*, edited by Zaiotti, Ruben (London: Routledge, 2016).

Section Three

DISCOURSES

So far, this edited volume has analysed two important contemporary but understudied topics related to migration by boat: data and methodology and geopolitics and legal regimes. This final section also reviews an important but understudied issue: how elite and media discourses represent migration by boat. Though many authors have examined how such discourses broadly and theoretically represent migration, only few have specifically looked in detail at migration by boat more generally. Given that existing research indicates that discourses play an important role in the legal, political and spatial classification of migrants, and that the previous section showed how such constructions affect everyday lives, a nuanced, empirical understanding of discourses of migration by boat is extremely useful. An additional relevance of such research is that it directly relates migrant outcomes and geopolitics to public opinion, something which scholars often assume but fail to demonstrate.

The following chapters by Elaine Burroughs, Marco Binotto and Marco Bruno and Andonea Dickson each empirically identify and explore discourses on migration by boat. In chapter 7, Burroughs demonstrates the emergence and construction of the narrative of migration as a 'crisis' through measuring its proliferation in the news media of the United Kingdom in 2015. Using this approach, she deconstructs discursive representations of the crisis to unravel their meaning and purpose with respect to debates on migration by boat. Bruno and Binotto conduct an in-depth analysis of how Italian media have depicted migration by boat since the 1990s using modern theories by media scholars. They show how media discourse built the representation of borders and spaces through a 'two-sided' narrative: buzz and crisis. In chapter 9, Dickson probes how the government of Australia and Australian media narrated the activities of Operation Sovereign Borders since 2014. She uncovers how elites use 'silences' to obfuscate borders and their effects on migration by boat; further, Dickson demonstrates how strategies of mobility control can serve to amplify such silences from the level of the state all the way to the body of migrants.

Through these chapters, Burroughs, Binotto and Bruno and Dickson contribute to migration by boat discourse in two key ways. First, they focus on discursive data and methods – that is, make use of empirical evidence related to discourses from news media, political outlets or online sources – rather than take solely take a theoretical approach. They specifically address questions to identify key discourses which construct migration by boat and their functions. Second, they extend existing approaches to analysing discourses on migration by explicitly linking empirical data on migration by boat and its governance with its discursive/visual representations. These chapters analyse the links between data on migration by boat and discourse, as well as the relationships between representations of migration by boat with border enforcement practices. By providing initial answers to these questions, this section gives critical insight into discourses on migration by boat.

Chapter 7

Deconstructions of the Migration 'Crisis' and Representations of Migration by Boat in the UK News Media

Elaine Burroughs

INTRODUCTION

The news media have significant influence upon the construction of discourses of ongoing events and in representing certain groups of people in particular ways (Machin and Mayr 2012). This is certainly the case when we examine discourses of current migration. In 2015, the migration 'crisis', as it is referred to, and migrants travelling by boat to the EU gained significant attention from the UK news media. This issue also became heightened within the EU and UK political milieu and, as a consequence, within public consciousness. While an increase in the number of migrants travelling by boat to the EU partly accounted for this amplified attention, multiple discourses of 'crisis' disseminated through the news media also contributed to the prevalence of the concept of a migration 'crisis'. Through a critical lens, this chapter concentrates on 2015 to deconstruct discursive representations of the migration 'crisis' and migration by boat that emerged in the UK news media. The aim of this analysis is to identify the various ways that this type of migration was represented and, most importantly, to reveal how these discourses functioned and to what end.

This chapter will show how the UK news media concentrated their reporting of migration on the topics of increasing numbers of migrants, descriptions and representations of boat sinkings and 'out-of-control' migration, the linking of migration to terrorism and claims that migrants are dangerous and have a negative impact on the economy. On the whole, these representations justified restrictions on refugee access to the United Kingdom, increased border controls and the implementation of quotas. Furthermore, these discourses contributed to a number of significant events that took place in the years to follow: (1) the destruction of 'the jungle' in Calais and (2) Brexit.

LITERATURE REVIEW

To date, the level of research into how migrants travelling by boat are represented in elite discourses is minimal, especially in the European context (Bacas 2013; Bruno 2016; Campesi 2011). Other regions have been examined to some degree: Australia, New Zealand (Bogen and Marlowe 2015; Holtom 2013; Kampmark 2006; McKay, Thomas and Blood 2011; O'Doherty and Lecouter 2007; Slattery 2003) and Canada (Ashutosh and Mountz 2012). Although the body of work on these regions is minimal, it does indicate that discourses play an important role in the categorisation of migrants and that discursive framings function to legitimise the governance of human migration at sea (McKay, Thomas and Blood 2011; O'Doherty and Lecouter 2007; Slattery 2003). The work undertaken by Kampmark (2006) indicates that negative representations of migration by boat (discursive framings of danger, security and cultural difference) have existed in Australia for decades. Bogen and Marlowe (2015) argue that discourses functioned to justify the detention of 'mass arrivals' in New Zealand.

The literature also indicates that this practice of categorisation occurs in the EU context, especially in relation to the discourse of the migration 'crisis'. For example, Bruno (2016) and Campesi (2011) found that the Italian political elite and the Italian media use discourses of emergency to justify border security practices that fall outside the regular legal and political framework. Significantly, Holtom (2013) argues that press and policy agendas intersect with public opinion to contribute to the ongoing exclusion of 'boat people'. This chapter aims to build upon this emergent body of work by specifically examining how the migration 'crisis' and migration by boat were represented in UK media discourses in 2015.

DATA AND METHODOLOGY

I utilised the online media aggregator LexisNexis to identify UK news articles from 2015. The UK news media proved to be a substantial source of data on this topic, as the online system identified 8,881 news articles that mentioned the term 'migration crisis'. These articles came from a range of broadsheet and tabloid newspapers, including both print and online publications. The key sources of data included *Daily Mail* (19 per cent) and *Express* (18 per cent). This was closely followed by *Independent* (15 per cent), *Telegraph* (13 per cent), and *Guardian* (12 per cent). By examining these data over the year (see figure 7.1), it is clear that there was a steady rise in the number of articles produced, from a mere 25 in January to 489 in July. The figures increased significantly to 1,214 in August and to 2,724 in September. The level decreased from October onwards but remained relatively high in comparison to the beginning of the year.

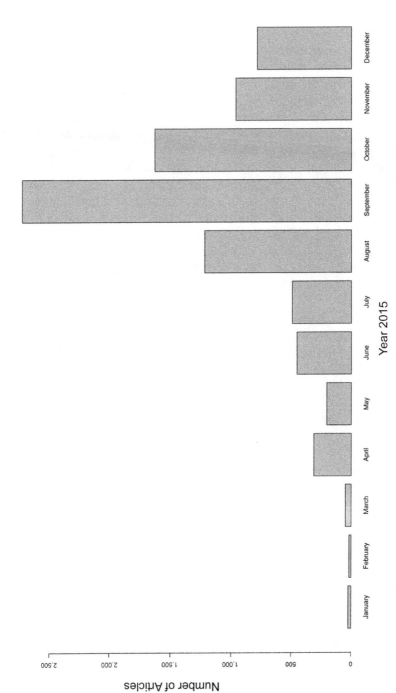

Figure 7.1.   Number of Articles throughout the Year 2015. *Source:* **authors own research.**

The research in this chapter is underpinned by a Critical Discourse Analysis theoretical framework and a critical approach to the analysis of discourses (Wodak and Meyer 2009). This was undertaken through a critical reading of the news articles and the deconstruction of dominant discourses. In other words, once the articles were identified, each article was read and analysed with the aim of identifying general trends in the narratives and identifying specific themes that dominated the cohort of data. Dominant discourses were noted, and extracts were compiled for further analysis. At this point in the chapter it is worth noting that the articles that were identified tended to be formulaic. Most articles were descriptive pieces, which outlined to the reader the fundamentals of what occurred (e.g., the boat sank and X number of migrants died). This was usually followed by a reaction from an elite or a number of elites, such as campaign or migrant groups (e.g., UNHCR, Save the Children), political leaders (e.g., mayors; UK, French or Spanish political leaders; the UK Prime Minister or UK opposition politicians) or religious leaders (e.g., the pope). Following this, a history of the situation or reasons for people migrating to the EU were listed, and the articles generally concluded with a call to action (e.g., the French authorities need to strengthen their borders). A further notable item was the repetitive use of certain phrases, one prominent example being: 'Mediterranean migrant boat crisis' (*Guardian* 2015).

This chapter begins by chronologically examining the various narratives of the migration 'crisis' that were produced in the UK news media throughout the year 2015. This is followed by the second core analytical component of this chapter, which specifically examines discourses of migration by boat that were produced within this 'crisis' framework. This chapter therefore first sets out the 'story' of the migration 'crisis' as it evolved over the year and, based on this analysis, identifies and explores the key themes through which migration by boat was discussed within this 'crisis' framework.

CHRONOLOGICAL ANALYSIS OF THE MIGRATION 'CRISIS' DISCOURSE

This section chronologically explores the various narratives of the migration 'crisis' that were produced in the UK news media in 2015. As referred to above, this research concentrated upon 2015, as the media and political elites placed significant attention on migration and an apparent 'crisis' during this time. The examination of a clustered narrative, such as the migration 'crisis', is important, as it demonstrates the way in which this discourse of 'crisis' was produced and how it evolved over time. Furthermore, it also offers a context for the next substantive section of this chapter, which specifically examines discourses of migration by boat and how this type of migration was represented through a number of particular framings.

January–March (2015)

A number of distinct discourses in the first three months of 2015 set the tone for the year to follow. The first of these discourses concentrated upon incidents of boat sinkings and migrant deaths in the Mediterranean Sea. Reporters expressed concern over the increasing number of refugees coming to the EU and to the United Kingdom. There was a particular focus on Syrian refugees travelling to the EU, and the media debated whether or not these migrants should be permitted access into the United Kingdom. There were general calls for fewer migrants to the United Kingdom, immigration reform and increased border controls. The media forwarded the concept that among these refugees were terrorists. Elites like Nigel Farage (the then leader of the UK Independence Party) championed this idea discussing it in relation to the forthcoming UK general election. During this time, and in this context of the migration 'crisis', a discussion on the possibility of the United Kingdom exiting the EU (Brexit) emerged. Within this environment of anxiety over increasing numbers of migrants and 'out-of-control' migration, the argument was forwarded through the media that migration to the EU was having a negative impact on the economy. The media justified this opinion through the discussion of the migrant camp in Calais, France. Although the situation in Calais was represented by the media as a 'crisis' on a number of levels (humanitarian, cultural, security), they tended to focus on the economic impact (e.g., reports on delays to cargo) and represented migrants as dangerous (e.g., reports of drivers travelling to the United Kingdom being attacked by migrants).

April–July (2015)

Between April and July, a number of individualised migrant stories were produced by the media; nonetheless, the overall tendency of the news media was to refer to migrants as a mass of people and to offer generalised representations. There were continued reports on deaths/drownings/rescue operations in the Mediterranean Sea. These included expressions of sympathy, with multiple references to 'desperate refugees' (Parker 2015). Rescue efforts at sea were debated, and it was suggested that instead of rescue operations, there should be blockades. There were also suggestions that UK naval ships should be taking part in these efforts. Often referred to as 'Burden Sharing' (*Guardian* 2015), the government of Germany urged its fellow EU member-states to permit increased numbers of refugees. In the United Kingdom, there was a high level of reluctance politically to do so. This reluctance was so strong that Britain made threats to pull out of EU over the migrant 'crisis'.

In May the then Home Secretary Theresa May suggested that a quota system be implemented for 'economic migrant boat people' (Hall 2015). Framing this type of migration in an economic sense has the result of delegitimising claims for asylum and justified the continued exclusion of migrants from the United Kingdom. Furthermore, migrants were also referred to as 'benefit tourists' (Groves 2015), a phrasing that also aims to delegitimise those seeking safe passage and refuge. Indeed, during these months, the focus on controlling UK borders increased, and there were further calls for migrant control. This debate took place within a milieu of concern/fear over increasing numbers of migrants, which were described as 'an influx' (Barnett 2015). Examples of extreme phrasings include 'Illegal immigrants flood in. 18,000 are now sneaking in' (Smith 2015); 'Invasion', 'Out of Control' (Sheldrick 2015); 'Swarming' migrants (Paris 2015) and 'Migrant Surge' (*Mail Online* 2015). The media continued to report on the unfolding situation in Calais, which was once again represented through an economic framing. Reports concentrated on 'contaminated' food stocks (Express.co.uk 2015) due to migrants gaining access to lorries and travelling to the United Kingdom in this manner. There was also a tendency to represent Britain as a target, by reporting upon the number of deaths of those trying to enter the United Kingdom through the Channel Tunnel (Allen and Tomlinson 2015; O' Neill 2015).

On the whole, the migrant 'crisis' was represented as having a negative economic impact on the UK economy, mainly how (1) the situation in Calais affected business and the economy; (2) asylum applications were an expense on the state; (3) delays at Calais were impacting on holidaymakers, for example, 'travel nightmare for Brits' (Wellman 2015); and (4) 'floods' of illegal immigrants were reported to be working on the black market in the United Kingdom, which some media outlets said affected the employment market. These discourses fed into and influenced the discussion on the soon-to-be-held UK general election, where UK government and opposition parties continually debated on how to 'handle the crisis' (Taylor, Wintour and Elgot 2015). Indeed, the practice of describing refugees as potential security threats was used by certain political parties (i.e., the UK Independence Party) to create a sense of fear and to push forward an anti-EU agenda. Compounding these discourses were reports that migrants travelling to the EU were a threat in terms of health/disease and in terms of criminality through the use of phrasings such as 'chainsaw-wielding' migrants (Sage 2015). Overall, during the first half of 2015 the key question put forward by the UK news media was: what can be done about the migrant 'crisis'? In the milieu of fearful discourses and increasing numbers of migrants, the key solutions offered included calls for (1) the EU to take action, (2) migrant quotas to be implemented and (3) a war on migrant traffickers.

August (2015)

Moving into the autumn of 2015, there was continued questioning of EU authority over the 'crisis', which was often described as 'chaos' (Fleig and Crossley 2015). This chaos was represented through dramatic accounts of boat sinkings, rescue efforts and deaths in the Mediterranean. Within this context of 'chaos' two key issues are identifiable. The first of these issues were reports of increasing numbers of migrants travelling to the EU, often referred to as a 'swarm' (Chapman 2015). Shocking and eye-catching numbers were quoted in the news media: 'Two migrants make it into Britain every hour' (Sheldrick 2015) and 'We must stop the flood of migrants heading here' (Express.co.uk 2015). The second major issue was the continued focus on the situation in Calais and the economic impact on residents, businesses and holidaymakers, rather than on the impact on the lives of migrants living in Calais. However, some news sources did report on the living conditions of migrants, and there were a number of descriptive pieces on life in the 'jungle' (Finan and Crossley 2015). In addition, reports continued to be produced on the number of migrants trying to enter the United Kingdom through Calais and on the number of migrant deaths.

September (2015)

Perhaps the most prolific and poignant incident that occurred within this migration 'crisis' discourse took place in early September 2015. Indeed, it was this incident that accounted for the large number of articles published during that month. The image of Alyan Kurdi spread across the world's media in September 2015. The photograph of this boy, who drowned in the Mediterranean and was found and photographed lying on a Turkish beach, went viral across the world. With this case one can clearly see the role of the media at large, where some outlets merely reported on this incident and others presented a range of opinion and analysis. Indeed, this played out differently in different venues (e.g., along the right-left spectrum). There were thus different valences around the death of Aylan Kurdi. Nonetheless, there were a number of broad reactions by the UK media that can be identified. First, there was an outpouring of sympathy for him, his family and for refugee children in general. Second, in the wake of this incident there were calls for exceptions to be made for refugee children. In reaction to this, the then Prime Minister David Cameron announced plans to take in thousands of refugees and to review the UK asylum policy. Last, the general public in the United Kingdom offered rooms in their homes to migrants.

Instead of focusing upon EU immigration policies and restrictive border controls, the news media blamed two entities for the migration 'crisis': (1) the war in Syria and (2) the facilitation of transport by traffickers and smugglers. Even though much sympathy was expressed by the media towards refugee children, the conservative view on migrant entry to the EU remained, and the focus turned to bringing an end to the war in Syria: 'If you really want to save Syrian children, save Syria' (Hartley-Brewer 2015). So large was the number of refugees travelling from Syria to the EU that there seemed to be an increased impetus to halt the war in Syria. It is arguable that this was not necessarily for the benefit of the Syrian people but to prevent continued migration to the EU and to the United Kingdom. A further layer to this discourse was the linking of refugees to terrorism. There were reports that terrorists were masquerading as Syrian refugees in order to gain access to the EU. This discourse functioned to delegitimise refugee claims. On the whole, the media concluded that traffickers were solely responsible for facilitating migration to the EU, and in the case of Aylan Kurdi, they were blamed for the tragedy.

Although the media expressed much sympathy in relation to the continually produced images of hundreds of people dying and children drowning, migrants were still represented as a threat, and the media continued to disseminate a message of chaos: 'Migrant crisis out of control' (*Daily Star* 2015); 'We can't cope with this tide' (Stevens 2015); 'Prepare yourselves: The Great Migration will be with us for decades; It is not war but money, that drives people abroad' (Nelson 2015). This discourse of chaos is important, as it is argued here that this discourse offered an opportunity to those in positions of power to govern in particular ways. For example, representations of chaos and increasing numbers of migrants justified the closure of borders in a number of EU member-states, including Hungary, Denmark and Germany. In the United Kingdom this discourse prompted the questioning of the continuation of the European Free Movement Policy: 'Euro dream over as border controls return in face of tidal wave of EU migrants' (Dawar, Ingham and Virtue 2015). These types of discourses formed the groundwork for the justification of the United Kingdom's exit from the EU.

October–December (2015)

As 2015 came to an end, the discourse that huge numbers of migrants were arriving in the EU continued: '218,394! The Euro migrant tide for one single month' (Little 2015). Indeed, it was speculated that this 'problem' would worsen in the future: '3m more migrants to flood Europe in 2016' (Little 2015). Furthermore, the fear of the 'crisis' intensified: 'Crisis getting even worse' (Express.co.uk 2015). The news media continued to call for control to be taken: 'Seize control' (*Sun* 2015) and for action: 'Send failed Asylum Seekers to African camps' (Holehouse 2015). Although articles that represented migrants as a single group dominated the UK news media, there were some individualised stories of migrant journeys to the EU, and sympathy was expressed towards these migrants, especially those travelling during the cold winter months.

The concept that the permitting of refugees to the EU was also a method of access for terrorists continued to be disseminated: 'Terrorist arrived in Greece as "refugee"' (Charter 2015). This discourse heightened with the terrorist attacks that took place in Paris in November. Indeed, reports that the suicide bomber in Paris had a Syrian passport proliferated through the media: 'Jihadist sneaked into Europe as fake Syrian refugees' (Gallagher 2015). In conjunction with this, migrants in Calais were represented as violent and desperate: 'Chaotic scenes in Calais as "massive invasion" of migrants leads to violence' (Allen 2015). Finally, the discourse that migrants affected the British economy and British trade continued: 'EU migrant deal will cost UK dear' (Stevens 2015).

Concluding Remarks

The research discussed so far has shown how the UK news media represented the migration 'crisis' through a number of key discourses during 2015. These included reports of increasing numbers of migrants, descriptions and representations of boat sinkings and 'out-of-control' migration, the linking of migration to terrorism and claims that migrants are dangerous and had a negative impact on the economy. These discourses were interlinked and fed into an overall discourse of 'crisis', which served a number of specific functions. In particular, these discourses functioned to justify the restriction of refugees to the United Kingdom, an increase in border controls, the implementation of quotas and formed the groundwork for a range of broader political actions in 2016.

THEMATIC ANALYSIS OF DISCOURSES
OF MIGRATION BY BOAT

This section examines media discourses of migration by boat that were produced within the migration 'crisis' framework discussed earlier. I thematically analysed this data to reveal the way in which the UK media represented migration by boat in 2015. A number of specific themes emerged in relation to this: individualised and generalised representations; descriptions of migration by boat; who is to blame for the 'crisis'?; and is there a solution to this 'crisis'?. Each of these themes will be discussed in turn.

Individualised and Generalised Representations

The first notable theme that emerged was the use of individualised narratives of migration by boat and, more commonly, the use of generalised representations of these migrants (where there is a concentration on large and increasing numbers of migrants). In articles that represented migrants as individuals, it was common practice for the reporter to name the migrant and tell their story. For example: 'Om Ali injured her leg while she was walking through mountains in Turkey. The family crossed from Izmir to the Greek island of Lesbos in a smuggler's rubber boat carrying 35 people, but the engine broke down. After waiting a few hours in the middle of the sea they were rescued by Greek coastguards' (Samaan 2015). The general trend of the news media, however, was to represent migrants who travel by boat as a mass of people. This was effectively carried out by the media through a discussion of numbers, which were constantly quoted in relation to migration by boat.

The number of migrants was an important aspect, as it was a method of creating a sense of 'crisis' about this issue and to portray migration as an uncontrollable invasion. This was done in a number of ways. First, there was a noticeable use of a whole range of numbers to describe arrivals, rescues and deaths: 'Migrant crisis: boat arrivals tops 100,000' (Squires 2015); 'Over 60,000 migrants have swamped the Mediterranean coasts of Italy and Greece this year. Thousands more have drowned attempting the precarious sea crossing in rickety boats' (Newton Dunn 2015). In some articles, there could be five to ten separate numbers quoted in relation to these migrants. For example, the *Mail Online* (Bloom 2015) listed the following array of numbers throughout one specific article: 2,000, 2,164, 100, 520, 900, 3,200 and 600. This practice was also undertaken by broadsheet newspapers: 'Up to 200 people still unaccounted for after migrant boat sinks off Libya; of estimated 600 migrants on board during Wednesday's capsizing 373 have been rescued' (Kirchgaessner 2015). Using numbers this way can bombard the reader with figures and inflate the situation, which can give an impression of chaos and 'out-of-control' migration. Indeed, do the numbers quoted in the news media even reflect reality? Or even offer a contextual view of the situation? As discussed in chapter 2 of this edited book by Williams, the collection of data on the number of migrants travelling by boat is extremely difficult to assess, and there are many gaps in the data. Given the great variance in the numbers reported, one can contend that it is highly likely that these figures are unsubstantiated. Nevertheless, the media continued to report on the number of migrants in 2015. Accuracy in numbers was not necessary for the story to function, and the overall impression that large numbers of migrants were arriving in the United Kingdom and in EU member-states dominated.

Furthermore, the general impression offered by the media was that the number of migrants arriving by boat was increasing. For example, 'A record 218,000 migrants crossed the Mediterranean in October – 2,000 more than the amount for the whole of 2014, UN reveal' (Malm 2015); 'Three million migrants coming to EU by end of next year; Migrant crisis shows no signs of easing according to latest European Commission projections' (Glaze 2015); and 'The relentless flood of migrants is continuing this year after 170,000 were rescued at sea by Italy in 2014 – a 277 per cent increase over the number in 2013' (MacFarlan 2015).

Reports of substantial increases in numbers led to impressions of mass invasion and a general sense of crisis: 'Minister warned of an "exodus without precedent"' (Bloom 2015); 'EU "is weeks away from falling apart": Dire warning as countries battle to cope with influx of migrants' (Doyle 2015). The argumentation was forwarded that EU member-states were overwhelmed by these migrants: 'Italy simply cannot cope with the daily influx of migrants' (Reid 2015). Representations of a migrant invasion was used by some to promote political agendas; this was particularly the case in relation to the Brexit vote: 'Why we need to get out of the EU: More than 1 million illegal migrants flood EU this year alone' (Dawar 2015). In conjunction with the use of numbers, the use of maritime language to describe the scale of this type of migration was notable, for example, 'wave of migrants'; 'illegal migrant tide'; 'tide of suffering' (Alexander 2015); 'Illegal migrants flood in' (Dawar 2015). This type of phrasing adds to an already exaggerated discourse of large numbers of migrant arrivals to the EU.

Descriptions of Migration by Boat

In addition to the general trend of the news media to depict migration by boat through general representations, the articles tended to be highly descriptive in format. Articles described multiple elements, including journeys by boat, sinkings, drownings, migrant deaths, the migrants themselves, boats and rescue operations (including the involvement of the navy). Examining articles that describe the journey by boat first, they mainly referred to conditions at sea, conditions on the boat, a lack of supplies for the migrants (e.g., drinking water) and the mistreatment of migrants (descriptions of kidnapping, beatings, imprisonment, starvation, police brutality, torture and rape). Second, there were also detailed descriptions of boat sinkings and migrant drownings, for example, 'Migrants frantically shimmied up rope dangling from a towering cargo ship and others jumped into the water grasping at lifesavers' (Thomas 2015).

Third, reports of migrant deaths dominated news media reports. For example, 'The dead bodies of desperate migrants who were bundled onto overcrowded boats destined for the EU, but capsize killing those on board, were washed up on Libya's beaches' (Stanton 2015). These descriptions varied from a belittling tone: 'They died like rats in cages' (Tomlinson, Fagge and Roberts 2015) to sympathetic: 'Stark photographs show the tide of death washing up on the shores of Lesbos as local fishermen say they dread what they will find on their nets' (Calderwood 2015). Indeed, it is notable how migrants were often described in extreme terms: 'Panic-stricken migrants' (Reid 2015), 'desperate people' (Mepham 2015).

Fourth, the boats that migrants used to reach the EU were a focal point of reports. The boats were mainly described as small, unsafe and unseaworthy, and their descriptions include 'flimsy boats' (McGreal 2015), 'crammed into unseaworthy boats' (Wyke 2015), 'ramshackle boats' (Tickle 2015), 'rickety boat' (Kingsley et al. 2015), 'dangerous boats' (Porter 2015), 'overcrowded boats' (Hall 2015) and 'leaky boats' (Travis 2015).

Last, the media described and tended to highlight the various rescue operations that took place at sea. Quite often these descriptions juxtaposed migrants as 'desperate' and in need of saving, while the various EU authorities were represented as heroes. For example, 'Tiny, sodden and limp-limbed after hours in the water, an infant in a baby pink life-belt is finally passed to safety by rescue workers, following the latest tragedy in the Mediterranean' (Roberts 2015). Furthermore, the media highlighted how the UK Navy personnel were involved in search and rescue operations: 'These are some of the lucky hundreds of migrants plucked to safety by personnel from the HMS Bulwark' (Brown and Pickles 2015). In recent years we have witnessed the increased militarisation of borders, not only in the United Kingdom and EU but also in Australia (see chapter 9 by Dickson). By invoking patriotic language the UK Navy personnel were portrayed as successful heroes: 'The Royal Navy's flagship has rescued more than 100 refugees adrift in the Mediterranean' (Halkon 2015) and 'Bulwark to the Rescue' (*Daily Mail* 2015). The media used descriptions of the navy, moreover, to function within a discourse of control: 'One of Britain's biggest warships, which is already playing a part in search-and-rescue efforts to save people at risk of drowning on rickety boats, could also be switched to combat role to help in any push to take on the smuggler networks' (Haynes 2015). This discourse, therefore, was quite functional as it could adapt to a discourse which held a 'search and rescue' sentiment, but also a 'military function and operation' undertone in order to justify the control of migration.

Who Is to Blame for the 'Crisis'?

The question of who caused the migration 'crisis' and the continued practice of people travelling across the Mediterranean by boat was a key concern of the news media. The UK news media's tendency during 2015 was to cast EU authorities and the British Navy into the role of hero and protector, while traffickers and smugglers were firmly blamed for facilitating migration 'by boat: 'EU launches naval operation in bid to curb Mediterranean migrant flow; Officials say plan will disrupt human-trafficking network rather than target migrants attempting to flee conflict' (Sehmer 2015) and 'We must target the traffickers who are responsible for so many people dying at sea and prevent their innocent victims from being tricked or forced into making perilous journeys [Philip Hammond, the then UK Foreign Secretary]' (Whittam Smith 2015). Traffickers and smugglers were firmly placed into a villainous role: 'And we have got to crack down on the terrible traffickers and people-smugglers who are at the heart of this problem' (Winchester 2015), 'ruthless human traffickers' (Dearden 2015) and 'the evil traffickers who are peddling whatever kind of utopian vision of Europe to the victims' (McGiffin 2015). Traffickers and smugglers were also associated with crime: 'gang of migrant traffickers' (Reid 2015) and 'Europe's migration crisis creating "unprecedented wave of criminality" as gangs across the continent converge around the "honeypot" of people smuggling, says head of Europol' (Freeman 2015). In some ways, this was a simple but effective narrative. This discourse diverted attention away from EU authorities, who actively prevented migrants entering the EU in a safe manner and whose migration policies forced some migrants to take alternative and often dangerous routes.

A further layer to this discourse was the claim that terrorists used the same methods and routes taken by those fleeing persecution to enter the EU. Migration by boat was not only presented as a problem in terms of numbers but also represented as a security threat: 'Italian Defence Minister Roberta Pinotti told the newspaper IL Messaggero that the risk of jihadists arriving in Italy on boats carrying immigrants from Libya cannot be ruled out' (Bloom 2015). By discussing migration by boat and terrorism in conjunction with one another, migrants were explicitly represented as a threat: 'Boat migrants represent a significant terror threat' (Express.co.uk 2015), 'Sadistic Islamic State leaders have openly bragged that they are sending evil Sunni Muslim jihadis to the UK and Europe hidden among migrant boats in order to carry out terrorist activities on our shores' (Austin 2015) and 'They use the boats for their people who they want to send to Europe as the European police don't know who is IS and who is a normal refugee' (Roberts 2015). In addition to this, it was claimed that migrants were actually being recruited into terrorism: 'Fears jihadi recruiters "grooming" migrants at refugee hotspots and turning them to terror' (Perring 2015). This was particularly highlighted in relation to the Paris attacks of November 2015: 'Face of a Paris suicide bomber: First picture of ISIS killer as its revealed two of the Jihadis sneaked into Europe via Greece by posing as refugees and being rescued from a sinking migrant boat' (Gallagher, Beckford and Robinson 2015). The discursive practice of combining terrorism with migrants fleeing persecution functioned to conflate the situation, to discredit pleas for safety, to reinforce a simple narrative that migration is bad and ultimately justifies practices of exclusion. The final aspect of this terrorism discourse was the highlighting of the religious faith of migrants. For example, one incident of an apparent altercation on a boat was described purely in religious terms: 'Muslims throw Christians overboard sinking ship for "refusing to pray to Allah"' (Baldwin and Barnett 2015). It is noteworthy that this event was reported upon in religion terms, rather than perhaps taking into consideration that travelling by boat is a stressful, dangerous situation where people may not be getting along for a variety of reasons within that particular context. Focusing upon the religious beliefs of migrants, and in particular the Muslim belief, may function to further represent migrants as the 'Other'.

Is There a Solution to This 'Crisis'?

The UK news media offered a number of solutions to the issue of migrants travelling by boat to the EU. The first of these was to control migration: 'We must reclaim Europe's borders to stop such tragedies' (Burleigh 2015) and to return people to their country of origin: 'such people should be shipped back' (Withnall 2015). It was also suggested that blockades be established and smuggler boats destroyed: 'We must stop this tide of misery at its source' (*Telegraph* 2015). At times, justifications for controlling migration were masked in a discourse of concern: 'Our immediate priority is to prevent more people from dying at sea. We have therefore decided to strengthen our presence at sea, to fight the traffickers, to prevent illegal migration flows and to reinforce internal solidarity and responsibility' (Johnston and Dawber 2015). At the extreme end, there were those that proposed to put 'boots on the ground' in North Africa and Syria: 'Europe's tide of migrant tragedy can be stemmed only in Africa' (Nougayrède 2015). On the whole, the UK news media suggested solving the 'crisis' of migration by boat through a variety of measures.

CONCLUSION

In 2015 the UK news media represented the migration 'crisis' through a number of key interlinking discourses. These included reports on increased numbers of migrants, descriptions and representations of boat sinkings and 'out-of-control' migration, the linking of migrants to terrorism and claims that migrants had a negative impact on the economy. Not only did these discourses feed into one another, but they also formed a basic thematic framework for the conceptualisation of migration by boat: (1) individualised and generalised representations of migrants that travel by boat, (2) highly descriptive pieces covering multiple aspects of migration by boat, (3) the seeking of entities to blame for migration by boat and (4) the seeking and offering of solutions to the migration 'crisis'. These various discourses of 'crisis' and thematic representations of migration by boat served particular functions and were highly influential. Indeed, the sheer scale of the coverage of this issue (approximately 9,000 articles produced in 2015) and the dissemination of similar and repetitive representations of this 'group' of migrants left little room for alternative discourses and allowed for dominant discourses that were overall negative in tone to proliferate through the news media. This had a significant impact on how people conceptualised the migration 'crisis' and migration by boat during 2015. Indeed, when repetitive discourses are disseminated through the media, they can become ingrained in the public consciousness. Although it may be argued that these news articles may have documented what was happening to these migrants and highlighted the situation they were in, it cannot be forgotten that these discourses were also highly politicised and were used in a number of ways to justify certain actions. The conceptualisation that there was a 'crisis' and that migration was 'out of control' and causing 'chaos' was used to justify political action.

As Mountz and Hiemstra (2014) argue, the logic of 'chaos' and 'crisis' creates a vacuum of exceptionalism – moments that allow for geopolitical influence to take place. States use these moments of exceptionalism to expand sovereign claims and powers. This can be seen in relation to border control in a number of EU member-states in 2015 and, in particular, in relation to the externalisation of asylum processing, the offshore interception and processing of migrants and the internal expansion of policing powers.

This chapter has identified a number of key narratives of migration that dominated the UK news media in 2015. It has shown how the discourse of 'crisis' was produced and how it evolved over a twelve-month period. It is clear from this research that the discourse of 'crisis' (including a broad anti-EU agenda) fed into representations of migration by boat and migration in general. Indeed, discourses of 'crisis' can cloak the implementation of geopolitical influence over the governance of migration (Mountz and Hiemstra 2014) and can be used to legitimise gatekeeping policies (Bernardie-Tahir and Schmoll 2014, 89). I contend that representations of the migration 'crisis' and migration by boat functioned to justify a number of specific political practices, namely, the continued restriction of access for refugees to the United Kingdom, increased border controls and the implementation of quotas. These discourses also contributed to the groundwork for a number of significant events that took place in the years to follow, chiefly the United Kingdom's exit from the EU (Brexit) and the eventual destruction of 'the jungle' in Calais, France.

BIBLIOGRAPHY

Alexander, Harriet, 'What can be done to end the tide of suffering?; As politicians in Europe wring their hands about the migrant crisis on the southern shores of Europe, it is time to actually do something about it – even if there is no easy solution', *The Telegraph*, 20 April 2015. LexisNexis Academic.

Allen, Peter, 'Chaotic scenes in Calais as "massive invasion" of migrants lead to violence – with British anarchist groups blamed; More than 100 migrants broke through fences and stormed the Channel Tunnel in what authorities described as an "organised attack"', *The Mirror*, 3 October 2015. LexisNexis Academic.

Allen, Peter, and Tomlinson, Simon, 'Two migrants hit by trains and seven others saved from drowning after trying to sneak into Britain as holidaymakers face yet more delays on both sides of the Channel', *Mail Online*, 28 July 2015. LexisNexis Academic.

Ashutosh, I., and Mountz, A, 'The geopolitics of migrant mobility: Tracing state relations through refugee claims, boats, and discourses', *Geopolitics* 17 (2012): 335–54.

Austin, Jon, 'EXCLUSIVE: Deserters from brutal Assad's army entering UK with Syrian migrants', Express.co.uk, 7 October 2015. LexisNexis Academic.

Bacas, J.L., 'Perceiving fences and experiencing borders in Greece: A discourse on irregular migration across European borders'. *Journal of Mediterranean Studies*, 22, no. 2 (2013): 319–36.

Baldwin, Paul, and Barnett, Helen, 'Muslims throw Christians overboard sinking ship for "refusing to pray to Allah"', Express.co.uk, 19 April 2015. LexisNexis Academic.

Barnett, Helen, 'Farage wages war on BBC: Cancels interview and warns Beeb has too much cash and influence' Express.co.uk, 1 May 2015. LexisNexis Academic.

Bernardie-Tahir, N., and Schmoll, C., 'Islands and Undesirables: Introduction to the Special Issue on Irregular Migration in Southern European Islands'. *Journal of Immigrant & Refugee Studies* 12 (2014): 87–102.

Bloom, Dan, 'Italy rescues another 2,000 Libyan migrants from packed boats in the Mediterranean as minister warns of "exodus without precedent" if ISIS is allowed to spread', *Mail Online*, 16 February 2015. LexisNexis Academic.

Bogen, Rachel, and Marlowe, Jay, 'Asylum discourse in New Zealand: Moral panic and a culture of indifference'. *Australian Social Work*, DOI: 10.1080/0312407X.2015.1076869.

Brown, Larisa, and Pickles, Kate, 'British Navy rescue 400 migrants from their sinking, overloaded ships in the Mediterranean . . . but diplomatic sources insist there is "no chance" they will be given asylum in Britain', *Mail Online*, 13 May 2015. LexisNexis Academic.

Bruno, Marco, 'Framing Lampedusa. Between alarmism and pietism – The landing issue in Italian media coverage of migration', in *Public and Political Discourses of Migration*, edited by Haynes, A., Power, M. J., Devereux, E., Dillane, A., and Carr, J. (London: Rowman and Littlefield).

Burleigh, Michael, 'We must reclaim Europe's Borders to stop such tragedies', *Daily Mail*, 21 April 2015. LexisNexis Academic.

Calderwood, Imogen, 'Stark photographs show the tide of death washing up on the shores of Lesbos as local fishermen say they dread what they will find in their nets', *Mail Online*, 7 November 2015. LexisNexis Academic.

Campesi, Giuseppe, 'The Arab Spring and the crisis of the European border regime: Manufacturing emergency in the Lampedusa crisis'. Fiesole: EUI working paper.

Chapman, John, 'Migrants swarm to Britain; Inside: The pictures that prove . . . Torrent of stowaway migrants on a typical day in borderless UK', *The Express*, 29 August 2015. LexisNexis Academic.

Charter, David, 'Terrorist arrived in Greece as "refugee" ', *The Times*, 16 November 2015. LexisNexis Academic.

Daily Mail, 'Bulwark to the rescue', 29 May 2015a. LexisNexis Academic.

Daily Star, 'Migrants crisis out of control', 2 September 2015b. LexisNexis Academic.

Dawar, Anil, 'Illegal migrants flood in: 18,000 are now sneaking into UK every year', Express.co.uk, 6 June 2015a. LexisNexis Academic.

Dawar, Anil, 'Why we need to get out of EU: More than 1million illegal migrant attempts this year alone', Express.co.uk, 11 November 2015b. LexisNexis Academic.

Dawar, Anil, Ingham, John, and Virtue, Rob, 'Euro dream over as border controls return in face of tidal wave of EU migrants', Express.co.uk, 3 September 2015. LexisNexis Academic.

Dearden, Lizzie, 'The darker your skin – the further down you go: The hierarchical system aboard Italy's migrant boats that governs who lives and who dies; Survivors have told of African migrants being forced below deck and threatened or killed if they try to escape', *The Independent*, 21 April 2015. LexisNexis Academic.

Doyle, Jack, 'EU "is weeks away from falling apart": Dire warning as countries battle to cope with influx of migrants', *Mail Online*, 26 October 2015. LexisNexis Academic.

Express.co.uk, 'Boat migrants represent a significant terror threat', 21 May 2015. LexisNexis Academic.

Express.co.uk, 'Expect dirty tricks as the referendum draws closer', 3 November 2015. LexisNexis Academic.

Express.co.uk, 'Laws target honest lorry drivers not real criminals', 17 July 2015. LexisNexis Academic. Express.co.uk, 'Songs of Praise in Calais is political propaganda', 9 August 2015. LexisNexis Academic.

Finan, Tim, and Crossley, Lucy, 'Brussels pledges £3.6m for MORE accommodation for 1,500 migrants in Calais . . . and yes, you're footing the bill', *Mail Online*, 31 August 2015. LexisNexis Academic.

Fleig, Jessica, and Crossley, Lucy, 'Calais chaos caused by blockade of just TWO small boats: Striking French ferry workers cause misery for thousands of holiday-makers', *Mail Online*, 31 August 2015. LexisNexis Academic.

Freeman, Colin, 'Migration crisis creating "wave of criminality" as gangs turn to people-smuggling; Europe's migration crisis creating "unprecedented wave of criminality" as gangs across the continent converge around the "honeypot" of people-smuggling, says head of Europol', *The Telegraph*, 19 September 2015. LexisNexis Academic.

Gallagher, Ian, Beckford, Martin, and Robinson, Martin, 'Revealed: Two of the Jihadis sneaked into Europe via Greece by posing as refugees and being rescued from a sinking migrant boat – and survivors say one of the attackers was a woman', *Mail Online*, 16 November 2015. LexisNexis Academic.

Glaze, Ben, 'Three million migrants coming to EU by end of next year; Migrant crisis shows no signs of easing, according to latest European Commission projections', Mirror.co.uk, 5 November 2015.

Groves, Jason. 'PM targets benefit tourists: He will demand EU allows Britain to ban payouts to migrants for first four years', *Mail Online*, 13 May 2015. LexisNexis Academic.

The Guardian, 'Europe's shame over migrant boat people', 16 April 2015. Lexis-Nexis Academic.

Halkon, Ruth, 'Royal Navy rescues 110 migrants floating in the Med in first mission since being dispatched; HMS Bulwark was deployed in wake of migrant crisis which has cost the lives of 1,800 people this year', *The Mirror*, 7 May 2015. Lex-isNexis Academic.

Hall, Macer, 'Support soars to quit the EU: Migrant crisis is fuelling surge, say Euros-ceptics', Express.co.uk, 17 September 2015a. LexisNexis Academic.

Hall, Macer, 'Theresa May says NO to taking 60,000 more economic migrant boat people from north Africa', Express.co.uk, 12 May 2015b. LexisNexis Academic.

Hartley-Brewer, Julia, 'If you really want to save Syrian children, save Syria; The only way to save children like Aylan Kurdi is to go to war against the psychopaths they're fleeing. Everything else is just empty noise', *The Telegraph*, 3 September 2015. LexisNexis Academic.

Haynes, Deborah, 'British forces to confront people traffickers in Med', *The Times*, 18 May 2015. LexisNexis Academic.

Holehouse, Matthew, 'Send failed asylum seekers to African camps', *The Daily Telegraph*, 9 October 2015. LexisNexis Academic.

Holtom, Bridget, '"Boat people" in Australia: Press, policy and public opinion'. Research Project BEES (BEES0007), 2013, available here: http://geoview.iag.org.au/index.php/GEOView/article/view/29

Johnston, Ian, and Dawber, Alistair, 'Migrant crisis: Cameron sends in Royal Navy', *The I*, 24 April 2015. LexisNexis Academic.

Kampmark, Binoy, '"Spying for Hitler" and "Working for Bin Laden": Comparative Australian Discourses on Refugees', *Journal of Refugee Studies* 19, no. 1 (2006.

Kingsley, Patrick, Abbott, Diane, Hannan, Daniel, Finch, Tim, and Wittenberg, Jona-than, 'How many refugees should the UK take in?; Yvette Cooper has suggested the UK should welcome 10,000 refugees from the Middle East, with each town housing 10 families. Our panellists give their verdict', *The Guardian*, 28 September, 2015. LexisNexis Academic.

Kirchgaessner, Stephanie, 'Up to 200 people still unaccounted for after migrant boat sinks off Libya; Of estimated 600 migrants on board during Wednesday's capsizing 373 have been rescued, pointing to largest loss of life in Mediterranean since April', *The Guardian*, 7 August 2015. LexisNexis Academic.

Little, Alison, '3m more migrants to flood Europe in 2016', Express.co.uk, 5 November 2015b. LexisNexis Academic.

Little, Alison, '218,394! The Euro migrant tide for one single month', *The Express*, 3 November 2015a. LexisNexis Academic.

MacFarlan, Tim, '5,800 saved in a weekend: Ten Med migrants die as rescue operations from boats near Libya overnight continue just weeks after hundreds lost their lives in deadly shipwreck', *Mail Online*, 4 May 2015. LexisNexis Academic.

Mail Online, 'Cameron says looking at bolstering UK-French border after migrant surge' *Mail Online*, 24 June 2015. LexisNexis Academic.

Malm, Sara, 'A record 218,000 migrants crossed the Mediterranean in October – 2,000 more than the amount for the whole of 2014, UN reveal', *Mail Online*, 2 November 2015. LexisNexis Academic.

Mayr, Andrea, and Machin, David, *How to Do Critical Discourse Analysis: A Multimodal Introduction*, London: Sage.

McGiffin, Carol, 'The death of little Aylan and Galip Kurdi will not be the last tragedy; Carol McGiffin says death of tots is a tragedy beyond words and not only because it didn't have to happen', *The Mirror*, 6 September 2015. LexisNexis Academic.

McGreal, Chris, 'The year of fear: Republicans and media stoked bigotry and anxiety in 2015; Donald Trump, politicians and the news kept us afraid of mass shooters, terrorist threats and the so-called "refugee crisis" – all of which were least likely to kill us', *The Guardian*, 30 December 2015. LexisNexis Academic.

McKay, F., Thomas, S., and Blood, R. W., ' "Any one of these boat people could be a terrorist for all we know!" Media representations and public perceptions of "boat people" arrivals in Australia', *Journalism* 12, no. 5 (2011): 607–26.

Mepham, David, 'David Cameron's rhetoric on the EU migrant crisis is cruel and misleading; Children are fleeing the escalating violence, forced recruitment and army conscription, and marriage', *The Independent*, 23 June 2015. LexisNexis Academic.

Mountz, Alison, and Hiemstra, Nancy, 'Chaos and Crisis: Dissecting the Spatiotemporal Logics of Contemporary Migrations and State Practices', *Annals of the Association of American Geographers* 104, no. 2 (2014): 382–90.

Nelson, Fraser, 'Prepare yourselves: The Great Migration will be with us for decades; It is not war, but money, that drives people abroad. That is not going to change any time soon', *The Telegraph*, 3 September 2015. LexisNexis Academic.

Newton Dunn, Tom, 'PM "Migration Force" to Africa; Elite Force', *The Sun*, 24 June 2015. LexisNexis Academic.

Nougayrède, Natalie, 'Europe's tide of migrant tragedy can be stemmed only in Africa; While the EU argues over those drowning in the Mediterranean, it overlooks the need to work with the sub-Saharan countries that people are fleeing', *The Guardian*, 15 May 2015. LexisNexis Academic.

O'Doherty, Kieran, and Lecouter, Amanda, ' "Asylum seekers", "boat people" and "illegal immigrants": Social categorisation in the media', *Australian Journal of Psychology* 59: 1–12.

O'Neill, Sean. ' "I'm happy to be in Britain . . . but I am hungry"; Thousands of migrants stormed the Channel Tunnel. The struggle will not end for those who made it through', *The Times*, 29 July 2015. LexisNexis Academic.

Paris, Henry Samuel, 'Video showing swarming migrants storming UK-bound truck in Calais goes viral; Shocked tourists witness hundreds of migrants seeking to stow away in a UK-bound truck in Calais, as cross-border migrant row worsens between France and Italy'. *The Telegraph*, 15 June 2015. LexisNexis Academic.

Parker, Fiona, 'Cam can't escape blame for deaths', *Daily Mirror*, 28 April 2015. LexisNexis Academic.

Perring, Rebecca, 'Fears jihadi recruiters "grooming" migrants at refugee hotspots and turning them to terror', Express.co.uk, 30 November 2015. LexisNexis Academic.

Porter, Lizzie, 'Refugee crisis in Greece: What can tourists do to help?; British tourists explain why they have spent their holidays on the Greek island helping refugees fleeing conflict in their home countries', *The Telegraph*, 25 September 2015. LexisNexis Academic.

Reid, Sue, 'Next stop, El Dorado UK! Last month this boatload of migrants was cynically abandoned in the Med – Now they're right on Britain's doorstep', *Mail Online*, 17 January 2015. LexisNexis Academic.

Roberts, Hannah, 'Freezing and barely alive, a baby in a pink life-jacket is passed to safety by rescue workers after being dragged from the Mediterranean in latest migrant boat tragedy', *Mail Online*, 7 August 2015a. LexisNexis Academic.

Roberts, Hannah, 'ISIS supporters post photos of notes showing group's logo and messages near famous Italian landmarks warning of counting down "till the zero hour" ', *Mail Online*, 17 May 2015b. LexisNexis Academic.

Sage, Adam, 'French police powerless to stop chainsaw-wielding migrants', *The Times*, 30 July 2015. LexisNexis Academic.

Samaan, Magdy, 'Walking with migrants: "Arrested, nearly knifed, but I've made it as far as Serbia"; A daily diary of migrants' stories as they travel from Greece to central Europe', *The Telegraph*, 27 September 2015. LexisNexis Academic.

Sehmer, Alexander, 'EU launches naval operation in bid to curb Mediterranean migrant flow; Officials say plan will disrupt human-trafficking network rather than target migrants attempting to flee conflict', *The Independent*, 22 June 2015. LexisNexis Academic.

Sheldrick, Giles, 'Calais crisis: Two migrants make it into Britain EVERY hour', Express.co.uk, 1 August 2015a. LexisNexis Academic.

Sheldrick, Giles, 'EXCLUSIVE: Migrant threat to kill truckers as UK drivers fear for their lives in Calais', Express.co.uk, 11 June 2015b. LexisNexis Academic.

Smith, Oli, 'British warship rescues 1,000 Med migrants as half a million more wait to cross', Express.co.uk, 7 June 2015. LexisNexis Academic.

Slattery, Kate, ' "Drowning not waving": The "children overboard" event and Australia's fear of the other'. *Media International Incorporating Culture and Policy* 109 (2003): 93–108.

Squires, Nick, 'Migrant crisis: Boat arrivals tops 100,000', *The Daily Telegraph*, 10 June 2015. LexisNexis Academic.

Stanton, Jenny, 'Exclusive: The Mediterranean's grim tide – shocking never before seen pictures of migrants' bodies washed up on beach in Libya', *Mail Online*, 17 August 2015. LexisNexis Academic.

Stevens, John, 'EU migrant deal will cost UK dear', *Daily Mail*, 3 November 2015. LexisNexis Academic.

Stevens, John, 'We can't cope with this tide! Europe's despairing leaders bring back border controls with free-movement zone on brink of collapse', *Mail Online*, 3 September 2015. LexisNexis Academic.

The Sun, 'Seize control', 31 October 2015. LexisNexis Academic.

Taylor, Matthew, Wintour, Patrick, and Elgot, Jessica, 'Calais crisis: Cameron pledges to deport more people to end "swarm" of migrants; Prime minister's vow comes as increased police presence and media attention discourage mass movement but hundreds still try to enter Eurotunnel terminal', *The Guardian*, 31 July 2015. LexisNexis Academic.

The Telegraph, 'There's only one way to stop the Mediterranean migrant crisis; Telegraph View: Calls for an official channel for refugees fleeing Libya will not help the situation. Instead, we must stop this tide of misery at its source', 22 April 2015. LexisNexis Academic.

Thomas, Trisha, 'Video shows desperate migrants in dinghies', *The I*, 6 May 2015. LexisNexis Academic.

Tickle, Louise, 'The refugee children making the journey to a new life, alone: "I expected I would die"; The risks facing any refugee crossing the Mediterranean are vast; for an unaccompanied minor they are inconceivable. Still, more and more children are being forced to take that risk – and from Sicily to Kent, the reception that awaits them in Europe is a dismaying one', *The Guardian*, 11 December 2015. LexisNexis Academic.

Tomlinson, Simon, Fagge Nick, and Roberts, Hannah, ' "They died like rats in cages": Horror of migrants' final moments as it emerges 300 were locked in Europe-bound ship's hold as it capsized – leaving up to 900 dead', *Mail Online*, 20 April 2015. LexisNexis Academic.

Travis, Alan, 'Refugee crisis: Britain can no longer sit out as EU prepares for greater numbers; Cameron celebrates keeping door shut but 2016 forecasts an even greater displacement of people that demands a response more like Angela Merkel's', *The Guardian*, 18 December 2015. LexisNexis Academic.

Wellman, Alex, 'Calais crisis: Travel nightmare for Brits as "migrant activity" at Eurotunnel causes massive motorway queues; Operation Stack has caused huge tailbacks on the M20 while ferry companies and Eurotunnel warn customers to "leave more time" for travelling', *The Mirror*, 24 July 2015. LexisNexis Academic.

Whittam Smith, Andreas, 'The Conservatives' compassion deficit is clear in their statements on migrants in the Mediterranean; Unfortunately, traffickers don't live round the corner from Downing Street', *The Independent*, 23 April 2015. LexisNexis Academic.

Winchester, Levi, 'Europe should TURN AWAY migrant boats and BAN refugees settling, Aussie PM urges', Express.co.uk, 21 April 2015. LexisNexis Academic.

Withnall, Adam, 'Mediterranean migrant crisis: Theresa May says people making journey "simply for economic reasons" should be sent back against their will; Home Secretary rejects potential EU plans for resettlement quota', *The Independent*, 13 May 2015. LexisNexis Academic.

Wodak, R., and Meyer, M, *Methods of Critical Discourse Analysis*. London: Sage.

Wyke, Tom, 'Motorists face TWELVE MILE tailbacks in Austria after police crackdown on migrants as hundreds pack into trains bound for Germany', *Mail Online*, 30 August 2015. LexisNexis Academic.

Chapter 8

Media Discourses of the Rescue and Landing of Migration by Boat in the Italian News Media

Marco Binotto and Marco Bruno

MEDIA DISCOURSES AND BORDERS

What are the media needed for? The media provide an image of reality, provide information on what happens beyond our visual space (McCombs 2013) and contribute to the social distribution of knowledge (Hannerz 1992). But it is also certain that the media system, especially the journalistic information system, *constructs a space* by defining dimensions, limits and ways of relating to our 'neighbours'.[1] This chapter aims to analyse how media discourses build representations of boundaries and the construction of space in the Italian news media. This understanding is required in order to act on the boundaries set between cultures, between people and between social *varieties*. The methodology employed here is the collection, processing and analysis via mixed methods (content analysis, lexical analysis, frame and discourse analysis) by the authors[2] – on press, television news and talk show content – and the review of some research carried out by many media scholars between 1989 and 2016.

The next section will summarise the recent history of this representation from the early 1991 crisis by examining the findings of media coverage of migration issues and major media events. Representations of seaborne arrivals permit a complete portrayal of immigration. Although there has been over twenty years of immigration into Italy, seaborne arrivals make up only a small part of the total arrivals. Photographs of boats overloaded with people arduously reaching the coasts are virtually *the only images* that can represent the crossing of borders. Together with representations of the actual apparatus of borders – walls, barriers, barbed wire, border guards – and that of their ('illegal', 'unauthorised') crossing, they become a metonymy for immigration itself. Media and political discourse make migration visible when it is legally invisible and deviant: the consequence is that in public perception immigration appears desperate, chaotic and unmanageable, condensed in time and space, en masse.

The following paragraphs will focus on the two-sided narrative of this representation. The first is constituted by the *background noise* of small news stories, usually crime or small landings on the Italian coast. The second has the aspect of a crisis or an *emergency* and – as we will see – has many similarities to moments of special attention, such as natural disasters or moral panics. Indeed, the police and border intervention itself transforms an otherwise silent movement into a spectacle, by the exhibition of the boats or by the description of the drama of droves of *clandestino*[3] waiting to be fed, identified or deported. The projection of a successful defence exhibits the danger of a rupture, even when this particular assault fails. Thus immigration by boat is represented as an emergency; as a border to defend from the arrival of masses of persons (van Dijk 1991; Welch and Schuster 2005). The political solution then retraces the same logic: to strengthen the border, close the space and prevent entry.

THE LANDING ISSUE IN THE ITALIAN MEDIA

The representation of arrivals thus becomes *the* metaphor for migration. It helps to illustrate a complex phenomenon through its iconic dimension, the aspect that best identifies it within the social imagination. Or, rather the media representation of arriving people better corresponds to the public image of other migration issues: always focused on the moment of movement, always in transit, always temporary and, of course, always an impetuous and catastrophic emergency, as previously shown in chapter 7 by Burroughs. Since its debut in the Italian public perception in the 1990s, the chronicling of landings – then from the coast of Albania – has always been 'discovered' by Italian public opinion via media events. In 1991 the crisis of that small ex-communist country brought several thousand people fleeing to the coast of Puglia in the far south-east of the Italian peninsula (Devole 1998; Mazzara 1998; Vehbiu and Devole 1996). Italy had already been a country of immigration for some years, but it happened so quietly that the discussion on the new regulations, approved between 1989 and 1990, came almost as a surprise in the public debate (Marletti 199; Sciortino and Colombo 2004).

Over time, landings have changed in their locations, their management and in the consistency of their flows but have consolidated as the symbolic image of migration. From a numerical point of view, various studies of coverage of the Italian news media offer data that are difficult to compare due to the survey methodology and periods analysed, since this is a type of news that depends much on its period of occurrence. For example, in our research conducted between 2002 and 2003, reports of landings reached 16.3 per cent of television news and 7.2 per cent of daily newspapers (Binotto and Martino 2004). When we conducted a similar study in 2008, we found that the reports reached almost 5 per cent of televised news and 3 per cent of printed news outlets. Looking at just the front page of print news produced similar data: about 5 per cent in 2010, 10 per cent in 2012 (Binotto, Bruno and Lai 2016). Reports for 'Carta di Roma'[4] of 2015 and 2016 data showed, respectively, 28 per cent and 27 per cent for television news programs, but in this case the reference category – 'migration flows' – included the news on boundaries, walls and land borders.

At least until 2010–2011, landing remained essentially a media icon of migration (Bruno 2004, 2016), omnipresent in news reports but quantitatively smaller compared to the reality of inflows (Ambrosini 2010, 99–100). These new sea entries were, for example, about 36,000 in 2008, 9,500 in 2009, 4,400 in 2010, and they rose to about 63,000 in 2011 (the year of the so-called Arab Spring) before declining again over the following two years (see Figure 8.1 and chapter 5 by Cuttitta).[5] It was in 2014 that the crisis increased with numerous arrivals by sea alongside land arrivals via the Balkans.

In essence, over the years the symbolic weight of sea landings remained unchanged, and, indeed, has some distance from the reality, as evidenced by the data and characteristics of incoming migration flows. Only in the recent years of 'crisis' and deep transformation of Italian migration has the phenomenon of immigration by sea changed in public perception: the allegorical

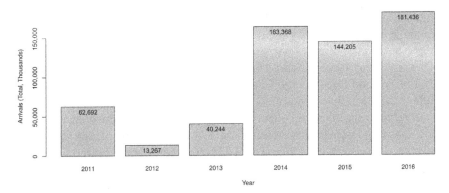

Figure 8.1. Arrivals by Sea in Italy, 2011–2016, by Year. *Source*: (ISMU, Italian Ministry of Interior and UNHCR, 2016).

representation of a larger problem becomes more and more of a problem in itself. If Italy is no longer a destination country and recipient of inflows, it thus becomes more and more an EU frontier, moored in the centre of a Mediterranean region with thousands of people fleeing civil wars, armed conflicts or murderous regimes like those in Syria, Libya, Eritrea or Egypt (see chapter 6 by van Selm). The status of these people as refugees, asylum seekers or persons in need of international humanitarian protection becomes clearer as these traditional routes – for example, to the islands of Malta or Lampedusa at the centre of the Strait of Sicily[6] – increasingly augment other land and sea routes to the EU.

With respect to how this is reflected within the media dimension and the representation of arrival by sea, it is significant to note the progressive importance assumed by the military's patrol and rescue operations. This is especially so since the mission 'Operation *Mare Nostrum*', activated by Italy following multiple incidents, most notably the October 2013 shipwreck off the coast of Lampedusa.

The militarisation of sea rescues[7] has also significantly changed the iconography of arrivals in the media, placing stress on security and border control which we discuss later.

The shipwreck topic – as we will see, referring to the arrival issue 'as a disaster' – recurs within the most significant moments of the media's history of Italian immigration by boat (table 8.1).

A TWO-SIDED NARRATIVE: NEWS REPORT
OR DISASTER

In public discourse, the problem then becomes one of management of these international crises: determining who will be saved and assisted, how it will be done and who will pay the costs and under what system of rules. In this representation and as shown in chapter 7 by Burroughs and chapter 9 by Dickson, then, the actors and emphasis change while the images, stereotypes and responsibility of the media and political coverage remain as have been established in previous decades. The 'landing-as-problem' often becomes a 'migration-as-problem' epiphenomenon: the causes and consequences appear similar, as the popular reaction is similar to the set of procedures for medial narration (Horsti 2003, 2007; Ter Wal 2002). The public figure of the economic migrant becomes very similar to that of refugee: this story cannot be left out of current analysis.

The narrative of the landings, as with the representation of immigration-as-theme and other social phenomenon, is built around a dual system: the

Table 8.1. A Chronology of Major Events Related to Landings in Italy

Date	Year	Event	Description
February–March	1991	Crisis in Albania	Thousands of landings in few weeks
8 August	1991	Bari – landing of the ship *Vlora*, from Albania	Approximately 20,000 people landed (up to now the largest number in a single ship); was the most significant of the landings in this period also for its symbolic and iconic impact.
8 September	1994	New Landings in Puglia	400 Albanians
25 December	1996	'Christmas Eve Massacre'	283 dead (Pakistanis, Indians and Sri Lankans) between Sicily and Malta after a collision between a Lebanese cargo ship and a motorboat
28 March	1997	The 'Good Friday Massacre'	81 dead in the sinking of the patrol boat *Kater i Rades* after a collision with the *Sibyl*, an Italian Navy corvette, in the Strait of Otranto between Italy and Albania
27 May	1999	Collision between a migrant boat and Italian Police boat	Off the coast of Otranto, Puglia, collision between rubber a dinghy operated by smugglers and police boat of the Italian *Guardia di Finanza*. Five dead, including two children
15 September	2002	Agrigento, Sicily: boat sinking	37 bodies recovered, 92 survivors
29 July	2006	Lampedusa, Sicily: boat found after 20 days adrift	Survivors reported that 13 had died during the crossing, and that they had dumped the bodies into the sea
19 August	2006	Lampedusa, Sicily: a boat is accidently rammed during rescue by the Italian Navy ship *Minerva*	10 bodies recovered; 40 remained missing, including 10 children
23 August	2007	Lampedusa, Sicily: boat sinking	A man overboard was rescued by the fishing boat *Ofelia* (from Mazzara del Vallo, Sicily). Boat sank, 45 drowned, 1 survivor
29 March	2009	Tripoli: a fishing boat overloaded with migrants sinks off the coast of Said Biilal Janzur after three hours at sea	20 bodies recovered, 210 lost at sea. At the same hour another ship with 350 passengers was saved by the Italian tugboat *Asso*

(Continued)

Table 8.1.   (Continued)

Date	Year	Event	Description
7 September	2012	Shipwreck off the coast of Lampedusa	One body recovered, 79 lost at sea
6 April	2011	Boat capsizes during rescue due to rough seas	213 people lost at sea, including many women and children
13 April	2011	Libya: Two boats headed for Lampedusa from Eritrea assumed lost at sea	335 passangers on one boat, 160 on the other
3 October	2013	Barge sinks off the coast of Lampedusa	Approximately 360 people drown
11 October	2013	Sinking of a boat headed for Lampedusa	50 people lost
13 October	2013	'Operation *Mare Nostrum*'	Operation *Mare Nostrum* launched: Italian Navy and Air Force begin large-scale patrol and rescue operations in the Sicilian Channel
18 April	2015	Shipwreck in the Sicilian Channel	58 confirmed dead and 700–800 lost in a shipwreck off the Libyan coast

Source: authors own research.

facts come to public attention according to the degree of *intensity* and *time*. At least through these two dimensions it is possible to observe and record the ways in which they fit into the medial circuit and bring collective interests to the surface. For a broader discussion of methodologies in studying and representing migration by boat, see chapter 2 by Mountz and chapter 3 by Williams in this volume.

Two possible extremes arise from this cataloguing: the view of the media can be traced in each of the two sides of a *continuum* of events, above all, the rhythm and structure of *media languages*. In fact, there are two wavelengths by which the complexity of reality and its effervescence dread unfold in the *media coverage*: *buzz* and *emergency*.

The former is the *background noise* of small everyday risks; the pointed fear of the news story; crime's daily aggression to the (social) body; the constant siege of immigration represented by the chronicling of single, small landings on Italian coast: the illustration of an (of course illegal) phenomenon of daily viral infiltration; and *finally* the attack of invisible pollution. The environment as house, neighbourhood, city and nation: these are the imaginary territories under attack in the daily representation of naturally anxiety-provoking information.

The crisis, the *emergency*, represents the climax, the exceptionally unbridled and extreme event symbolic of this (otherwise) unnoticed, almost subliminal attack. It is the moment that danger materialises in an opportune or disproportionate manner, but also the moment in which subterranean fear condenses: accumulated tension requiring an action, a defence, a reply. The 'tragedy in the sea' is the amplified expression of something that already happens in a more ordinary way. Because of the seriousness of the facts, there is a moment of greater intensity and spectacle in the media over a shorter period of time (Couldry, Hepp and Krotz 2009; Pantti, Wahl-Jorgensen and Cottle 2012). This is especially the case of migration by boat, where the difference now lies only in the number of people involved or the victims of the act, both corresponding to the event's ability to gain simultaneous and collective attention from the news media.

The way of telling this story is quite comparable. Both elements share a set of established formats and consolidated scripts, now extending from the everyday landings (the buzz) to the more serious or tragic emergency (crisis). The only differences are in intensity, the quantity of news and topics and their duration and depth; the tone, conventionality or quality of the narrative remains the same (Riegert and Olsson 2007; Tuchman 1978). In the following section we will illustrate, through examples and data, these two narratives, defining the consequences in agenda-building process and the way in which the migration issue is shaped and framed. The first side permits the observation of how a story's form is built slowly and cyclically via the network of news sources and paths. The second allows us to identify how the news event becomes a problem to explain, resolve and be remembered.

MIGRANT BOAT ARRIVALS AS A NEWS REPORT

In the first case, the daily accounting of the same type of occurrences over time builds a language: a set of terms and *phrases* and a repertoire of images and narrative traditions recognisable and ready to use and understand. At the same time, it modifies the chain of information, making clear the importance of sources to the content and the very existence of news. The 'sensory network' (Giacomarra 1997, 95) that allows the timely conveyance of news to editors reaches the landing places in the south of the country and builds a long-standing system of relationships and professionalism (Cohen and Young 1973; Ericson, Baranek and Chan 1987; Fishman 1980, 1981; Gans 1979).

If one of the main criteria of newsworthiness derives from the information sources' territorial distribution, then new arrivals and landings become easily newsworthy (Binotto 2004). They come from a series of recurring and exclusive institutional sources: the Italian agencies involved in border control for specific incidents and the Italian Ministry of the Interior, EU and international organisations for more general information. The news media organisations, which build a web of conventional sources of, for example, agreements with local broadcasters over time, have been a source of exceptional events of undoubtedly spectacular dimension and, in the case of accidents, of unquestionable newsworthiness. This network of sources and channels provides a constant flow of elements and images enhancing the regular opportunity to make a small arrival into publishable news. The information industry, then, constructs territory, along with the relief and unquestionable reliability provided by official sources of information, causing emphasis to be placed on some news items over others. All of these mechanisms constitute the same bias, which are characteristic of production and reproduction of stereotypes and referred to as the *selective perception*: the cognitive process by which individuals perceive the messages and experiences coherent with their viewpoints (Allport 1979; McCombs and Shaw 1972).

The presentation of the news also reflects its kind. Disembarkation becomes everyday news. Every landing is described as 'yet another landing'. Often the descriptions of these events include the theme of recurrence: each landing is 'a new landing', a landing that 'continues' a precedent. The use of numbers that show with precision and insistence the amount of people arriving at various ports also recurs. Some examples:

> 'The landing of migrants continues inexorably' (*TgCom24*, 5 November 2016); 'Landings begin again | another 90 refugees in Puglia' (*La Repubblica*, 12 April 1997); 'Every other day a new landing, Three thousand intercepted as of January' (*Corriere della Sera*, 11 March 2002); '150 Migrants land in Latina, foiling border controls' (*L'Unità*, 5 October 2010, front page); 'Still more landings and fear' (*Avvenire*, 18 June 2008, front page); 'Night landing of hundreds of clandestines [illegal immigrants]'[8] (*Corriere della Sera*, 25 August 1997); 'Illegal immigration: A boat carrying 230 clandestines [illegal immigrants] was rescued by the Italian Coast Guard and the Navy' (*Tg3*, 25 April 2008); 'Still more landings and victims among migrants' (*Tg1*, 20 August 2016)

Prevailing alongside this is the typical *news-media logic* of reference to some quantification, the use of numbers (in this case of landed persons) as an element of reification (Bruno 2016, 20), giving veracity and a supposed dose of neutrality to the story.

A quick review of article titles – as found in our research data – dramatically confirms the sense of a representation that persists unscathed over the inexorable passage of time. It is difficult to distinguish between the titles that have appeared over the past three decades: we witness the 'Tragedy in the Sicilian channel: bodies being counted. Bodies of 14 illegal immigrants recovered as the search continues' and the 'Thousands of people on the coast ready to flee in case of conflict' to alarm 'Italian coasts taken by assault' and to concern 'The Interior Ministry fears an invasion of illegal immigrants'. The first title dates back to 18 July 2007, the second and the third to the crisis in Albania in 1997 and the last to the Libyan crisis in 2011.[9] The titles are interchangeable not only because they refer to similar events, but because they use a similar manner of explanation, warn of the urgency of impending danger and offer solutions. Also recurrent are allegories of constant emergency, an 'exodus' and a perpetually announced tragedy.

MIGRANT BOAT ARRIVALS AS DISASTER

Stanley Cohen (1980), in his seminal book on the relationship between social change, deviance and media, places moments of moral panic in direct correlation with natural disasters. Public reaction to catastrophic situations, or situations presented as such,[10] is particularly useful for understanding social behaviour: 'Disaster researchers have constructed one of the few models in sociology for considering the reaction of the social system to something stressful, disturbing or threatening' (ibid., 15). In fact, Cohen's analysis of the attention paid to British subcultures in the early 1970s derives from the phases and categories developed in disaster studies. The medial and social reaction to juvenile delinquency followed the same attention curve and characteristics as reactions to 'events as earthquakes or floods' (ibid., 15). While this similarity could be allusive and indirect, it appears to be particularly suitable for the analysis of the reaction to migrations by boat (McRobbie and Thornton 1995; Ungar 2001).

The involvement of numerous people at the same time, the presence of numerous victims and emergency relief structures, the need for an extended period to recover equilibrium or achieve stable adaptation to the changes brought by the disaster join the moment of special attention to landings to that of natural disasters. Also similar is the presence of a moment of 'Threat Warning' during which institutions and the media warn people of impending tragedy. Articles providing the size and numbers of the incoming landings are also recurrent:

> A boarding occurred within the last twenty-four hours. While it is true that the arrivals, with boats cradled by the sea and protected by our rescue ships as they approached the 'Lampedusa Mirage', took place in a 'controlled regime', it makes an impression to read the number of landings occurred between Thursday and Friday: *twothousandthreehundredthirtythree* [*duemilatrecentotrentatré*].[11]

In the warning phases, as in the time of the disaster itself, media behaviour has many commonalities with the widespread public alarm accompanying hurricanes, volcanic eruptions, earthquakes or epidemics (see chapter 7 by Burroughs). We observe the perception and description of danger, preparation, countermeasures and crisis management (Critcher 2003). In some cases, a single landing becomes a media event that draws extraordinary attention due to its importance or character. As with a news wave or media hype, in these cases the media coverage behaves differently than normal. The criteria of newsworthiness are changed, offering the topic of arrivals and immigration in general 'exceptional' or 'explosive' levels of attention (Boydstun, Hardy and Walgrave 2014; Vasterman 2005). Some of these disasters at sea have taken on the character of key events. In fact, these focused 'the attention of readers, listeners and viewers on a certain topic', thereby building a news wave on the subject (Kepplinger and Habermeier 1995, 374). They also constitute the trigger event for media and collective representation of the problem; they become pivotal moments in describing the situation and tell the story while causing a visible change in their management at the level of policy. The October 2013 sinking of a barge off the island of Lampedusa was one of the most significant examples of these key events: public attention around the tragedy led to Operation *Mare Nostrum*.

It is interesting to note that the changes in visibility of these key events over time are not only in relation to the number of people involved or the number of victims of the tragedy. As we know, the number of people affected is just one of significant dimensions that define the newsworthiness of a story (Gans 1979; Tuchman 1978). All these elements are present in the recent history of migrant boat arrivals in Italy.

We can identify some examples of this dynamic by analysing the public attention given to some of these events. The tragedy of 3 October 2013, which occurred off the coast of Lampedusa, for example, shows how the symbolic dimension, especially grief, intersects directly with the political and institutional action. The wreck and the scale of the tragedy were immediately very clear. Unlike other shipwrecks, it gained a very strong symbolic importance and not just for purely quantitative reasons. For example, a shipwreck in April 2015 that killed between 700 and 900 people – though only about 60 were confirmed dead – received less media attention (Bruno 2014a). The central symbolic role of this event in the Italian public discourse of migration is evidenced by the institutionalising of a yearly 'National Day of the victims of immigration'.[12]

The news coverage of the sinking was extensive and characterised by a strong element of drama from a lexical and iconographic point of view; the dimension of the human drama was evidenced on the front pages the day following the tragedy. The terms most used in the titles were 'slaughter' and 'shame'. At the same time, it relies on strictly political debate (also in terms of reference 'voices') as its main and sometimes only form of theming.[13]

It must be said that this focus on the dimension of tragedy places migrants in an absolutely passive position (Carta di Roma 2014). These accounts necessarily carry the 'human' dimension and empathic participation; however, although death is present, it appears detached from the materiality of migrant bodies, as a process of 'symbolic rarefaction' (Nicolosi 2017), especially when compared with the perception of strong *embodiment* that appears in the representation of the rescuers and the people of Lampedusa.[14]

The first phase, in which the narrative of the event has immediately gained a highly symbolic dimension through the frame of mourning and tragedy, clearly triggered a priming effect with respect to the debate on the issue, conditioning consequences both inside but especially outside the perimeter of the media. In particular, the first reactions of the political actors, statements and visitors to the island, including then Prime Minister Letta, the President of the European Commission Barroso, and ministers, who insisted on a keyword like 'shame',[15] are part of this *symbolic phase*.

This visibility of this political and institutional component maintained high attention on Lampedusa for the entire month of October (on the front page 181 times in 252 editions in the period analysed, on nine daily newspapers: Belluati 2014, 66–67); moreover, this visibility triggered and fuelled a later *regulative phase* through which the Italian law on migration and the entrance of migrants was changed. The Parliament abolished the so-called crime of illegal immigration and launched maritime interdiction operation *Mare Nostrum*. A broader discussion of maritime interdiction operations occurs in chapter 2 by Mountz.

In a further example, just before dawn on 6 April 2011, a boat crowded with people disembarked from Libya and began to take on water, capsizing shortly later. Only 51 people were recovered alive by rescue ships and over 250 remained missing. 'Massacre at Sea' of April 2011 showed, indeed, other dynamics in the representation of landings. As we have seen, the presence of a catastrophic event is characterised by massive attention of the news media, a prominent coverage characterised by a certain homogeneity in the behaviour of news organisations not usually known for a similar editorial line and to focus on the theme immigration. A disaster is news that you 'cannot not cover'.

The day after the tragedy, the front pages of all major Italian newspapers showed the event among the main news with similar titles and initial comments. Even the iconographic choices were similar: the same photograph appears on many front pages – a symbolic image of suffering and survival, accompanied by the presence of a rescuer, emblematic of the topic of sentiment as studied by Luc Boltanski (1999; Chouliaraki 2013).

The language used in the media is typical of reporting of natural disasters: carnage (*Corriere della Sera*), apocalypse (*La Repubblica*), humanitarian shipwreck (*Liberazione*), Final Solution (*Il Fatto quotidiano*), Mediterranean Inferno (*L'Unità*) and Massacre at Sea (*QN*). This type of lexicon consolidates the decades-old image of migration as an inevitable cataclysm however tragic, and epochal however inexplicable.[16]

Immigration disasters clearly show one of the more peculiar thematic characteristics in media representation of disasters and calamities: the search for those responsible. The ritual, as in times of moral panic, consists precisely of identifying the culprits and figuring out who is to blame (Cottle 2006; Liebes and Curran 1998). In the definition of *news frame*, from the work of William Gamson, and the public problem, in the seminal work of Gusfield, two crucial dimensions refer to the causes attributed to a phenomenon: the first concerns causes and, therefore, origins; the second refers to responsibility and, therefore, blame.

> *The first usage looks to a causal* [emphasis mine] explanation of events. The *second looks* to the person or office charged with controlling a situation or solving a problem. The *first* answers the question, How come? The second answers the question, What is to be done? The first – strict liability – is a matter of beliefs or cognition, an assertion about the sequence of events that is in fact the existence of the problem. The second – political responsibility – is a matter of policy. (Gusfield 1981, 13)

The policy response to these narratives forms around these two questions. The dominant frames of the *migration by boat* narrative simultaneously define how the phenomenon is explained – *why do they come?* – and the preferred solution – *what do we do; how do we stop them?* The former is substantially obscured precisely by the metaphor of the migratory catastrophe – an 'exodus' or a 'tsunami' is not caused by human activity – and each time political responsibility remains to be defined: *who is or is not managing their (apparently) uncontrolled influx?* It was precisely in the weeks of the tragedy that the political debate centred around the origins and the way to put a stop to the most recent 'wave of migration'. The *lead* comment by Franco Cangini published on the front page of the major Italian newspaper *Quotidiano nazionale*, titled 'The atrocious impunity', was emblematic: 'It is open season on those responsible for the terrible shipwreck in the Sicilian Channel, but let's be careful not to target incorrectly. The criminals profiting from human trafficking are responsible'.[17]

For once, however, the news organisations closer to the centre-right, then in the national government, could not attribute what had happened to the laxity of the majority party in office; therefore the 'usual suspects' – smugglers, criminals, folk devils – became both the 'new slave traders' – the southern Mediterranean countries unable to hinder the departure of the vessels – and the governments of other NATO's European countries for having waged war against Muammar Gaddafi's regime. In its usual direct and vernacular style, the newspaper *Libero* explicitly blames those responsible for these 'barbarian invasions': it is the Tunisian government which 'drowns the illegals' by 'doing nothing to stop human trafficking'.

A treaty with Tunisia for the management of migration flows was in fact under discussion in those weeks, while there was a dispute with France over Tunisians crossing into its territory via Italy after having received Italian temporary residency permits.

The response of the newspapers 'close to the opposition' was simpler, as they could easily attribute to the ineffectiveness of the treaty with Tunisia to the Berlusconi government. Political responsibility is identified with politicians (of the government). According to an established script of journalistic rhetoric, these would naturally be inept, inadequate, unable to foresee, manage or plan ahead making 'Italy a boat adrift without rudder'.[18] As summarised by the first-page editorial of the conservative daily *Il Tempo*, in the face of the complexity of the international situation and the importance of the issues, the list of which can be easily formulated, the national government and its policy class always seem unprepared: 'This list is sufficient to understand that we are facing a cataclysm, and the political class – and not only that, unfortunately – is largely devoid of the cultural tools to understand and deal with it'.[19]

THE POLITICS OF NARRATION: THE 'GAME' OF THE RESPONSIBLE AND THE SYMBOLIC CONSTRUCTION OF THE BORDER

If the field of policy response can be characterised as discussed before, with debate structured around the differing attitudes of newspapers alternatively supporting government or opposition forces; in this case the corresponding references to causes and external enemies are transverse and uniform. Meanwhile, the figure of the 'smuggler' persists and takes on the character of folk devil: a ruthless and often faceless criminal. Framed as the true culprit of all that happens, this devious image easily brings together the language of disaster with the rhetorical crime-news stereotypes of *law and order* in representing the 'already landed' immigrants (Hall et al. 1978; Maneri 2011; Maneri and Ter Wal 2005; Palidda 2011). In these solutions, we see the mix of militaristic language of the emergency landings frame with the identification of a public enemy to fight, as is evident in the words of the then Minister of the Interior, reported by the main national news:

> Traffickers continue to work undisturbed on the other side of the Mediterranean. To really fight them, international agreements are needed, reminds minister Alfano: '[We must] respond with a declaration of war on human traffickers. We have long called on the international multilateral bodies to ensure that, within the bounds of international law, an offensive against this gruesome travel agency is unleashed'.[20]

In this way the double articulation of the typical boundaries of immigration media representation are joined (Binotto 2015; Binotto, Bruno and Lai 2016). The *external* boundary, represented by the arrival by boat, identifies the 'human trafficker' as responsible, while the *inner* boundary identifies him as a criminal to identify and subdue. In these terms, the narrative of the disaster can become that of a moral panic, with the urgent need to 'do something' and a villain to oppose. To this *molecular* enemy – in the end, the usual erratic response from the black market to a mass need – the *moral* enemy is easily associated: distant or neighbouring countries, the south or the European Union who, through their denial of aid or assistance, 'leave Italy alone' in the face of danger.

On the one hand, we have a crime story discourse: the fight against crime and 'combating trafficking', on the other, the timeless rhetorical appeal of the 'wounded nation' and of the muscular or military confrontation between states. In both cases we see a Manichaean confrontation between good and evil, on one side virtue, humanity, scrupulousness, and on the other crime or selfishness: that language that unites nations and builds walls through the liquid boundary of the media.

CONCLUSION

This chapter has explored almost thirty years of media discourses on migration flows in the Italian news media. Since its beginning in the early 1990s, representations of rescues and the landing of migrants by boat have become a metaphor to describe migration more broadly in Italy and Europe. This chapter has shown how the Italian news media have built up and re-used a certain set of representations of boundaries and space over a significant period of time (1989–2016), which focus on migration by boat. Over time, the symbolic weight of sea landings remained significant and unchanged, and, most importantly, these representations continued to have some distance from reality. Through the analysis of news media coverage and the discourse analysis of some case studies, we identified the two-side narrative of the landings. Indeed, this representation is built around a dual system: (1) what we call the *buzz*, the background noise that daily landings feed; and (2) the plain attention to a tragic emergency (*crisis*).

If every narrative has a set of consolidated scripts and formats, then we find different common figures and frames in this representation. The militarisation of the sea policy coincides with the military language of the *emergency* news frame, as well as the *attack/invasion* one. This language in the small news reports corresponds to that related to crime news and *law and order* rhetoric so characteristic of the media representation of migration in Italy and other countries. The emotions created by this language – fear, anxiety, alarm – correspond to the one related to the search for 'someone to blame' and for an immediate resolution. The solution is easily identified among those typical frames, those same enemies, internal or external. If, in fact, media discourse builds 'in the sea' the symbolic boundary between who is in a territory and who would want to enter, then these frames also build the separation between those who want to curb this emergency and who causes it, ultimately determining who becomes friend or foe.

NOTES

1. The way of representing and subdividing the near from the distant, between us and the foreigners, refers to 'metaphorical' spaces constructed within precise anthropological dimensions (Binotto 2006).

2. Some of this research is conducted in partnership with the University Network for 'Carta di Roma' Observatory (see note 4) (Binotto and Martino 2004; Binotto, Bruno and Lai 2016).

3. The term (in Italian) *clandestino* is frequently used by the Italian media; hence it is a focus of attention and much criticism from civil society and experts.

4. The 'Carta di Roma' is the journalist's code of conduct on Immigration, signed by the National Council of Journalists and the National Federation of the Italian Press in June 2008. Since 2011, the Association 'Carta di Roma' has published periodical reports on the representation of immigration in Italian media. https://www.cartadi-roma.org/who-we-are/.

5. Data from ISMU (Iniziative e Studi sulla Multietnicità; Initiatives and Studies on Multi-ethnicity), elaborated by the Italian Ministry of Interior and UNHCR. Moreover, 2016 is a tragic year of record deaths in the Mediterranean Sea: according to UNHCR, 5,011 people have died trying to reach European shores in 2016, which is 1,300 more than 2015, in which 3,771 perished (http://data.unhcr.org/mediterranean/regional.php).

6. On this topic, see also chapter 5 in this volume, in particular for the Central Mediterranean as a 'uniform migratory space'.

7. On this topic, see also chapter 4 in this volume. For a summary and analysis of this military approach to the 'humanitarian' field, see Musarò (2017).

8. On the term 'clandestino', see note 2.

9. Reported, respectively, by *La Stampa* (Colombo 2007, 351), *Il Messsaggero* and *L'Unità* (Devole 1998) and the *Corriere della Sera* (Fiorenza Sarzanini, 20 February 2011, 3).

10. In fact, he added, 'many workers in the field claim that research should not be restricted to actual disasters – a potential disaster may be just as disruptive as the actual event. Studies of reactions to hoaxes and false alarms show disaster behavior in the absence of objective danger' (16).

11. Guido Ruotolo, *La Stampa*, 23 March 2014. The author writes in the article the number in full, with the obvious purpose of accentuating its meaning.

12. The day was instituted with Law Number 45/2016, approved in Parliament on 20 March 2016.

13. The empirical basis used here for this specific event is the collection, processing and analysis via mixed methods (content analysis, lexical analysis, frame and discourse analysis) by the authors (on television and talk show content), in partnership with the University Network for 'Carta di Roma' Observatory (and particularly with Marinella Belluati at the University of Turin). Extended reports on this research are also available in Carta di Roma (2014).

14. On this topic, see interviews conducted by Nicolosi (2017).

15. The retreat to this term and its semantic field can undoubtedly be associated with the fact that Pope Francis had dealt precisely with this concept during his visit to Lampedusa last summer, showing once again the strong centrality of this religious figure on the horizon of almost all Italian media, even those of a more 'secular' appearance (2017).

16. One of the reasons within the behavior of mass media can be easily identified: the focus on domestic policy and lack of attention paid to international crises such as inequalities in development or the politics of international aid. These potentially obscure the causes of most migratory phenomenon from public perception.

17. See Franco Cangini, 'L'atroce impunità', *Quotidiano nazionale*, 11 April 2011, p. 1.

18. From the front-page editorial by Antonio Padellaro in the opposition newspaper, *Il Fatto quotidiano* (7 April 2011).

19. Mario Sechi, 'Disordine nostro. Esodo altrui', *Il Tempo*, 7 April 2011, p. 1.

20. Giulia Palmieri, 'Migranti, continuano gli sbarchi', *Tg1*, aired 3 September, 2015. http://www.rai.it/dl/RaiTV/programmi/media/ContentItem-32eba8d2-a8c4-45da-a8a9-b9adc6b03148-tg1.html

BIBLIOGRAPHY

Allport, Gordon Willard, *The Nature of Prejudice* (New York: Basic Books, 1979).

Ambrosini, Maurizio, *Richiesti e respinti. L'immigrazione in Italia. Come e perché* (Milan: Il Saggiatore, 2010).

Belluati. Marinella. 'Lampedusa, 3 ottobre 2013. Cronaca di una tragedia', in *Carta di Roma: Notizie alla deriva. Secondo rapporto annuale Associazione Carta di Roma* (Rome: Ponte Sisto, 2014).

Binotto, Marco. 'Le fonti', in *FuoriLuogo. L'immigrazione e i media italiani*, edited by Binotto, Marco, and Martino, Valetina (Cosenza: Pellgrini/Rai-ERI, 2004).

Binotto, Marco, Marco, Bruno, and Lai, Valeria (ed.), *Tracciare confini. L'immigrazione nei media italiani* (Milan: Franco Angeli, 2016).

———, 'Invaders, Aliens and Criminals: Metaphors and Spaces in the Media Definition of Migration and Security Policies', in *Destination Italy Representing Migration in Contemporary Media and Narrative*, edited by Peter Lang (Edinburgh: University of St. Andrews Press, 2015).

Boltanski, Luc, *Distant Suffering: Morality, Media and Politics* (Cambridge: Cambridge University Press, 1999).

Boydstun, Amber, Hardy, Anne, and Walgrave, Stefaan, 'Two Faces of Media Attention: Media Storm versus Non-Storm Coverage', *Political Communication* 31, no. 4 (2014): 509.

Bruno, Marco, *Cornici di realtà. Il frame nell'analisi dell'informazione* (Milan: Guerini e Associati, 2014b).

———, 'Frame e discorsi televisivi nel racconto del dolore. Il naufragio di Lampedusa nei talk italiani', in *Carta di Roma: Notizie alla deriva. Secondo rapporto annuale Associazione Carta di Roma* (Rome: Ponte Sisto, 2014a).

———, ' "Framing Lampedusa". The Landing Issue in Italian Media Coverage of Migrations, between Alarmism and Pietism', in *Public and Political Discourses of Migration: International Perspectives*, edited by Haynes, Amanda, Power, Martin, Devereux, Eoin, Dillane, Aileen, and Carr, James (London: Rowman and Littlefield, 2016).

———, 'L'ennesimo sbarco di clandestini', in *Fuoriluogo. L'immigrazione e i media italiani*, edited by Binotto, Marco, and Martino, Valentina (Cosenza: Pellegrini-Rai ERI, 2004).

Carta di Roma, *Carta di Roma: Notizie alla deriva. Secondo rapporto annuale Associazione Carta di Roma* (Rome: Ponte Sisto, 2014).

Chouliaraki, Lilie, *The Ironic Spectator: Solidarity in the Age of Post-Humanitarianism* (London: John Wiley & Sons, 2013).

Cohen, Stanley, *Folk Devils and Moral Panics: The Creation of the Mods and Rockers* (Oxford: M. Robertson, 1980).

Cohen, Stanley, and Young, Jack, *The Manufacture of News; Social Problems, Deviance and the Mass Media* (London: Constable, 1973).

Cottle, Simon. 'Mediatized Rituals: Beyond Manufacturing Consent', *Media, Culture & Society* 28, no. 3 (2006): 411.

Couldry, Nick, Hepp, Andreas, and Krotz, Friedrich, *Media Events in a Global Age* (London: Routledge, 2009).

Critcher, Chas, *Moral Panics and the Media* (Buckingham: Open University Press, 2003).

Devole, Rando, *Albania. Fenomeni sociali e rappresentazioni* (Rome: Agrilavoro, 1998).

Ericson, Richard, Baranek, Patricia, and Chan, Janet, *Visualizing Deviance: A Study of News Organization* (Toronto: University of Toronto Press, 1987).

Fishman, Mark, *Manufacturing the News* (Austin: University of Texas Press, 1980).

————, 'Crime Waves as Ideology', in *The Manufacture of News: Social Problems, Deviance and the Mass Media*, edited by Cohen, Stanley, and Young, Jack (London: Constable – Sage, 1981).

Gans, Herbert, *Deciding What's News: A Study of CBS Evening News, NBC Nightly News, Newsweek, and Time* (Chicago: Northwestern University Press, 1979).

Giacomarra, Mario, *Manipolare per comunicare: lingua, mass media e costruzione di realtà* (Rome: Palumbo, 1997).

Gibson, James, *The Ecological Approach to Visual Perception: Classic Edition* (Hove: Psychology Press, 1978).

Hall, Stuart, Critcher, Chas, Jefferson, Tony, Clarke, John, and Roberts, Brian, *Policing the Crisis: Mugging, the State, and Law and Order* (London: Macmillan, 1978).

Hannerz, Ulf, *Cultural Complexity: Studies in the Social Organization of Meaning* (New York: Columbia University Press, 1992).

Horsti, Karina, 'Global Mobility and the Media: Presenting Asylum Seekers as a Threat', *Nordicom Review: Nordic Research on Media and Communication* 24, no. 1 (2003): 41.

————, 'Asylum Seekers in the News: Frames of Illegality and Control', *Observatorio (OBS) Journal* 1 (2007): 14,561.

Kepplinger, Hans, and Habermeier, Johanna, 'The Impact of Key Events on the Presentation of Reality', *European Journal of Communication* 10, no. 3 (1995): 371.

Liebes, Tamar, and Curran, James (ed.), *Media, Ritual and Identity: Communication and Society*. (London: Routledge, 1997).

Maneri, Marcello, 'Media Discourse on Immigration. The Translation of Control Practices into the Language We Live By', in *Racial Criminalization of Migrants in the 21st Century*, edited by Palidda, Salvatore (Farnham: Ashgate, 2011).

Maneri, Marcello, and Ter Wal, Jessika, 'The Criminalisation of Ethnic Groups: An Issue for Media Analysis', *Forum Qualitative Sozialforschung/Forum: Qualitative Social Research* 6, no. 3 (2005).

Marletti, Carlo (ed.), *Extracomunitari. Dall'immaginario collettivo al vissuto quotidiano del razzismo* (Torino: Eri Rai-Vqpt, 1991).

Mazzara, Bruno, 'Stampa e migrazione: due casi a confronto', in *Relazioni etniche stereotipi e pregiudizi*, edited by Delle Donne, Marcella (Roma: Edup., 1998).

McCombs, Maxwell, *Setting the Agenda: The Mass Media and Public Opinion* (John Wiley & Sons, 2013).

McCombs, Maxwell, and Shaw, Donald L., 'The Agenda-Setting Function of Mass Media', *The Public Opinion Quarterly* 36, no. 2 (1972): 176.

McRobbie, Angela, and Thornton, Sarah, 'Rethinking "Moral Panic" for Multi-mediated Social Worlds', *British Journal of Sociology* (December 1995): 559.

Musarò, Pierluigi, 'Mare Nostrum: The Visual Politics of a Military-Humanitarian Operation in the Mediterranean Sea', *Media, Culture & Society* 39, no. 1 (2017): 11.

Nicolosi, Guido, 'Lampedusa, 3 October 2013: Anatomy of a Social Representation', *International Journal of Cultural Studies* (first published online: 16 February 2017).

Palidda, Salvatore, *Racial Criminalization of Migrants in the 21st Century* (Farnham: Ashgate, 2011).

Pantti, Mervi, Wahl-Jorgensen, Karin, and Cottle, Simon, *Disasters and the Media* (London: Peter Lang, 2012).

Riegert, Kristina, and Olsson, Eva-Karin, 'The Importance of Ritual in Crisis Journalism', *Journalism Practice* 1, no. 2 (2007): 143.

Sciortino, Giuseppe, and Colombo, Asher, 'The Flows and the Flood: The Public Discourse on Immigration in Italy, 1969–2001', *Journal of Modern Italian Studies* 9, no. 1 (2004): 94.

Ter Wal, Jessika (ed.), *Racism and Cultural Diversity in the Mass Media. An Overview of Research and Examples of Good Practice in the EU Member State, 1995–2000* (Vienna: European Monitoring Centre on Racism and Xenophobia (EUMC), 2002).

Tuchman, Gaye, *Making News: A Study in the Construction of Reality* (New York: Free Press, 1978).

Ungar, Sheldon, 'Moral Panic versus the Risk Society: The Implications of the Changing Sites of Social Anxiety', *The British Journal of Sociology* 52, no. 2 (2001): 271.

van Dijk, Teun, *Racism and the Press: Critical Studies in Racism and Migration* (London: Routledge, 1991).

Vasterman, Peter, 'Media-Hype: Self-Reinforcing News Waves, Journalistic Standards and the Construction of Social Problems', *European Journal of Communication* 20, no. 4 (2005): 508.

Vehbiu, Ardian, and Devole, Rando, *La scoperta dell'Albania: gli albanesi secondo i mass media* (Milan: Edizioni Paoline, 1996).

Welch, Michael, and Schuster, Liza, 'Detention of Asylum Seekers in the UK and USA Deciphering Noisy and Quiet Constructions', *Punishment & Society* 7, no. 4 (2005): 397.

Chapter 9

Silencing Migration by Sea: Unveiling Technologies of Exclusion in Australian Maritime Borders

Andonea Dickson

INTRODUCTION

Through recent changes in migration flows, maritime geographies are increasingly central to states' bordering agendas and, as such, receive unprecedented attention in public discourse and policymaking. In contrast to this public attention, the regulation of migration in maritime geographies transpires at an innate distance from population centres and hence from the public gaze, allowing border operations to transpire with a distinct lack of public scrutiny. This distance, I argue, is amplified by strategies of mobility control that conceal the specificities of regulation at sea, from their spaces of operation to the strategies of interdiction and deterrence. Australia's former Immigration Minister Scott Morrison explicitly demonstrated this when he denied any transparency into Australia's border agenda Operation Sovereign Borders (OSB) and the number of boats it has intercepted and turned around at sea, declaring its 'secrecy' as integral to its success (Murphy 2013). This chapter explores how silence is employed in practice and in policy in mobility control in Australia and the ways it actively contributes to the discourse on maritime migration, especially since the institutionalisation of Australia's militarised border regime, OSB, in late 2013.

The chapter will begin by briefly espousing how silence will function as a field of study in this chapter, before analysing three specific themes in the manifestation of silence in mobility regulation at sea. First, the chapter will explore the function of 'Silence in Practice', examining the month-long detention of Tamil asylum seekers at sea by Australian border agents in June 2014. Second, 'Silence in Policy' will be examined through the analysis of Australia's Border Force Act 2015, which explicitly demands a silence surrounding bordering practices. Third, the chapter will analyse 'Silence through the

Body', exploring the ways in which the quantification of deaths in maritime borderscapes by the media and by politicians functions to both annul the gravity of the lives lost at sea and conceal the operations and technologies operating to secure these spaces. These sections will function together to reveal the multitudinous and complimentary ways silence permeates public discourse on maritime migration. The nature of silence, its impact on rights and its relationship to the militarisation of spaces are rarely examined in border and migration studies. Due to the limitations of this chapter, the ambition here is not to unpack the problematic of opacity and power at sea, but, rather, generate a prospective model through which the nascent study of silence in border politics can be examined. This chapter's ambition is hence to be an agenda-setting piece, suggesting ways to analyse this concept and the need for further research.

SILENCE AS A STUDY

The study of silence in academia has largely existed within the context of sociolinguistic and societal studies, in which scholars situate language as building community, such as in relation to shared identity, or collective ideology. In this context, scholars frequently frame silence as the 'unstated antithesis' of language, the 'lacuna' between words (Ferguson 2003, 51). Adding criticality to the role of absences in language, feminist studies have exposed the nature of silence in relation to power and agency to illustrate how 'silences are no more free of organization by power than speech is' (Brown 2009, 87) and the need to reassess the language of governing powers (Brown 2009; Brownmiller 2013; Elshtain 1982; MacKinnon 1989; Olsen 2014). Similarly, Michael Foucault (1998) has addressed how silence is co-constitutive of knowledge.

Silence intermittently emerges elsewhere in the study of power in relation to language and politics (Brummett 1980; Dauenhauer 1980; Ferguson 2003; Glenn 2004; Picard 1952; Spivak 1988). Correlatively, secrecy has been regarded as having a functional role within the state, especially within the rubric of securitisation. Cole et al. argue that national security frameworks, and indeed constitutional democracies at large, rely as much on transparency as on the concealment of information (2013, 1). There has hence been analysis of the role of privacy and secrecy in policy and constitutional law, as well as the legal proliferation of secrecy across agencies after 11 September 2001 (Lippert and Walby, 2016; Pozen 2009; Roach 2013). Yet, as illustrated by Lippert and Walby in their legal analysis of public video surveillance in Canada, privacy has not yet been explored as a method of governing (2016, 336). It is the governing *through* an absence of information that this work seeks to explore as a method of border control, which in relation to the practice of control and exclusion remains a nascent field of research. It is relevant to articulate in the context of this research, distinct to legal analyses, how the terminology of 'silence' and 'secreting' will be used. The term 'secret', or the act of secreting, is a practice of removing from sight. Etymologically, the word comes from the Latin term *secretus*, meaning to separate or set apart. The practice of separating migrants from public knowledge is an enabling mechanism for governments, permitting bordering agencies to develop a monopoly over the epistemology of this landscape. Secreting, in this case, is synonymous with obfuscating and indicates the practice-based aspect of the border, the distancing from sight and from knowledge, whereas silence is the outcome of such separation.

Silence does not denote an absence of discourse but rather a field of knowledge wherein certain aspects of structural violence are not represented. As Dauenhauer writes, 'silence is not the correlative opposite of discourse, but rather establishes and maintains an oscillation or tension among the several levels of discourse' (1980, 82). While reports on operations in the maritime border may emerge in the media, demonstrating a discourse on this space, these reports fail to detail the many aspects of exclusion within this border made inaccessible to them. Silence therefore does not reference the elimination of all discourse on a subject, geography, or practice but rather signifies a regulating power whereby specific functions and spaces of operation of the maritime border are, by design, withheld from the public. This gravely impacts on the nature of debarment experienced by migrants, as many of the practices employed to secure the border against unsanctioned migration are removed from public scrutiny. The silence denoted here is thus one which functions alongside language and particular representations of the maritime border and, in so doing, becomes integrated into the knowledge of this space. As will be demonstrated in the successive sections, silence has an active function: it is productively employed in practice, in policy and in the representation of migrants in order to obfuscate the maritime as a bordering space.

SILENCE IN PRACTICE

Australia's border programme, OSB, relies upon an integrated system dependent upon the efforts of federal agencies including the Australian Border Force, which contains the Maritime Border Command, and the Australian Federal Police. Implemented by the Liberal Government in September 2013, the operation has contributed to a greater militarisation of the Australian maritime border than any prior border agenda. While Australia's border is increasingly structured by an ad hoc approach in which practice often precedes policy, through framing the border agenda as a military operation, these ad hoc tactics of border defence and mobility control are largely concealed from public scrutiny. For example, on 31 January 2014 there was a senate hearing scrutinising the secrecy surrounding OSB and the public interest immunity the Minister for Immigration and Border Control had claimed surrounding the demand for the provision of information and documentation detailing the operation.

OSB was, at the time, under the dual operational command of the Australian Customs and Border Protection Service[1] and the chief of the defence force. Both agencies were present at this inquiry, as was the former Minister for Immigration and Border Security Scott Morrison. In response to the demand for documentation on the operation, Morrison declared secrecy to be central to the success of the programme, stating that the disclosure of any information would put the current and future operation at risk, as well as the safety of those involved in the programme and, ultimately, the safety of the nation (The Senate 2014, 13). Mr. Morrison, in describing the type of operational information concealed from the public, explained a broad range of details, including, but not limited to, 'on water tactics, training procedures, operational instructions, specific incident reports, intelligence, posturing and deployment of assets, timing and occurrence of operations, and the identification of attempted individual voyages, passenger information, including nationalities involved in those voyages' (The Senate 2014, 31).

This discourse of secrecy has only been further compounded by recursive public announcements by past and present immigration ministers and prime ministers defending both the militaristic and secreted approach of OSB. In reference to Australia's maritime border, Scott Morrison declared that 'this is a war against people smuggling and you've got to approach it on that basis' (*7.30 Report* 2013). Similarly, former Prime Minister Tony Abbott stated in early 2014 that the secrecy surrounding the operation was justified, premised on the grounds that they have no desire to make public 'information that is of use to the enemy' (ABC 2014). OSB is commonly referred to as a warlike operation, in which the enemy is situated as 'people smugglers'. This is not distinct to the representation of smugglers as the central 'culprits' of the tragedy in the Mediterranean, as Binotto and Bruno articulate in chapter 8 in this book, and the sense of a 'public enemy' that subsequently legitimises a militarised response.

Through framing the border agenda as requiring a militarised response, the actions and practices of this space are justifiably extracted from public consideration. As Shapiro notes, in international politics, where the technomilitancy of the West reigns as an informing structure, the 'scientific/military standpoint' becomes 'valid knowledge' (1989, 21). Framing the maritime border as requiring a militarised response enables a technocracy that not only expunges certain actions at sea from requiring justification but also legitimises the concealing of information premised upon the discourse of threat management. This landscape is consequently seen to be determined by 'logistical thinking' (Shapiro 1989, 21) and as a result, decisions at sea ascertain a condition of being publicly incontrovertible. As such, the government and its bordering agents ascertain a monopoly over the knowledge production of the maritime border. Thus, while there is constant discourse produced in relation to maritime migration, there is a marked absence surrounding the practices defining this borderspace. Since the implementation of OSB, it has become difficult to estimate the influence of operational silence on the extent of exclusion at sea as the government will not reveal how many boats have recently entered the Australian territory, as this type of information is said to infringe the success of the operation. As Mr. Morrison stated, 'It would not be in our national interest or the public interest to disclose this information that would impede our ability to stop the boats' (Glenday 2014).

While it is difficult to estimate the extent of this silence through the number of boats that are being interdicted and returned, the impact of such silence on the nature of exclusion is clearly evidenced by the case of the detention of 157 Tamil asylum seekers at sea during 2014. On 29 June 2014, a boat carrying 157 Tamil asylum seekers was intercepted 27 kilometres off Christmas Island, inside Australia's contiguous zone. The asylum seekers on board were transferred to an Australian Customs vessel, where they were detained for the period of one month, from 29 June 2014 until 27 July 2014. On 7 July, after over a week detained at sea, an interim injunction issued by the High Court halted the return of the Tamil asylum seekers to the Sri Lankan Navy (Laughland and Dehghan 2014). The group of lawyers acting on behalf of the asylum seekers were only able to ascertain the names of forty-eight of those on board the customs vessel, as authorities had withheld the names of the others. The High Court provided this injunction on the grounds that there stands a 'grave concern' for returning Tamils, a persecuted ethnic minority in Sri Lanka, to the Sri Lankan authorities. Through this injunction it was also exposed that the government of Australia had recently returned forty-one Tamil asylum seekers to Sri Lanka, where they faced criminal charges for departing their country illegally, a national criminal offence in Sri Lanka carrying a penalty of two years of imprisonment.

Throughout the detainment of the Tamil asylum seekers, the government obstinately refused to disclose to the public how many were being detained at sea,[2] where the boat detaining them was located, what the purpose of the detention was, what the conditions were and the health and safety of those on board.[3] On 11 July, after close to two weeks at sea, a Senate Inquiry questioned Lieutenant General Angus Campbell, former Commander of OSB, over the conditions and location of the asylum seekers. Campbell persisted in refusing to disclose any relevant information on the grounds that he had not spoken directly to those in charge on the boat and was hence unaware of specific details. He also claimed that it was inappropriate to comment as the legitimacy of the detention was being disputed in the High Court (Farrell 2014). While on board the customs vessel ACV *Ocean Protector*, the asylum seekers were not given access to an asylum procedure, they had limited access to legal counsel, and it was later exposed that during this extended period they were kept in windowless rooms for twenty-two-hours of each day (Doherty and Farrell 2015). After the injunction prevented the return of the asylum seekers to Sri Lanka, the Australian government attempted to return the asylum seekers to India, as India had been a transit country in their journey. India, however, did not comply. On 27 July, they were removed to Curtin Immigration Detention Centre in Western Australia. During 1–2 August the asylum seekers were removed once again to the Nauru Regional Processing Centre.

In January 2015, one of the asylum seekers subject to this protracted detention at sea took the case to the Australian High Court, where it was ruled, through retroactive changes to the Maritime Powers Act 2013 and the Migration Act 1958,[4] that detention at sea for indefinite periods of time when in transit is considered lawful.[5] During this case one of the seven judges, Justice Patrick Keane, proclaimed that 'Australian courts are bound to apply Australian statute law even if that law should violate a rule of international law'.[6] As such domestic law, informed by ad hoc tactics of border defence and employing tactics of arbitrary detention and attempted *refoulement*, was given priority over international rights. This legislation not only amplified the nature of exclusion at sea through ruling in favour of indefinite detention in transit, it also indirectly legitimised practices enshrouded in secrecy to become an ordering structure of Australia's maritime border.

The Australian government, in propagating the success of its militarised border agenda, frequently propounds the narrative that people have stopped attempting to seek asylum in Australia. In contradistinction, the government increasingly relies upon a tactic of secreting boats that appear near this border. For example, in November 2015, a boat of asylum seekers was interdicted off the coast of Christmas Island. Locals reported to the media that it was between 100 and 200 metres from the entry of the harbour (Safi and Doherty 2015). The Australian authorities who intercepted it promptly covered the boat in tarpaulin in order to prevent a headcount and towed the boat back out to sea (Safi and Doherty 2015), encouraging the media to refer to the boat as 'the disappeared'.[7] When questioned about it, Prime Minister Malcolm Turnbull responded with a phrase repeatedly used by Liberal ministers since the institutionalisation of OSB: that being that the Government does not comment in regard to 'on water operations' (Davidson 2015). These narratives demonstrate the pattern of repetitive and recursive silences, legitimised by the technocratic discourse of threat management defining Australia's ad hoc tactics of border defence.

The maritime can be mobilised to hide in its folds and creases the lives of those that are *othered* from the state. As Shapiro argues, 'geography is inextricably linked to the architecture of enmity' (1997, xi). Gregory expands upon this to explain that 'architectures of enmity are not halls or mirrors reflecting the world – they enter into its very constitution' (2004, 20). The secreting capacity of the ocean is an enabling materiality of the maritime border. While space is never neutral, some geographical landscapes possess an oppressive character that can be harnessed for political motives, allowing geography to function as an 'alibi' of the state (Doty 2011). The maritime, in this context, functions as a secreting landscape, facilitating the obfuscation of arrivals and interdictions in Australia's maritime borderspace.

The secrecy surrounding maritime practices exposes the propensity of border agendas to use opacity and distance to prevent asylum seekers from accessing international systems of protection and hence ensure the insularity of the state and the militant sealing of the maritime border. The mechanism of secrecy in ad hoc practices enforces a distance in which the state has knowledge over a landscape, yet, through propagating a silence, obfuscates this geography from the public. This strategy of concealment is not a condition of this border geography confined to practice and speech acts by political leaders; it is also, as of 2015, fixed in policy.

SILENCE IN POLICY

Succeeding the detention of these Tamil asylum seekers at sea, the Australian government introduced the Border Force Act 2015, which came into full effect on 30 July 2015. The secrecy employed in practice in Australia's maritime borderspace became, through this Act, a justified procedure at the border. The policy has encouraged silence to have greater scope, allowing the government to engineer who can speak about this space as well as the influence of alternate discourses, so that even when counter-narratives emerge on maritime borderspaces, they are often annexed or annulled by the predominating state narrative.

Under Section 42 of the Border Force Act, succinctly titled 'Secrecy', the disclosure of information relating to Australia's border is criminalised. In detail, Section 42 prohibits an 'entrusted person', meaning the Secretary, the Australian Border Force Commissioner and any employee of the Department of Immigration and Border Protection,[8] including those employed by a foreign government or agency or providing a service to the Department through a contractor, from disclosing 'protected' information to the public with a penalty of two years of imprisonment. 'Protected information' is broadly defined in this context as 'information that was obtained by a person' in their capacity working in relation to Australia's border. It is also stipulated that the act has extraterritorial application, and thus 'extends to acts, omissions, matters and things outside Australia'.[9] This thus generates a vast geography and number of agencies that are legally prohibited from revealing practices in relation to Australia's border agenda. While there is a provision to enable the disclosure of information where there is a threat to life or health, the wide scope of Section 42 acts as a powerful dissuasion against whistleblowers, health workers and advocates arguing for human rights and visibility within Australia's detention network.

The Border Force Act does not eliminate speculation of practices in media and public about what happens at sea and the correlating discursive digressions from the state's ambition of secrecy. Yet, the policy mandating secrecy contributes to a monopolisation of knowledge so that often what is reported upon in the media does not challenge the epistemology of this geography. In reporting on ostensible events, the media not only fail to critically appraise the information disseminated by authorities, but they also fail to critique the role of borders, from their increasingly militarised discourse to the naturalisation of exclusion. Even when details of experiences of exclusion at sea are published, such as the pictures *The Guardian* released of the customs vessel where the Tamil asylum seekers were detained for a month, evidencing the bleak confinement that was experienced (Doherty and Farrell 2015), it does not counter-narrate the image of the hermetic sealing of the border and the implicit impenetrability of this space. Such images hence function to reify the institution of the border, aiding the work of those propagating the draconian nature of its impenetrability. The representations of this space in the media do not, therefore, rupture the state discourse being produced on this space.

In many ways, the news articles published on mobility control at sea are an asset to the government as they both advertently and inadvertently propagate the 'success' of stopping migrant boats. They thus function to verify the capability of the government to its domestic audience, as well as supplement the state-based propaganda dissuading migrants internationally from engaging in maritime journeys to Australia. Consequently, the details that emerge of Australia's maritime border in the media become incorporated into the discourse framing this landscape as militarised and war-like. These alternative voices to the state, potential counter-narratives, are 're-codified' by the dominant practice of this space. The knowledge in place, or what Foucault may refer to as the 'unitary knowledge', is ready to 'annex' such counter-systems of knowledge, 'to take them back within the fold of their own discourse and to invest them with everything this implies in terms of their effects of knowledge and power' (1994, 44). In other words, the knowledge that is 'disinterred' fails to successfully counter the technocracy of this border geography. It is important to emphasise that silence does not exist as a static absence of words, an aperture in language. Rather, it works with and through various discourses. As Foucault espouses, silence 'is less the absolute limit of discourse, the other side from which it is separated by a strict boundary, than an element that functions alongside the things said, with them and in relation to them within over-all strategies' (1998, 27).

There are thus many silences within the discourse on the maritime, each of which perpetuates an obfuscation of maritime migration and thus fails to effectively counter the muted nature of exclusion at sea.

This is not to say that resistant discourses become inconsequential in the heterogeneity of this space. In June 2015, over forty health care professionals, teachers and humanitarian staff who have worked in Australia's onshore and offshore detention centres signed an open letter in defiance against the institutionalisation of the Border Force Act and the forced concealing of human rights abuses. Although small in scale, it was a significant act against secrecy. Yet, while contestation of the secrecy of the Border Force Act may exist, the predominate system of power prevails in generating a widespread understanding of the maritime, so that even when contestations arise they are primarily in relation to the hierarchisation of knowledge and a system of silence.

Most absent from the discourse of the maritime is the voice of migrants. The discursive criminalisation of migrants internationally has had a significant impact on their absence of voice. Engaging in unsanctioned transgressions of borders, migrants travelling in an 'irregular' manner are branded by the government as participating in activities that threaten the security of the state. This is reinforced by their claimed association with the criminalised industry of people smuggling, as well as with the potential threat of terrorism. In Australia, the smearing of the reputation of asylum seekers was cultivated by John Howard's government (1996–2007), which frequently framed asylum seekers as 'bogus' and as potential terrorists (Pickering 2001; Wilson and Weber 2008). More recently, the widespread demonisation of people smugglers functions as a de facto criminalisation of asylum seekers for their participation in the industry. As such, the voice of asylum seekers and migrants, not only for reasons of security but also public legitimacy, has become part of the 'subjugated knowledges', 'disqualified' from the public arena, through being situated as 'beneath the required level of cognition or scientificity', in this case a scientificity related to order and militarisation (Foucault 1994, 41). In consequence, the knowledge that emerges on the maritime space is always only ever about migrants rather than by migrants. Gayatri Chakravorty Spivak (1988) recontextualises the epistemic violence Foucault espouses to have emerged with the 'redefinition of sanctity at the end of the European eighteenth century' to the production of knowledge on the 'Other' in imperialism (281). Through this production *on* rather than *by* a group of people, Spivak elucidates an 'asymmetrical obliteration of the trace of that Other in its precarious Subjectivity' (1988, 281). This notion of the subject, made at once invisible in their individual capacity as actors, and visible as others excluded from the political community, embodies the multi-faceted way in which migrants are locked out of the state in maritime borders.

Failing to be visible can be an asset in covert migration (Pezzani 2013; Pezzani and Heller 2013); however, when there is a militarised border enforcement agenda in place, being secreted from the public has the effect of greatly exaggerating the very physicality of the distance across maritime borders. The policy of silence has the effect of distancing asylum seekers from institutions of rights. In sanctioning an operational secrecy at Australia's borders, the Border Force Act expunges the capacity to review actions that occur at sea and thus enables ad hoc tactics to predominate without scrutiny, such as 'enhanced screening',[10] and practices of *refoulement*. While the secrecy surrounding Australia's border has been operational for some time, the procedure of interdicting and turning around boats in silence has become, through the Border Force Act, a naturalised practice, allowing the government to centralise the impenetrability of the border while eliminating the capacity for transparency.

SILENCE THROUGH THE BODY

A necessary outcome and objective of silencing bordering agendas is a silence that is enacted through the body of the asylum seeker. The absence from public discourse of the use of names in discussing maritime tragedies, as well as the concomitant numerical aggregation of those deceased at sea, functions to remove from public knowledge the corporeal existence of migrants both in life and in death. This is a problem raised by Judith Butler (2006) in *Precarious Life*, in which Butler elucidates how lives exist with different social gravity, so that the death of some will be enough to 'mobilize the forces of war', while the deaths of others 'will not even qualify as "grievable"' (32). As such, the deaths of those who are not deemed worthy of public recognition, or indeed in death of mourning, vanish 'in the ellipses by which public discourse proceeds' (Butler 2006, 35). The emphasis of this research is not on the politics of death of those whose lives Butler considers 'already negated', but how further obscuring such deaths, both through the lack of social value they may have and the further opacity added by aggregating fatalities, contributes to an opacity of the technologies which enact exclusion at sea. By limiting the sense of human loss within this space, the systems and technologies in place escape scrutiny.

The information on maritime migration diffused by the government and non-governmental agencies, and recapitulated by the media, is largely that of a numerical quantification of death. This is propagated by domestic campaign platforms claiming the need to securitise borders as well as by non-governmental organisations who, in arguing the urgency of such borderspaces, rearticulate a quantification of death. In this way, humanitarian organisations reaffirm the nature of borders by becoming part of their technology. As Walters argues, the 'humanitarian border' employs a governmentality which functions to 'manage political crises' and order bodies (2011). For example, UNHCR propounds 2016 to be one of the worst for maritime borders, with titles such as 'Mediterranean death toll soars, 2016 is deadliest year yet'. In a corollary sense, articles in *The Guardian* declared the 2016 death toll the 'highest ever on record'. The mortality of this geography, discussed principally in its aggregated significance, loses a profound sense of humanity.

In examining the recording of deaths of Iraqis in the war in the Middle East, Jennifer Hyndman argues that the 'fatality metrics' of war is, in itself, a site of conflict and contestation. Numbers are politically loaded devices, and while the function of 'Counting bodies is important', it fails to 'account for the remarkable destruction of lives' (Hyndman 2007, 38). Knowledge production within the political is a 'masculinist practice' that implies universality and truth (Hyndman 2007, 37). Hyndman problematises the namelessness of those deceased in Iraq, arguing that such aggregates exaggerate the distance between the observer and the human reality. Although the recording of deaths in war in a cumulative manner is both necessary and at times helpful, it also transforms the deceased into 'abstract figures' and, in so doing, obscures the social and political violence enacted upon bodies. Numerics profoundly impact the interpretation of violence, as Hyndman writes, the 'political and social meaning of the lost lives is effaced by the numbers' (2007, 40).

The quantification of death at the border has a similar function, used to critique borders or inspire new agendas (Walters 2011, 149). The number is whole within itself, a political device that has a specific function, rather than an indication of the sum of its parts: the individual lives caught within the debarment of borders. Inserting such metrics into the public discourse on maritime borderspaces shifts the focus away from lives in need of protection and the human need at sea. What gains principal attention is the seemingly objective need to respond to the border by deploying more thorough mechanisms at sea, including more thorough systems of management. Burroughs, in this edited book, analyses the tendency of the media in the United Kingdom to refer to migrants travelling by sea and those who perish in the Mediterranean both numerically and as 'masses'. Burroughs argues that the effect of the media inundating readers with numbers is the exaggeration of a climate of 'crises' surrounding migration. The Australian maritime borderscape does not suffer the same fatality as the Mediterranean, yet the collective terminology frequently used in Australian discussion of the maritime border can be seen to function in a similar way to numerical representations of the fatality metrics seen in the Mediterranean. The frequently used term 'boat people' in public discourse in Australia annuls the individuality of the lives of those involved in this borderspace, but most pertinent to this research, it distances observers from the programme that effectuates their debarring.

Butler argues that obituaries function 'as the instrument by which grievability is publicly distributed' (2006, 34). This research is not suggesting that names will instantly invoke an interest or humanisation of those deceased in border geographies. Nor is it the intention to ignore the role of the public in becoming desensitised or being disinterested in the deaths of those presently as well as historically 'othered'. It does argue, however, that using names in reporting on deaths in maritime borders, when possible, will contribute to a greater sense of transparency and culpability. As Burroughs notes, the avoidance of the use of names to refer to migrants in the media is specifically pertinent to migrants travelling by sea. The ambition of naming those who perish at sea is thus not to emphasise the need for collective mourning, grieving or empathy, but rather for the technology of borders to ascertain transparency. The gravity of the loss of this landscape will not be instilled through fear-inducing numbers, yet recognising the unique and individual lives lost could evolve critical recognition of the systems in place contributing to the violence of the maritime.

The anonymity of death quantified numerically exaggerates a distance between the 'us' and the 'other'; like 'gravity's rainbows'; it enables a knowledge to 'fold distance into difference' (Gregory 2004, 249). While the numerical representation of deaths, is not a secreting as such, it is an action of *separating* as is, functions to remove or reduce the notion of these lives from the cognizance of the polity. The separating of the value of these lives, in allowing a certain technology of power to proliferate and tactics of exclusion to persist without review, contributes to silence.

This chapter thus argues that in the numerical representation of deaths there is a dehumanisation which allows for a different yet just as profound opacity surrounding migration and exclusion in maritime borders. Not only are the lives reduced to aggregates but, in so doing, the systems that allow for such fatalities are made equally distant. There are, as Foucault writes, 'not one but many silences, and they are an integral part of the strategies that underlie and permeate discourse' (Foucault 1998, 27). The dehumanised representation of life lost at sea, in instilling a separation from the polity, functions to mute the tragedy of exclusion. Through losing a sense of humanity the events and structures that lead to death are expunged of review, encouraging the perpetuation of the layered silence of this geography. As Hockey writes, the body is largely interpreted 'as a terrain of signs and discourses which is to be read as a text, with the material flesh seemingly dissolved' (2009, 478). The proclivity of states and border agencies of using numerical representations and collective terminologies to refer to those travelling by sea not only effaces lives but also is integral to the strategies of silence in practice and in policy seen in maritime borders as it functions to further distance the actions that transpire at sea from scrutiny and from public knowledge.

CONCLUSION

Author Toni Morrison (1993) stated in her acceptance speech of the Nobel Prize for Literature at the Swedish Academy, 'Oppressive language does more than represent violence; it is violence; does more than represent the limits of knowledge; it limits knowledge'. This chapter has demonstrated how, within the agenda of Australia's border security, silence has become part of the mechanism of mobility control at sea. This silence functions in and through discourse to obscure this space and, as a result, distances migrants from systems of rights and protection. It is important to recognise that the impact of the silence that engulfs particular bodies rarely ends at the site of the border. For example, the silence that ensues when migrants are detained in domestic detention centres, in third-party detention centres or in the prisons within the countries they may be returned to perpetuates this distancing of migrants from systems of protection (Nethery and Holman 2016).

The 'on water' aspect of Australia's border defence is secreted through a profound separation from view, allowing the political to remove itself from having to provide details on events through formulating a technocracy whereby trained professionals protecting the state regulate the border environment and present the disclosure of information as a threat to the success of their agenda. The geography of this border, being both distant and transient, allows the government to veil operations with ease. While much of this obfuscation transpires in an ad hoc, practice-driven way, as seen with the detention of Tamil asylum seekers at sea, policy has had to retroactively adjust to incorporate an agenda of secrecy as a determining logic of Australia's maritime border.

Through reaffirming this functional use of silence in policy, a mandate of secrecy emerges separating from view what happens at sea. As a result of the Border Force Act, silence has come to hold an explicit and state-sanctioned role in border defence in Australia. This secreting allows a hegemonic knowledge of Australia's maritime space. This is not to suggest that discourse on mobility control at sea itself becomes uniform or unidirectional, but that a 'unitary' knowledge emerges premised upon a silence that works with and through discourse, preventing both the voice of asylum seekers and other resistant voices from gaining public traction or presenting impactful variant narratives. This is facilitated not only by framing the maritime as regulated by strategies of threat management but also by creating a condition where migrants are talked *of*, yet are forced themselves to remain unheard, a condition aided by the widespread criminalisation of migrants.

The removal of border operations from sight does not orientate exclusively around the concealing of practices; the silence of bordering practices is also realised through the body of migrants, negating their unique experience and existence through depicting mobility trends and fatality metrics as numerical aggregates. It is necessary to recognise how understanding migrants in this geography as represented in an aggregate manner dissolves the individual significance of their lives and the specific violence of their exclusion and thus functions to conceal the mechanisms enforcing their debarment. As a result, the technology enacting the exclusion of these migrants is removed from view. Maritime borders are specific political landscapes, and studies on the architectures of exclusion in these geographies remain nascent. What this study demonstrates is the way silence is emerging as an integral technology in the regulation of unsanctioned transgression of state borders. The effect of this silencing is not only a greater exclusion from rights and protection faced by asylum seekers but also an obfuscation of the nature of this exclusion.

NOTES

1. Australian Customs and Border Protection Service (ACBPS) was dissolved in 2015, when ACBPS was merged with the Department of Immigration and Border Protection, to produce the agency Australian Border Force.

2. It was only through the interim injunction on 7 July that an accurate number of those being detained was exposed. In fact, the injunction was the first time that the Australian government publicly acknowledged the very existence of the boat they had interdicted and those they had then detained.

3. It is important to acknowledge that while at sea a group of academics and lawyers warned that such bordering practices were not in compliance with international law and minimum stands of asylum procedures. They also emphasised that '[h]olding asylum seekers in this manner also amounts to incommunicado detention without judicial scrutiny' (Farrell, Laughland and Davey 2014).

4. These changes occurred under the Migration and Maritime Powers Legislation Amendment (Resolving the Asylum Legacy Caseload) Act 2014. Specifically,

detention at sea for indefinite periods when in transit is in reference to Subsection 72(A)5 Migration and Maritime Powers Legislation Amendment Act.

5. Domestic law previously allowed for a maritime officer to detain a person at sea and take the person to a place inside or outside of Australia. The new law stipulates that the destination that a person is being taken to may change 'at any time' (Migration and Maritime Powers Legislation Amendment, Subsection 72(4)(B)) and persons detained at sea may remain so for 'any period of time' while their place of destination is being determined or changed (Subsection 72A). The act further adds that the restraint on mobility is not considered an 'arrest' and is not classified as unlawful (Subsection 75) and that the restraint and removal of asylum seekers is not to be considered invalid as a result of a failure to recognize Australia's obligations to international law or to the domestic law of other countries (Subsection 75A).

6. *462 - CPCF v. Minister for Immigration and Border Protection* [2015] HCA 1 (28 January 2015).

7. It is unclear who exactly these authorities were, whether it was the Australian Navy or Australian Border Force.

8. Part 1, Section 4 of the Border Force Act explains an entrusted person to be a widely inclusive term, from Australian public service employees to authorised officers as stipulated by the Migration Act 1958 and the Customs Act 1901, as well as employees of state or territory, or an agency of any state, territory of the Commonwealth. The *act* also stipulates an officer or employee of any foreign government or an agency of any foreign government is also included in the definition of an entrusted person, as are consultant and contract employees.

9. Pt. 1, Sect. 6 of Border Force Act 2015.

10. In late 2012, the Australia government naturalised a process of 'enhanced screening' for Sri Lankan asylum seekers. These enhanced procedures included screening people without adequately informing them of their right to asylum, brief and often insufficient interviews, a lack of information on the right to legal assistance and the inability to request the independent review of a case. Additionally, these interviews often took place on boats via teleconference, with allegedly as few as four questions asked (Whyte 2014). Typically, enhanced screening can be used only when a '[c]ountry of origin information suggests that the cohort is not generally considered to be "at risk" in that country' (Pearson 2013) which is not the case for Tamil asylum seekers.

BIBLIOGRAPHY

Australian Broadcasting Corporation (ABC). 'Prime Minister Tony Abbott Likens Campaign against People Smugglers to "War"', accessed 15 February 2017. http://www.abc.net.au/news/2014-01-10/abbott-likens-campaign-against-people-smugglers-to-war/5193546

Brown, Wendy, 'Freedom's Silence', in *Edgework: Critical Essays on Knowledge and Politics* (Princeton: Princeton University Press, 2009).

Brownmiller, Susan, *Against Our Will: Men, Women and Rape* (New York: Open Road Media, 2013).

Brummett, Barry. 'Towards a Theory of Silence as a Political Strategy', *Quarterly Journal of Speech* 66, no. 3 (1980): 289.

Butler, Judith, *Precarious Life: The Powers of Mourning and Violence* (London: Verso, 2006).

Cole, David, Fabbrini, Federico, and Vedaschi, Arianna. *Secrecy, National Security and the Vindication of Constitutional Law* (Cheltenham: Edward Elgar Publishing, 2013).

Dauenhauer, Bernard, *Silence: The Phenomenon and Its Ontological Significance* (Lafayette: Indiana University Press, 1982).

Davidson, Helen. 'Christmas Island Asylum Seeker Boat "Disappeared" after Being Towed by Navy', *The Guardian*, accessed 15 February 2017. https://www.theguardian.com/australia-news/2015/nov/25/christmas-island-asylum-seeker-boat-disappeared-after-being-towed-by-navy

Doherty, Ben, and Farrell, Paul. 'Detention of 157 Tamil Asylum Seekers On Board Ship Ruled Lawful', *The Guardian*, accessed 15 February 2017. https://www.theguardian.com/australia-news/2015/jan/28/detention-157-tamil-asylum-seekers-on-board-ship-ruled-lawful

Elshtain, Jean. 'Feminist Discourse and Its Discontents: Language, Power, and Meaning', *Signs: Journal of Women in Culture and Society* 7, no. 3 (1982): 603.

Eng, David, and Kazanjian, David, *Loss: The Politics of Mourning* (Los Angeles: University of California Press, 2003).

Farrell, Paul, 'Operation Sovereign Borders Chief Unable to Answer Asylum Questions', *The Guardian*, accessed 15 February 2017. https://www.theguardian.com/world/2014/jul/11/operation-sovereign-borders-chief-unable-to-answer-asylum-questions

Farrell, Paul, Laughland, Oliver, and Davey, Melissa, 'Asylum Seekers Will Be Handed to Police on Return, Sri Lanka Confirms', *The Guardian*, accessed 15 February 2017. https://www.theguardian.com/world/2014/jul/07/asylum-seekers-will-be-handed-to-police-on-return-sri-lanka-confirms

Ferguson, Keenan, 'Silence: A Politics', *Contemporary Political Theory* 2, no. 1 (2003): 49.

Foucault, Michel, 'Genealogy and Social Criticism', in *The Postmodern Turn: New Perspectives on Social Theory*, edited by Seldman, Steven (Cambridge: Cambridge University Press, 1994).

Foucault, Michel, *The History of Sexuality. Vol. 1: The Will to Knowledge* (London: Penguin Books Limited, 1998).

Glenday, James, 'Asylum Seekers: Releasing Operation Sovereign Borders Details Not in the National Interest, Scott Morrison Tells Senate Committee', Australian Broadcasting Corporation, accessed 15 February 2017. http://www.abc.net.au/news/2014-01-31/morrison-appears-before-senate-committee/5230836

Glenn, Cheryl, *Unspoken: A Rhetoric of Silence* (Chicago: Southern Illinois University Press, 2004).

Government of Australia. The Senate, *Legal and Constitutional Affairs References Committee: A Claim of Public Interest Immunity Raised over Documents* (March 2014) (Canberra: Commonwealth of Australia, 2014).

Gregory, Derek, *The Colonial Present: Afghanistan, Palestine, Iraq* (Malden: Blackwell Publishing, 2004).

Hockey, John, ' "Switch On": Sensory work in the Infantry', *Work, Employment and Society* 23, no. 3 (2009): 477.

Hyndman, Jennifer, 'Feminist Geopolitics Revisited: Body Counts in Iraq', *The Professional Geographer* 59, no. 1 (2007): 35.

Laughland, Oliver, and Dehghan, Saeed, 'Handover of 153 Asylum Seekers to Sri Lanka Halted by High Court', *The Guardian*, accessed 15 February 2017. https://www.theguardian.com/world/2014/jul/07/high-court-injunction-halts-hand over-asylum-seekers-sri-lanka

Lippert, Randy, and Walby, Kevin, 'Governing through Privacy: Authoritarian Liberalism, Law, and Privacy Knowledge', *Law, Culture and the Humanities* 12, no. 2 (2016) 329.

Lloyd, Moya, 'Towards a Cultural Politics of Vulnerability: Precarious Lives and Ungrievable Deaths', in *Judith Butler's Precarious Politics: Critical Encounters*, edited by Carver, Terrell, and Chambers, Samuel (London: Routledge, 2008).

MacKinnon, Catharine, *Toward a Feminist Theory of the State* (Cambridge: Harvard University Press, 1989).

Morrison, Toni, 'Lecture and Speech of Acceptance, upon the Award of the Nobel Prize for Literature', delivered in Stockholm on 7 December 1993, accessed 15 February 2017. http://www.americanrhetoric.com/speeches/tonimorrisonnobel lecture.htm

Murphy, Katharine, 'Asylum Seeker "Secrecy" Is Challenged by Senate', *The Guardian*, accessed 15 February 2017. https://www.theguardian.com/world/2013/nov/14/ asylum-seeker-secrecy-challenged-senate

Nethery, Amy, and Holman, Rosa, 'Secrecy and Human Rights Abuse in Australia's Offshore Immigration Detention Centres', *The International Journal of Human Rights* 20, no. 7 (2016): 1,018.

Olsen, Tillie, *Silences* (New York: The Feminist Press at CUNY, 2014).

Pearson, Elaine, ' "Enhanced Screening" Means Enhanced Trauma for Asylum Seekers', *The Guardian*, accessed 15 February 2017. https://www.hrw.org/ news/2013/11/25/enhanced-screening-means-enhanced-trauma-asylum-seekers

Pezzani, Lorenzo, 'Mapping the Sea. Thalassopolitics and Disobedient Spatial Practices', in *Architecture and the Paradox of Dissidence*, edited by Weizman, Ines (London: Routledge, 2013).

Pezzani, Lorenzo, and Heller, Charles, 'A Disobedient Gaze: Strategic Interventions in the Knowledge(s) of Maritime Borders', *Postcolonial Studies* 16, no. 3 (2013): 289.

Picard, Max, *The World of Silence* (Chicago: Henry Regnery, 1952).

Pickering, Sharon, 'Common Sense and Original Deviancy: News Discourses and Asylum Seekers in Australia', *Journal of Refugee Studies* 14, no. 2 (2011): 169.

Pozen, David, 'Deep Secrecy', *Stanford Law Review* 62 (2010): 257.

Roach, Kent, 'Managing Secrecy and Its Migration in a Post–9/11 World', in *Secrecy, National Security and the Vindication of Constitutional Law*, edited by Cole, David, Fabbrini, Federico, and Vedaschi, Arianna (Cheltenham: Edward Elgar Publishing, 2013), 115.

Safi, Michael, and Doherty, Ben, 'Asylum Seeker Boat Towed Away after Coming within 200m of Christmas Island', *The Guardian*, accessed 15 February 2017. https://www.theguardian.com/australia-news/2015/nov/20/asylum-seeker-boat-reported-approached-christmas-island

7.30 Report, 'Scott Morrison Describes "War against People Smuggling"', 18 July 2013, accessed 15 February 2017. http://www.abc.net.au/7.30/content/2013/s3806305.htmShapiro, Michael, 'Textualizing Global Politics', in *International/ Intertexual Relations*, edited by Shapiro, Michael, and Der Derian, James (New York: Lexington Books, 1989).

Shapiro, Michael, *Violent Cartographies: Mapping Cultures of War* (Minneapolis: University of Minnesota Press, 1996).

Spivak, Gayatri, 'Can the Subaltern Speak?', in *Marxism and the Interpretation of Culture*, edited by Nelson, Cary, and Grossberg, Lawrence (Chicago: University of Illinois Press, 1988).

Strik, Tineke, 'The "Left-to-Die Boat": Actions and Reactions', Council of Europe Committee on Migration, Refugees and Displaced Persons, 2014, accessed 15 February 2017. http://repository.ubn.ru.nl/bitstream/handle/2066/156284/156284.pdf

Walters, William, 'Foucault and Frontiers: Notes on the Birth of the Humanitarian Border', *Governmentality: Current Issues and Future Challenges* (2011): 138.

Whyte, Sarah, 'Immigration Department Officials Screen Asylum Seekers at Sea "via teleconference"', *Sydney Morning Herald*, accessed 15 February 2017. http://www.smh.com.au/federal-politics/political-news/immigration-department-officials-screen-asylum-seekers-at-sea-via-teleconference-20140702-3b837.html

Wilson, Dean, and Weber, Leanne, 'Surveillance, Risk and Preemption on the Australian Border', *Surveillance & Society* 5, no. 2 (2002): 124.

Chapter 10

Conclusion: Problems, Answers and Ways Forward in Studying Migration by Boat

Elaine Burroughs and Kira Williams

GENERAL CONCLUSIONS

This edited volume focused on three crucial, yet understudied, issues in contemporary migration by boat: data and methodology, legal regimes and geopolitics and discourses. In doing so, it presented challenges to traditional theories, understandings and methodologies in migration studies. This resulted from its focus on an understudied medium of movement, strong empirical focus and emphasis on tying often disparate subjects in the field into one place. Through its three sections, each covering one of these themes, contributors approached these issues using empirically focused, novel methods in specific case studies. Building from its beginning, the book combined new data sources and methodologies to study the legal regimes and geopolitics and discourses of migration by boat. It specifically unfolded by interlacing and relating these complex but often separately studied subjects.

In this concluding chapter, we reflect on the book's core conclusions for studying migration by boat and migration studies more generally. We briefly explain our perspective on the book's major benefits. Finally, we provide our summaries of key problems and answers in studying migration by boat based on our three themes.

In section 1, which covered data and methodology, Alison Mountz and Kira Williams found that current data on migration by boat are often missing or insufficient to adequately describe it. Drawing from her research related to island detention and migration at sea, for example, Mountz showed how at the onset of her projects her research team could neither find nor agree upon a previous definition of what was a migrant boat. Williams likewise explored how even basic requests for information about migration by boat to states could become many times more complicated and obfuscated than expected.

175

Examples like these turn out to be all too common in studying migration by boat. In her chapter, Williams identified more general data-related problems in the field: differences in definitions, differences in recording, power relations, reluctance to report and even intentional data destruction. Mountz discussed the complex vulnerability and ethical concerns surrounding working with such data for migrants, bureaucrats and scholars alike. These barriers raise a daunting challenge to future researchers.

Mountz and Williams each continued by identifying and expanding on new methodological paths for research on migration by boat. Mountz specifically formulated ten innovative strategies with examples of how they have been used by recent scholarship. She poignantly argued and elaborated on how and why these strategies could overcome current methodological issues while not exposing migrants to further harm. Williams took a slightly different approach: she formed a basis for a more generalised approach to studying migration by boat combining a number of existing methodologies. Through this approach, she demonstrated how a combination of methodologies not only addresses the limitations of individual methodologies but also most of the data-related issues identified earlier. Section 1 ultimately helped contribute to future research on migration by boat by taking on two strong barriers to current scholarship: data gaps and methodologies limitations. In doing so, they helped form the basis of further discourse and research.

In section 2, reviewing legal regimes and geopolitics, Giuseppe Campesi, Paolo Cuttitta and Joanne van Selm revealed that the micro-level, corporeal realities of migrants who move by boat are empirically tied to multi-scalar, complex legal and political structures. Campesi relayed how the long-term construction of Italy's maritime border control not only framed its geopolitics with the wider European Union (EU) and Libya but also modified the legal regimes and spaces in which migrants, boats and maritime interdiction operations found themselves. As it turned out, the positionality and lived experiences of migrants became deeply entangled with their physical, legal and political locations and the constructed personhoods which followed therefrom. Cuttitta conceptualised and empirically showed how international governmental organisations, states and even non-governmental organisations worked together to build migrant legality via political location. In Italy's maritime border control policies, he found that such legal regimes impact the lives of migrants, the boats in which they move and enforcement through logics of inclusion and exclusion.

Van Selm took a wider analysis of how the EU's political construction and handling of the 'migrant crisis' since 2014 affected both asylum seekers making their way through the sea and Balkans and individual EU member-states. She thereby showed that it is not only migrants who become empirically harmed by ineffective border control policies but also entire populations of states, like Greece, which became the 'front line' border. Political death could thus happen to migrants, state populations and, as Van Selm showed, the entire EU project through the relationships between legality, geography and migration by boat. By its end, then, section 2 addressed a number of critical questions in current studies of migration by boat about the relationships between legality, geography, politics and migrant outcomes at sea. Its chapters thereby contributed to previous scholarship by connecting the analytical and empirical gaps between the legal regimes, geographies and migration by boat.

Section 3 included chapters by Elaine Burroughs, Marco Binotto and Marco Bruno and Andonea Dickson. Each contribution empirically identified and explored discourses on migration by boat. In chapter 7, Burroughs demonstrated the emergence and construction of the narrative of migration as a 'crisis' through measuring its proliferation in the news media of the United Kingdom in 2015. Using this approach, she deconstructed discursive representations of the 'crisis' to unravel their meaning and purpose with respect to debates on migration by boat. Bruno and Binotto conducted an in-depth analysis of how the Italian media depicted migration by boat since the 1990s using modern theories by media scholars. They showed how media discourse built the representation of borders and spaces through a 'two-sided' narrative: buzz and crisis. In chapter 9, Dickson probed how the government of Australia and Australian media narrated the activities of Operation Sovereign Borders since 2014. She uncovered how elites used 'silences' to obfuscate borders and their effects on migration by boat; further, Dickson demonstrated how strategies of mobility control served to amplify such silences from the level of the state all the way to the body of migrants. Through these chapters, section 3 contributed to migration by boat discourse in two key ways. First, it focused on discursive data and methods – that is, made use of empirical evidence related to discourses from news media, political outlets and online sources – rather than taking a solely theoretical approach. Second, they extended existing approaches to analysing discourses on migration by explicitly linking such empirical data on migration by boat and its governance with its discursive/visual representations.

This edited volume gave three key benefits to a wider audience with respect to these critical, yet understudied, issues in migration studies. First, the exploration of migration by boat in contemporary society is an under-researched area within migration studies. We designed this book to specifically address aspects which themselves remain insufficiently studied in migration by boat, and we made a unique contribution by bringing aspects into one place. Second, the book provided initial scientific evidence to better understand how migration by boat works, especially in relation to its surrounding geographies, politics and discourses. Policymakers and publics alike will benefit from access to such empirical work to inform evidence-based policy and opinion. Third, looking at gaps in studying migration by boat provided critical insight into social theory and human rights law. As migration by boat is so often a place where powerful social forces converge, unpacking how they affect movement at sea with novel evidence invariably sheds light on migration theory itself.

SOME PROBLEMS IN STUDYING MIGRATION BY BOAT

Throughout this book, contributors have taken on key problems within studying migration by boat and migration studies more broadly. Here we present a general summary of identified problems for the benefit of future researchers. In terms of data and methodology to study migration by boat, data themselves remain difficult to access or construct and fraught with methodological problems. As Williams noted, data are often completely unavailable or absent, deeply affected by the power relations which construct them and suffer from extreme selection bias and divergences in recording. Further, many state authorities even go so far as to actively destroy data in order to reduce their political consequences. Mountz showed that migration studies lack basic definitions and concepts to migration by boat, especially in contexts where social forces obscure people and data. These findings indicate that simply having adequate data to study migration by boat is one of its most important problems.

Finding appropriate methodologies, particularly in different contexts, to study migration by boat is also one of its most critical issues. Mountz revealed how many approaches clearly raise concerns about participant vulnerability and ethics, effects of which can geopolitically scale by reproducing social forces like racism and xenophobia. From Williams's perspective, any single methodology is effectively insufficient to adequately study migration by boat. She identifies how qualitative methodologies, for example, experience downsides such as insufficient specification, inability to demonstrate causation, significantly skewed sampling, neglect of empiricism and absence of proper documentation. She likewise pointed out that quantitative approaches exhibit just as many, if different, faults. Williams also showed how available solutions typically cannot address all methodological issues, which means that future researchers will have to make difficult decisions about how to study this subject.

Contributors additionally found a large number of problems with previous studies of the legal regimes and geopolitics of migration by boat. In his chapter, Campesi uncovered how the securitisation of migration and its politics obscures its study. He further revealed that current literature presents an insufficient understanding of border 'militarisation' and how that relates to previously 'civilian' threats, as well as how understanding the border is becoming more difficult due to its increasing complexity and proliferation of actors. Cuttitta paralleled Campesi in demonstrating current deficiencies in understanding the construction of legal geographies related to migration by boat, including how formal legal frameworks work in practice through space. While many migration studies scholars take concepts like 'territory' and 'sovereignty' as given, Cuttitta astutely displayed how legal geographies are relatively disparate at sea; therefore, future researchers may need to reconsider how migration and enforcement spaces were examined through previous theory. Van Selm amplified these concerns by exhibiting that such theory has yet to change state behaviour and that states have failed to learn from history despite repeated migrant influxes at sea. Previous scholars have inadequately connected differing geopolitical and policy scales to nuance *who* migration policy affects, *how* and *how* such outcomes might be changed. Differences in attention and priorities in study of scholars, policymakers and publics alike between migration by sea and land compound these issues.

Authors confirmed that research on discourses of migration by boat has serious problems. Burroughs, for instance, showed that there is generally little empirical evidence of how migration by boat narratives are constructed at all, especially with respect to 'crisis'. She additionally revealed how previous scholars have failed to tie such narratives to geopolitics or their social consequences on migrants themselves. According to Burroughs, current literature also insufficiently addresses how the media and states interplay in building narration on migration by boat. Bruno and Binotto poignantly demonstrated that such gaps may result from the lack of in-depth understanding of media by migration studies researchers. There is particularly a missing link between media and social narration and construction of legal and political spaces. The two went so far as to demonstrate how migration studies' typical understanding of the 'border' as physical and militarised is highly limited. Dickson accented this reality by displaying that states, media and populations manifest borders *ontologically* and that ontological distancing itself can be a bordering tactic. From this, it seems clear that migration studies will need to very carefully rethink what the border is and how to study it.

SOME ANSWERS IN STUDYING MIGRATION BY BOAT

This book's authors provided some initial answers to the problems related to studying migration by boat they posed throughout their chapters. On the subject of data and methodology, despite the issues identified, Mountz argued that this kind of research is vital and that we ought to explore and commit to studying it instead of shying away. Williams proposed that one way to do this was to employ mixed methods to triangulate date and reduce limitations of individual data sets or methodologies. She reasoned that many of our current data and methodological issues can be answered through a focus on identification of causal mechanisms and verification and updating of theory using collected data. This process, in itself, could then lead to further data collection on new evidence, snowballing into a wealth of data and perspectives. One advantage of this approach for migration studies is that it allows most previous migration theories to be used; one disadvantage is that it requires skills in both qualitative and quantitative methodologies, which only some scholars typically have. Mountz likewise advocated for the use of novel methodologies and exemplified how they have been previously used; future researchers should look to her list when first considering how to approach their studies of migration by boat. Core conclusions, then, are that scholars should expand their methodological repertoires and look to a broader range of work to more critically and carefully approach the field.

With respect to legal regimes and geopolitics, contributors agreed that more critical analysis and empirical work needs to be done to answer challenges in studying migration by boat. From Campesi's perspective, proper understanding of border and migration regimes first requires thorough historical and policy analysis of it. These analyses should be tied into empirical descriptions of the legal basis and institutional framework of enforcement and, in particular, surveillance. Cuttitta also called for strong investigation of bordering *practices* as opposed to purely looking at formal legal frameworks. He implicitly argued that future researchers must show the complex interactions of an array of actors in shaping legal and political spaces instead of simply assuming them. Further, he proposed that this analysis should be related to the spatial outcomes of migrants, including through logics of inclusion and exclusion. Last, van Selm held that a proper way to investigate important nuances of who migration and enforcement policies affect is to connect varying geopolitical and policy scales, from the state all the way to the body of migrants. Such connections must understand migration at sea *and* on land, particularly in how actors differently build, frame and implement their regimes. All authors concur that future research on migration by boat needs to better explore and describe spaces, as well as how such spaces work on/through various geographic scales and actors.

Finally, while demonstrating substantial problems in research on discourses of migration by boat, contributors additionally gave answers on how to move forward on these topics. Burroughs argued that the impact of the media and its narration on migration must be measured, particularly with respect to construction of ontologies of migration and threat. She argued that these ontologies should not be taken by scholars as static or given, but rather that we must understand how they themselves feed into media and political representations of migration by boat. Bruno and Binotto agreed that it will be necessary to empirically dissect and tie the media role in relation to cultural knowledge of migration by boat. Further, they advocated that the border must be complicated by showing how media itself can become a sort of bordering process by building cultural and political boundaries. Likewise, Dickson showed that our understanding of bordering remains incomplete so long as we fail to relate ontological distancing with bordering itself along with public participation therein. In parallel with Williams, she uncovered how absences can be as powerful and telling, empirically and conceptually, as presence; therefore, we ought to explain migrant outcomes as results of physical *and* ontological presence/absence. These proposed responses point to a need of future scholarship to more critically and empirically engage the media and its consequences on migration by boat.

In sum, critical studies of migration by boat can potentially do much to challenge and forward migration studies as a whole. Specifically, future researchers and studies can incorporate or begin to think about the following ways forward. First, in order to deal with major data and methodological limitations, we need to expand our methodological knowledge and practice; we should also draw on the work of as many other scholars as possible to help in this process. Second, in order to understand how legal regimes and geopolitics work in practice, we must better explore and describe space itself, as well as describe how such spaces work on/through various geographic scales. Last, in order to cope with the relative absence of elite and media narration in our studies, we should more critically and empirically engage the media and its consequences on migration by boat.

In conclusion, the broader impact of the research and analysis brought together in this edited book is noteworthy. This book has shown how, as a subsection of migration studies in general, migration by boat challenges a range of established concepts (both theoretical and methodological). It challenges concepts of regularity and easily definable objects that can be categorised, analysed and governed. Migration by boat also forces us to question preconceptions of space, of legal spaces and of legal/illegal bodies. In other words, this topic forces us, as researchers, to think beyond the norm and to create novel methods of research, data gathering and analysis. In essence, migration by boat highlights the messiness of migration: how it is difficult to define, how it is difficult to collect accurate data and how it is difficult to regulate/manage the movement of people across the sea. Furthermore, the stories that are told about migration by boat don't always reflect reality and are highly politicised, resulting in significant consequences for migrants and the broader populous. Therefore, this edited book fits well into the 'Challenging Migration Studies' series as it not only challenges the status quo and current ways of thinking about and talking about migration by boat, but it also offers a number of informed and innovative ways to study migration by boat.

Index

Note: Page references for figures and tables are italicised.

About the Authors

Marco Binotto is an Adjunct Professor of Communications in the Department of Communication and Social Research, Sapienza Universita di Roma, Italy. Currently, he coordinates research on security, immigration and asylum in Italian media.

Marco Bruno is a Researcher in the Department of Communication and Social Research, Sapienza Universita di Roma, Italy. His research explores journalism, media and diversity, particularly with respect to migration and Islam, political and electoral communications and political participation.

Elaine Burroughs works in Maynooth University, Ireland and is the author of "Political and Media Discourses of Illegal Immigration in Ireland" (2015). Her work focuses on migration in the Irish, UK and European contexts.

Giuseppe Campesi is a Researcher in the Department of Political Science, Universita Degli Studi di Bari, Italy. His research concerns contemporary social theory, critical legal theory, critical security studies and the relationship between migration, freedom and security in the contemporary world.

Paolo Cuttitta is a Member of the Faculty of Law, Vrije Universiteit, Amsterdam, the Netherlands. He carries out his recent research activities within the widely published 'The Human Costs of Border Control' project and also studies the Euro-African border and migration regimes.

Andonea Dickson is a PhD candidate in the School of Politics and International Relations, Queen Mary University of London. Her work focuses on the complex relationships of migration, borders, and the militarisation of maritime frontiers.

Alison Mountz is a Professor of Geography with the Department of Geography and Environmental Studies, Wilfrid Laurier University, Canada. Her multi-faceted research covers illegalised migration, migration detention, islands and war resisters.

Joanne van Selm is an Independent Consultant on Migration and Refugee Issues, who also serves as Associate Director for Research at Eurasylum. Her distinguished work investigates migration and asylum/refugee policy.

Kira Williams is a Post-Doctoral Fellow with the Department of Political Science, University of Waterloo, Canada. Her research studies migration by boat, analytical methodology and migration governance.